1/12

THE BIG-ASS BOOK OF CRAFTS 2

BY MARK MONTANO

G

GALLERY BOOKS

NEW YORK   LONDON   TORONTO   SYDNEY   NEW DELHI

Also by Mark Montano
Pulp Fiction: Perfect Paper Projects
The Big-Ass Book of Home Décor
The Big-Ass Book of Crafts
CosmoGirl: Cool Room
Dollar Store Décor
Super Suite
Window Treatments & Slipcovers for Dummies
While You Were Out: The Rooms, the Cast, the Dreams

G

Gallery Books
A Division of Simon & Schuster, Inc.
1230 Avenue of the Americas
New York, NY 10020

First Gallery Books trade paperback edition October 2011

GALLERY BOOKS and colophon are registered trademarks
of Simon & Schuster, Inc.

For information about special discounts for bulk purchases,
please contact Simon & Schuster Special Sales at 1-866-506-1949
or business@simonandschuster.com.

The Simon & Schuster Speakers Bureau can bring authors to your
live event. For more information or to book an event contact the
Simon & Schuster Speakers Bureau at 1-866-248-3049 or visit our
website at www.simonspeakers.com.

Designed by Jane Archer (www.psbella.com)
Photography by Auxy Espinoza and Jimmy Cohrssen

Manufactured in the United States of America

10 9 8 7 6 5 4 3 2 1

Library of Congress Cataloging-in-Publication Data

Montano, Mark.
   The big-ass book of crafts 2 / by Mark Montano.
      p. cm.
   Includes index.
   1. Handicraft. 2. House furnishings. 3. Interior decoration. I. Title.
   TT157.M63473 2011
   745.5—dc23
                              2011029548

ISBN 978-1-4516-2780-0
ISBN 978-1-4516-2783-1 (ebook)

CONTENTS

This book is dedicated to
Walter, my surrogate guardian
and my dearest friend

HELLO AGAIN, my creative friends!

It's good to be back with a whole new book of ideas that I hope will inspire you. While I know that not every project in this book will fit everyone's style, I can assure you that if you take a look at each project, you'll find a technique or process that will enhance your already wonderful creative abilities. After all, isn't that why you bought this book in the first place? I thought so.

Recently I tried to figure out when my creative soul took flight. It may have been the first time my grandmother let me sew a button on a piece of fabric or when my aunt Lulu taught me some basic macramé knots and let me go nuts with her stash of twine and cord. It's tough to pinpoint a specific project that sparked my crafty interest. All I know is that from early on, being creative made me feel good. I loved that I could take my creative challenges into my own hands, and that gave me a sense of pride and accomplishment; if I wanted a lamp or a piece of art or a scarf or a new top for my dresser, I could make it myself. I also learned that when I create, I'm happy. It's that simple. I don't think I'm the only one who feels that way, either. I believe that if everyone took a little more time to express themselves by creating, we'd all be a little happier.

I wish you the very best in your craft adventures, and I hope they bring you as much happiness as mine have brought me. And if you have any questions about the projects in this book or just want to say hello, you can always email me at MarkMontanoNYC@aol.com.

TWO IMPORTANT THINGS TO REMEMBER AS YOU EMBARK ON YOUR CRAFTING JOURNEY: Newspaper is crucial! Always have a stack on hand to cover your workspace. It will make cleanup a breeze and ensure that you don't get paint and glue on your tables and floors. And always remember to use safety glasses or goggles to protect your eyes when using power tools.

ometimes when I see a good accessory display at a store I get upset. I'm going to admit it: Wearing beautiful, colorful, and sparkly things is just plain fun, and it's unfair that as a man I don't get to partake in as many fabulously embellished pieces as my female counterparts. In any case, I always try on my crafts, even if I'm not the intended recipient, and revel in their lacy, glittery intricacies. As someone who tends to dress fairly plainly during the day, I really appreciate the impact that a cool necklace or scarf can have on an outfit, and I hope you find that the following projects will allow you to feel a bit fancier in your everyday wear. (Oh, and don't worry about me. I can rock a ribbon scarf like nobody's business!)

BEADED FRINGE NECKLACE

My friend Shaye wears the most amazing jewelry you've ever laid eyes on. I made this necklace with her in mind. It's a showstopper, just like she is, and just like you will be when you wear it out and about.

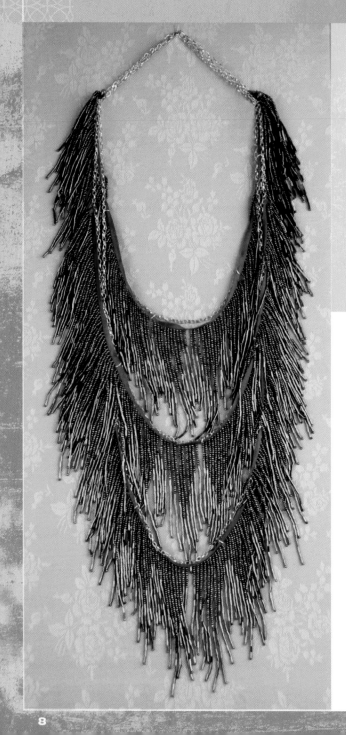

YOU'LL NEED

- 100 inches of gold or silver chain
- Wire cutter or needle-nose pliers with wire cutter
- 1 yard of beaded fringe on a ribbon
- Needle and thread that matches the ribbon on the fringe
- 14 jump rings
- Needle-nose pliers
- 1 lobster claw closure

HERE'S HOW

1. With wire cutters, cut 3 lengths of chain: 1 piece 25 inches, 1 piece 34 inches, and 1 piece 41 inches long.

2. Cut 3 lengths of beaded fringe, each 21 inches long.

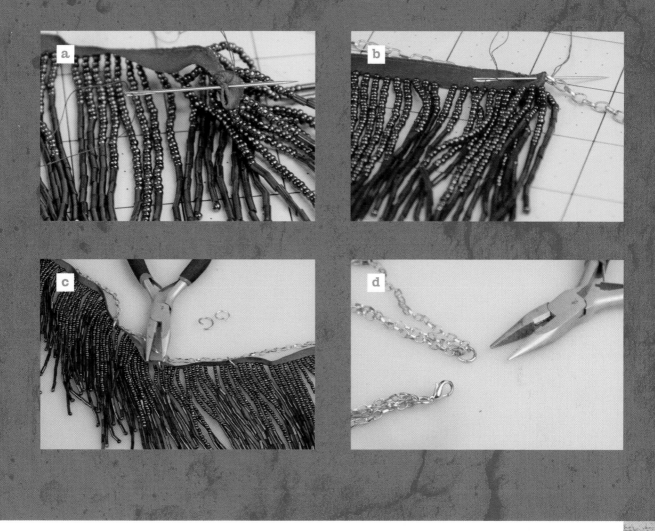

3. Fold the ends of each ribbon over $\frac{1}{4}$ inch and then $\frac{1}{4}$ inch again, and stitch the folds closed with needle and thread so that you have finished edges.

4. Center a length of beaded fringe on each chain, then sew the finished ends of the ribbons to the links of the chains at even intervals with needle and thread.

5. Evenly space 4 jump rings every 4 inches along each chain. Put each ring through a link of the chain and around the ribbon part of the beaded fringe, then close the rings up using your pliers. (This will hold the fringe in place and keep it from getting tangled.)

6. Arrange your chains in 3 rows, with the shortest on top and the longest on the bottom. Then link 1 end of all 3 chains together with a jump ring, and close the ring.

7. Put a jump ring through the lobster claw closure, then link the other ends of your chains together with the same jump ring and close it.

ZIPPER NECKPIECE

I wore this to a costume party once and by the time I left everyone wanted one. I think it's something Lady Gaga would go for, don't you? Or, if Queen Elizabeth I were alive, she might rock this, too. Either way, it's dramatic and I hope it sparks your creativity.

YOU'LL NEED

- 12 to 16 zippers, each 7 inches long (the number of zippers you'll need depends on the measurement around your neck)
- Sewing machine with zigzag stitch and black thread
- 3 inches of ¼-inch-wide black elastic
- 1 large button (should be about 1 inch in diameter)

HERE'S HOW

1. Lay 2 zippers side by side on your sewing machine, and attach them by sewing 3 inches of zigzag stitches along the center of the line where the sides meet.

2. Repeat until all of your zippers are stitched together.

3. Fold the elastic in half to form a loop. Pin it to one end of your neckpiece, right in the center along the edge, then stitch the ends of the loop to the back of the zipper.

4. Stitch the button on the outside of the other end of the neckpiece so it's positioned exactly opposite the elastic loop.

5. Wrap the piece around your neck and stretch the elastic over the button to close it.

6. Unzip each zipper as much as you want, and show off your dramatic neckpiece.

MELTED PLASTIC JEWELRY

I've been melting plastic for ages—even before I should have (my mother used to get mad at me for playing with the stove, and I deserved it). I can't help it—what's not to like? Put some plastic bottles over a flame, and suddenly fantastic shapes start to emerge!

YOU'LL NEED

FOR BOTH

- Heavy-duty scissors
- Needle-nose pliers
- Candle
- Soap and water
- Dry cloth
- Gold enamel paint
- Small paintbrush

FOR THE NECKLACE

- Gold chain with clasp
- 1 thick plastic bottle (such as a 64-ounce Ocean Spray bottle)
- 25 jump rings that will fit through your chain
- Additional pair of needle-nose pliers
- Drill with very small drill bit (a 1/16-inch drill bit should work)

FOR THE MATCHING BRACELET

- 1 thick plastic bottle (such as a 64-ounce Ocean Spray bottle)
- Minwax Polycrylic Protective Finish
- 1-inch paintbrush
- About 1/8 cup black faceted beads (bugle beads work, too)

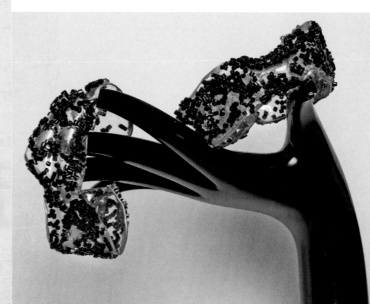

IMPORTANT

Make these projects outside!

HERE'S HOW
FOR THE NECKLACE

1. Cut out 25 ovals from your plastic bottle, varying in length from 1 to 3 inches.

2. Holding an oval with your needle-nose pliers, wave it over the candle to melt it into whatever shape you want. (See photos on page 14.)

3. Melt the rest of the ovals, wash them in soap and water to remove any soot, and dry completely.

4. Paint the edges of your ovals with gold paint and let dry.

5. Drill a hole in one end of each oval.

6. With pliers, add a jump ring to each oval, then connect the largest oval at the middle of your chain. Attach the rest of your ovals to the chain, using smaller ovals as you work each end toward the clasp.

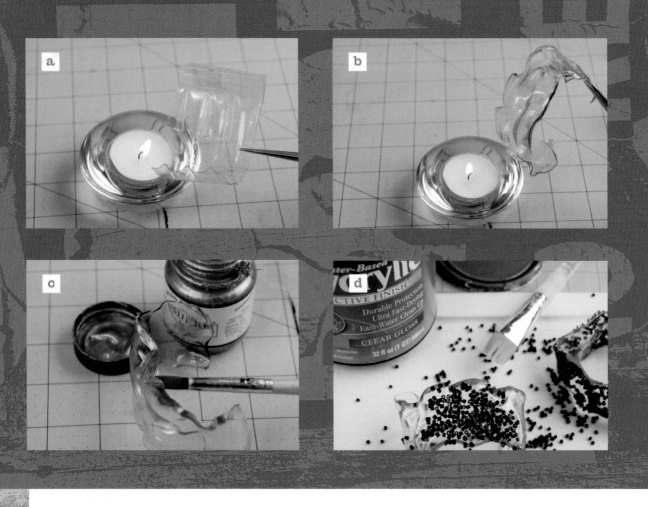

HERE'S HOW
FOR THE MATCHING BRACELET

1. Cut a ring of plastic from your bottle 1¹/₂- to 2-inches wide.

2. Cut an opening in the ring to form a cuff bracelet shape.

3. Holding the plastic ring over the candle flame with pliers, melt a little bit of the center section of the ring, observing how it reacts to the heat.

4. Continue melting and shaping the ring to form your bracelet.

5. Cut off any excess plastic at the cuff opening and melt the ends so they have a smooth edge and won't scratch you when you put on your bracelet later.

6. Clean the cuff with soap and water to remove any soot, then dry it completely.

7. Paint the edges with gold paint and let dry.

8. Coat the outside of your cuff with the clear coat, then dip it in a pile of loose beads, rolling it to get beads all over the cuff. Let the clear coat dry.

9. Apply several additional layers of clear coat, allowing each coat to dry before adding the next, until the beads seem very secure and there are no "bald" spots.

STRIPED RIBBON SCARF

A friend of mine came over the other day and said that a rainbow-colored ribbon scarf I'd just made looked like the decorations at his wife's circus-themed
baby shower. I responded by giving him a look that caused a tear to run down
his face. (I don't think he'll be commenting on my projects from now on!) I think
you'll love this project, whether you make it boldly colorful or subtle.

YOU'LL NEED
- Sewing machine with zigzag stitch
- 8 pieces of 1-inch satin ribbon, each 4 feet long
- Matching thread

HERE'S HOW

1. Lay 2 pieces of ribbon on your sewing machine side by side so they overlap a tiny bit. Starting about 8 inches from one end, zigzag stitch them together until you're about 8 inches from the other end, then stop stitching. (See photos on page 252.)

2. Continue adding ribbons, leaving 8 inches loose at either end to create a fringe, until you've used all of your ribbon.

3. Toss your new scarf in the washing machine to soften it up a bit before wearing.

...IDED BRAIDED YARN SCARF

No, I'm not drunk, I braided this scarf twice on purpose. (That said, there's nothing better than a glass of wine at the end of a tough day.)

YOU'LL NEED

- Skeins of yarn in several different colors
- Scissors
- Sewing machine
- Needle and thread
- 1 large button
- *Optional:* 1 bottle of cheap wine (no glass required)

HERE'S HOW

1 This scarf is made out of 9 braids, each made from 6 strands of yarn. To make a braid, cut 6 strands of yarn, each 40 inches long, bundle the strands together, and tie a knot 3 inches from one end. Then divide the yarn into 3 sections of 2 strands apiece and braid them together, knotting the braid at the end so it doesn't unravel. Repeat until you've made all 9 braids.

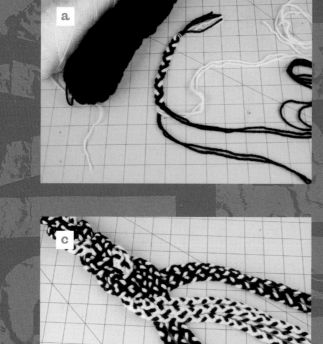

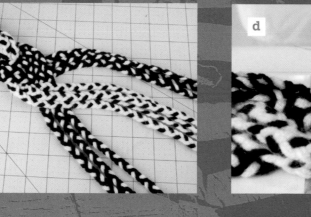

2 Line up your braids, gather them tightly together, and then sew across the braids about 8 inches from one end, using a sewing machine or needle and thread.

3 Starting at the stitch line, braid your individual braids together, using three braids per section. Finish braiding about 8 inches from the end. You should now have about 8 inches of loose braids at each end of your scarf, with a fat braid in the middle.

4 Gather the loose ends of your big braid together and stitch, with a sewing machine or by hand, across the bottom of the big braid.

5 Wrap the scarf around your neck to figure out where the button you'll use to close it will go. Using needle and thread, stitch the button on through several layers of yarn so that it's very secure.

6 Put your scarf on, slip the button through the braid, and enjoy your handiwork!

COUTURE RESIN JEWELRY

Have you ever seen footage of the huge Paris fashion shows? The dresses are works of art, but I love the jewelry even more. I am always inspired by the creativity I see on the runways, and these pieces reflect those inspirations.

YOU'LL NEED

FOR BOTH

- Plastic bottles with flat sides (Ocean Spray bottles work well)
- Scissors
- Newspaper
- 5 lids or caps from plastic juice containers or water bottles
- Mylar confetti or glitter
- Plastic jewels
- Resin
- Drill with small drill bit (a 1/16-inch drill bit will work)
- Pliers
- *Optional:* E-6000 glue

FOR THE SMALLER PIECE

- 80 inches of silver chain (plus more for added zing, if desired—see page 21)
- 7 jump rings (plus extra for added zing—see page 21)
- 1 lobster claw closure

FOR THE LARGER PIECE

- 100 inches of silver chain
- 2 pieces of 1/4-inch ribbon, each 18 inches long
- 2 pieces of 1/2-inch ribbon, each 18 inches long
- 1 lobster claw closure
- 1 large jump ring
- *Optional:* A piece of aluminum flashing and E-6000 glue

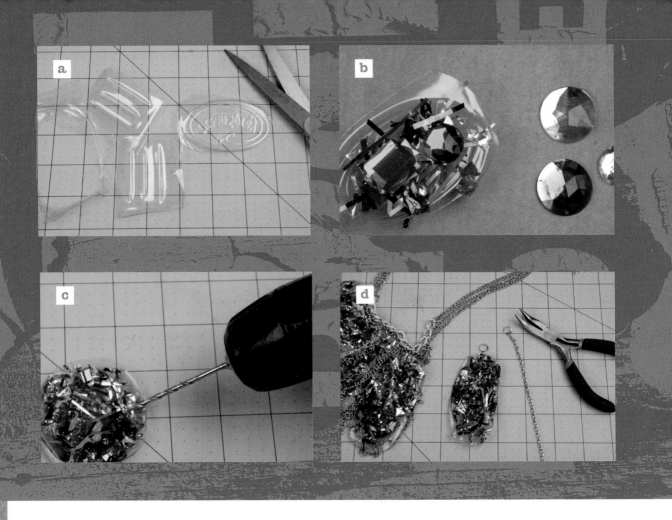

HERE'S HOW
FOR THE SMALLER PIECE

1. Cut 5 egg shapes that are each 3 to 4 inches long out of the flat parts of a plastic bottle.

2. Go outdoors for the next steps, and bring lots of newspaper to protect your work surface.

3. Lay each of your plastic eggs on top of a lid to elevate them, so when you pour the resin, it will drip off the eggs and won't stick to the newspaper.

4. Sprinkle some mylar confetti or glitter onto your egg shapes, and add some jewels for good measure.

5. Mix the resin by following the instructions on the package. Pour it over your pieces and let it set.

6. When the resin is hard, drill a small hole through 1 end of each egg, then thread a jump ring through each hole.

7. Cut 5 pieces of chain, each 16 inches long. Connect the ends of the chains with a jump ring (one ring per side), and add a lobster claw closure to 1 of the jump rings.

8. Connect the resin pieces to your chain choker with the jump rings on your resin pieces.

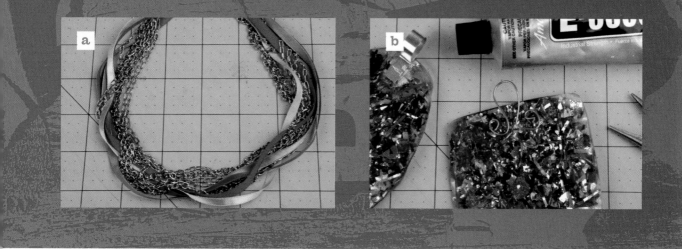

For even more zing, use some jump rings to add a few extra lengths of chain between your resin pieces.

Instead of using a jump ring to connect your resin piece to the chain necklace, try hanging it from a metal loop by cutting a 3-inch long strip of $1/4$-inch-wide metal, then fold it in half to make a loop and glue it to the back of your resin piece with E-6000. Just remember to thread your chains through the loop before you complete step 3.

HERE'S HOW
FOR THE LARGER PIECE

1 Cut 1 large egg shape out of a plastic bottle.

2 Follow the instructions from the previous page for the resin eggs and let set.

3 Cut 5 pieces of chain, each 20 inches long. Twist the 4 18-inch-long pieces of ribbon around the pieces of chain as shown in the photo, then tie the ribbon ends to the ends of the chains.

4 Connect the ends of the chain by adding jump rings and a closure, as described previously in step 7.

5 Drill a hole in 1 end of your large resin piece and insert a large jump ring. Add the resin piece to the center of the chain necklace, and close the jump ring.

DRAMATIC CHAIN SCARF

Add a little flair to your next outfit with this chain-adorned scarf. Pick a fabric that you really like and that matches your personality, then tap into your inner drama queen and start adding some chain bling!

YOU'LL NEED

- ¼ yard of fabric
- Scissors
- Sewing machine
- Needle and thread
- 2 yards of silver chain
- 2 yards of gold chain
- Needle-nose pliers with wire cutter
- Jump rings

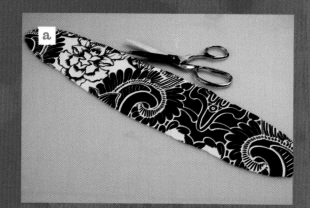

HERE'S HOW

1 Cut 2 identical pieces of fabric, each 22 inches long and 3 inches wide. Taper the ends so the pieces look like skinny ovals, as in the photo.

2 Sew the pieces together with right sides facing, using a ¼-inch seam allowance, and leaving a 2-inch opening in 1 side.

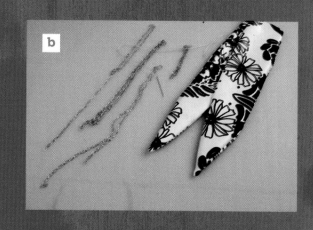

3 Turn the fabric right side out through the opening, then stitch the hole closed, either on the sewing machine or with needle and thread.

4 With wire cutters, cut your chain into various lengths (mine varied from 3 to 8 inches).

5 Attach a jump ring to a link near the middle of each chain with pliers, then affix the chains to the ends of your scarf by sewing the jump rings to the fabric with needle and thread.

NAUGHTY KNOTTY NECKLACE

Sometimes I want to make something with the items I already have in my craft kit. I'm just not always up for running out for supplies or spending all afternoon trying to find the perfect little something to make a project sing. I made this necklace with a little bit of leftover fabric and chain and was thrilled with the results of my no-hassle crafting.

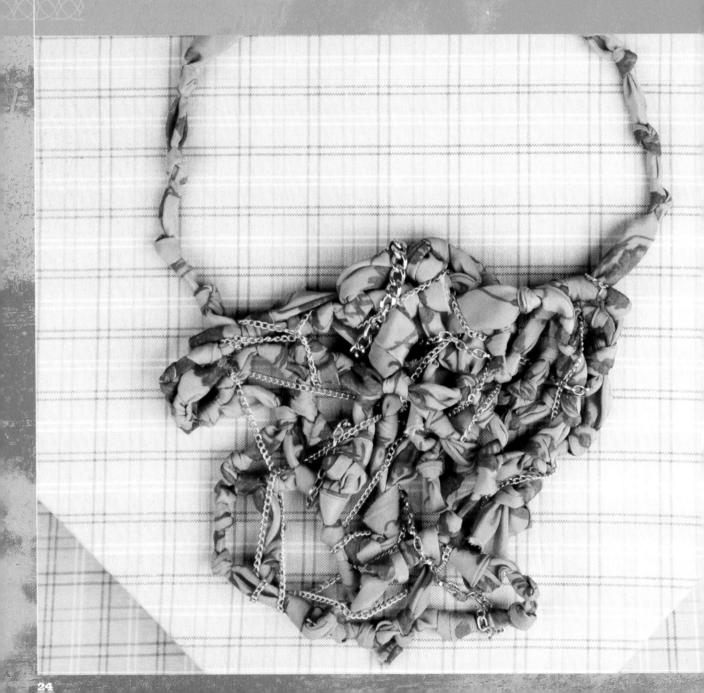

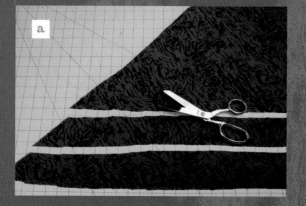

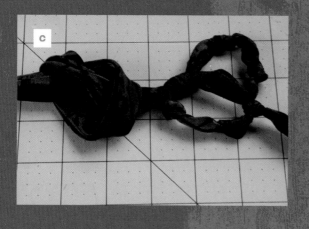

YOU'LL NEED

- ¼ yard of thin fabric
- Scissors
- Jump rings
- Needle-nose pliers
- Sewing machine
- 2 feet of chain or an old chain necklace
- Tube turner or wire hanger

HINT

You can make a tube turner by cutting a wire hanger and bending it into a straight line with a hook at one end and a circle at the other.

HERE'S HOW

1. Cut 5 strips of fabric on the bias, each 2 inches wide.

2. Sew your strips into long, skinny tubes by folding right sides together and using a ½-inch seam allowance.

3. Pull your tubes right side out using a tube turner.

4. Tie a few knots in a section of 1 of your tubes, then tie the section of knots in a big loop to form a circle of knots.

5. Create a total mess of knots with the tube, then take 1 end of your tube and tie it to a circle.

6. When you finish knotting 1 tube, tie another on the end and cut off the excess fabric from the ends, leaving little fabric stubs. Keep knotting and tying until you have formed a cool knotted centerpiece for your necklace out of 3 tubes.

7. Attach a tube to each end of your knotted centerpiece to tie around your neck.

8. Using your pliers, attach a jump ring to the end of your chain, then attach the ring to the knotted centerpiece.

9. Weave the chain in and out and around the centerpiece until you're satisfied.

10. Attach another jump ring to the other end of the chain and secure it to the centerpiece.

PRETTY PRINGLES NECKLACE

I was eating Pringles the other day while staring at my sewing machine, hoping that inspiration would hit me. Suddenly, like magic, an idea popped into my head: I should sew some fabric potato chips! Yes, folks, this is how these projects happen. Here's my munchie-induced homage to Pringles and leftover fabric scraps.

YOU'LL NEED

- Fabric scraps
  (I think this project looks best when you use a variety of patterns and colors)
- Scissors
- Sewing machine
- Contrasting thread
- Jump rings in different sizes
- Several feet of jewelry chain
- Needle-nose pliers
- *Optional:* Large, heavy bead and flathead pin

HERE'S HOW

1. Cut out 18 fabric chips as follows: 6 of 3" × 2", 6 of 4" × 2½", and 8 of 1" × 1½".

2. Using your sewing machine on zigzag, create your pretty Pringles pieces by stitching three layers of various-size chips together, going around

and around the edge and spiraling into the middle. Be sloppy—it looks really great when you let your stitches run wild.

3 Using sharp scissors, poke a hole in each end of your chips and wriggle a jump ring through each end of each chip, but don't close the jump rings yet!

4 Attach a few lengths of chain between your jump rings (I used 6 lengths of 5-inch chain), and close the jump rings with your needle-nose pliers.

OPTIONAL

Insert a flathead pin through a large bead (the flat end of the pin should be bigger than the hole, and the pin needs to be longer than the bead). Make a loop at the pointy end of the pin, then hang your bead on a small length of chain and attach it to your necklace using a jump ring. This will give your necklace some weight.

BEDAZZLED, BEDECKED, BEJEWELED

In New York I lived near a wonderful lady who also happened to have a beard. Not just a little fuzz, but a full-on, Abraham Lincoln, B-E-A-R-D! In addition to her amazing facial hair, she wore some fantastic jewelry, and I thanked the heavens every day for that. Why, you might ask? Well, let's face it. Accessories have the magical ability to take the focus off something that makes you want to squint ... like an unfortunate hairpiece, a too-tight pair of pants, or even a lady's beard. They also give you something to comment on when you're at a loss for words. For example, "Oh my, look at how pretty your earrings are!" or, in response to a child who hasn't quite blossomed yet, "Darling, your daughter's headband is just beautiful!" It's a bait-and-switch, and it gets the job done.

Even if you don't need to create a distraction or something to ease your eyes, accessories are just superfun to wear. So get some crafty ideas from the next few pages and then go forth and accessorize, my friends!

MUFFY ALEXIS HEADBAND

This headband was inspired by, and made for, my good friend Muffy. Okay, her real name is Alexis, but she's obsessed with headbands, so I call her Muffy. Don't worry, she's used to it now. Anyway, she needed something fancy to match a particular sweater set she was wearing to a party, so I whipped this up and enjoyed every minute of crafting it. (BTW, she loves it, too.)

YOU'LL NEED

- 1 yard of 1-inch satin ribbon
- Scissors
- Sewing machine or needle and thread
- ¼ yard of netting
- Straight pins
- Small rhinestones in different sizes
- E-6000 glue
- Toothpicks
- A couple of feathers
- Hot glue gun and glue sticks
- Plain headband

HERE'S HOW

1 Cut 4 pieces of ribbon, each 7 inches long.

2 Join the 2 ends of 1 of your ribbon pieces, and with the ends slightly overlapping, stitch a line through the ribbon loop where the ends overlap, so your ribbon is now

sewn into 2 equal loops. Repeat for the remaining 3 pieces of ribbon.

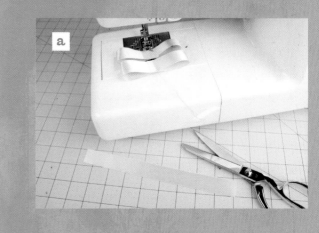

3 Crisscross the 4 ribbon loops so they form a bow, and stitch them together in the center.

4 Cut out 2 circles of netting, each about 6 inches in diameter.

5 Fold a ⅜-inch pleat in the center of each circle of netting, pin the pleats, and stitch them in place.

6 Stitch the netting poofs on top of the ribbon bow.

7 Cut out a 2½-inch-diameter circle from the netting. Using a toothpick and E-6000, carefully arrange your rhinestones on the netting circle. You can form a heart, fleur-de-lis, a starburst (like I made), or even your initials. Let the glue dry.

8 Glue your embellished circle on top of the netting poof with E-6000 and let the glue set.

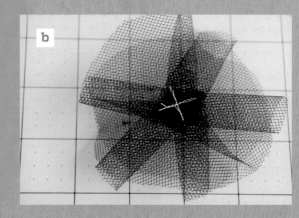

9 Affix a couple of feathers to the bow with E-6000.

10 Hot-glue your creation onto a headband, let the glue dry, then put on that cute sweater set.

DON'T WORRY

> Your fancy bow will cover up the glued ends of the feathers.

NECKTIE OBE BELT

What could be more glamorous than a woman wearing two men's neckties around her waist? Nothing!

YOU'LL NEED

- 2 men's neckties
- Straight pins
- Pencil
- ¼ yard of stiff fabric
- Scissors (I find my Gingher scissors work very well on heavy-duty fabrics)
- Sewing machine
- Contrasting thread

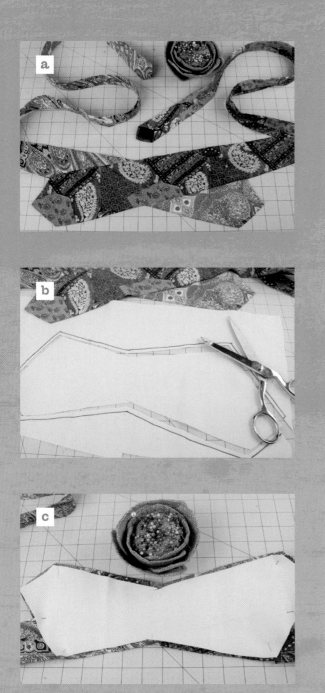

HERE'S HOW

1. Crisscross the fat ends of the neckties, as shown in the photo, and pin them together. This will be the center of your belt.

2. Trace the center of the belt on a stiff piece of fabric and cut out the fabric shape, but shave about $\frac{1}{4}$ inch off each side.

3. Pin the fabric on the back of the neckties.

4. Lay the center of your belt fabric side down on your sewing machine, and stitch around the outer edges of your crisscrossed ties.

5. Keep stitching in a spiral, working your way toward the center of the neckties and leaving about $\frac{1}{4}$ inch between the rows of stitches.

6. To get the look seen in the photo, position the center of your belt at the front, cross the loose ends behind your back, and then tie the loose ends in a funky bow in front.

PAPER DAISY EARRINGS

I could make these earrings all day long. Not only are they super-simple to put together, they cost only pennies to make and there are so many different things you can do with this technique—spray-paint them in different colors, make them in different sizes, change the shape . . . the possibilities are endless.

YOU'LL NEED

- Pages from an old magazine
- Scissors
- Elmer's glue
- Needle-nose pliers
- Minwax Polycrylic Protective Finish
- 2 large jewelry jump rings
- Earring wires
- *Optional:* Pencil

HERE'S HOW

1. Cut some magazine pages into 5 strips, each 6 inches wide and 12 inches long.

2. Roll the strips into 6-inch-long straws and glue down the loose end with a thin line of Elmer's glue.

3. When the glue is dry, cut the straws into tubes $3/8$ inch to $1/4$-inch-long, making sure to have one $1/4$-inch-long tube per earring. (The ends are going to be pinched, but don't worry, that's what you want.) These will be your petals.

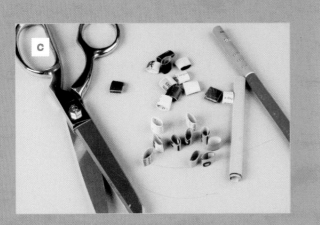

4. To make the spirals, cut 2 strips from a magazine page, 1½ inches wide and 11 inches long. Roll them into long, skinny tubes, and glue the ends with a tiny dot of Elmer's so they stay in place. Then grab the end of the tube with the tip of your needle-nose pliers and twist the tube around it to create a spiral. Dab a dot of Elmer's on the end of your tube to keep the spiral intact.

5. Glue the petals to the outside of your spirals, making sure to include at least one ¼-inch-long petal on each spiral.

6. Cover your flowers with clear coat to make them sturdy.

7. Loop a jump ring through a ¼-inch-long petal on each flower, add an earring hook, and feel the flower power.

HINT

I find that rolling the strips around a pencil makes the process easier and yields uniform straws.

COMB AND BUTTON BROOCHES

In the tradition of many great artists, I use things generally found in the bathroom to make jewelry. Oh, you think I'm kidding? Alexander Calder and Anni Albers both used hairpins in their work. So there!

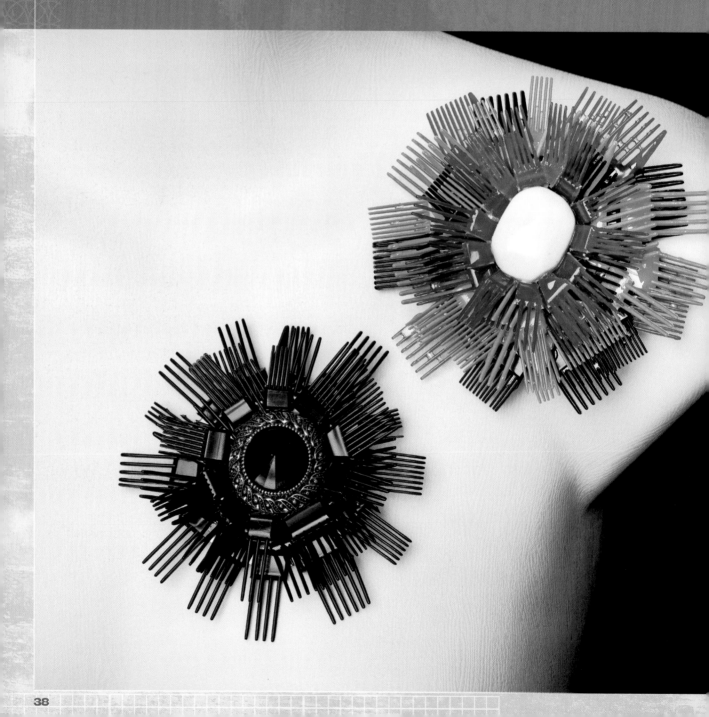

YOU'LL NEED

- A piece of tin flashing
- Tin shears or heavy-duty scissors
- Dremel tool
- E-6000 glue
- Large button
- Wire cutters
- About 3 pocket-size hair combs
- Jewelry pin back

HERE'S HOW

1 Using your heavy-duty scissors or tin shears, cut out a tin disk 2 inches in diameter from your flashing.

2 With the Dremel, sand off the shank on the back of the button so it lies flat on your tin circle. (The shank is the loop that you sew thread through to attach a button to fabric.)

3 Glue the button in the center of the tin disk with E-6000.

4 Using wire cutters, cut combs into $\frac{1}{2}$-inch-long pieces.

5 Using a good amount of E-6000, glue a ring of combs all around the edge of the disk.

6 Glue another ring of comb pieces just inside the first ring.

7 Glue a final ring of comb pieces right at the edge of the button. If you notice any holes between the rings, add more comb pieces.

8 Once you're satisfied with the placement and the glue is completely dry, turn the disk over and glue on the pin back.

ZIP TIE EARRINGS

As I was making these, I thought they were the perfect project for kids at summer camp. They're easy to make and bursting with color, and I think the kids would be up all night trying to become the next big jewelry designer. That doesn't mean they're not great for grown-ups, too. I think a funky black-and-white pair or a chic all-black set would look terrific on the right woman.

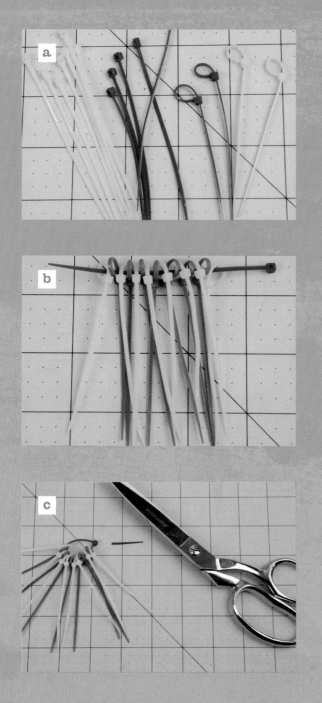

- 34 (3½-inch) zip ties
- Scissors
- 2 jump rings
- Set of earring wires

HERE'S HOW

1. Bend 30 zip ties into tiny loops by pulling the tails of the ties nearly all the way through the heads.

2. String 15 loops on another zip tie, alternating the directions of the loops, as shown in the photo.

3. Close up the zip tie that's holding the 15 ties, making the loop about ¾-inch long, then cut off the end.

4. Thread a zip tie through the big loop, bend it into a ½-inch loop, and cut off the end.

5. Add a jump ring and earring wire to the loop you just added. Repeat steps 1 through 5 to make your second earring.

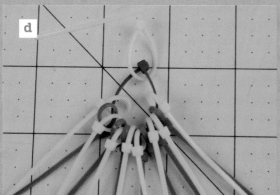

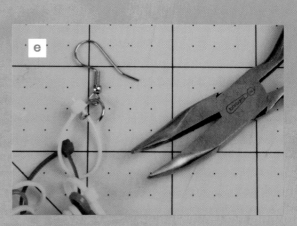

HOTTIE KNOTTY BELT

This belt is made completely of fabric and it's so easy to put together. In fact, if you're good with a needle and thread, you don't even really need a sewing machine to make it.

YOU'LL NEED

- ⅛ yard of 2 different knit fabrics
- Scissors
- Sewing machine or needle and thread

HERE'S HOW

1 Cut 2 rectangles from your fabric, each 8 inches wide and 54 inches long.

2 Place one piece of fabric on top of the other. On 1 side, make a 3-inch fold at the end.

3 Stitch down the fold to create a loop at the end of the fabric pieces.

4 Working your way from the loose ends of the fabric pieces up toward the sewn loop, cut the fabric into 1-inch strips.

5 Tie knots in each strip at random until you've reached the desired knotted effect.

6 Wrap the belt around your waist and slip the knotted strips through the loop to secure it.

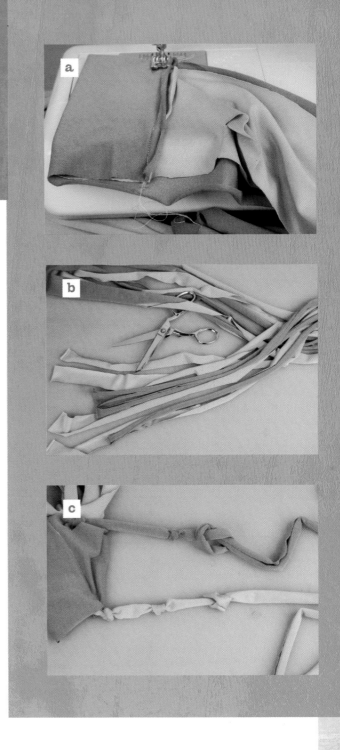

ZIPPER CORSET

This corset would look amazing over a simple dress or white cotton blouse. Plus, it feels even better than it looks! I put mine on the minute I finished making it.

YOU'LL NEED

- 26 (8-inch) zippers
  (this will fit a 26- to 34-inch waist)
- Sewing machine with black thread
- 1 yard of ¼-inch black ribbon
- Scissors
- Pins
- 2 yards of 1-inch black ribbon

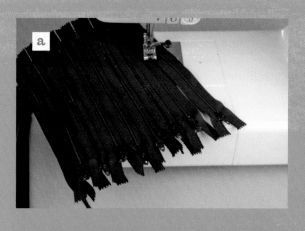

HERE'S HOW

1. Stitch 24 zippers together, side by side, overlapping them just a tiny bit. You can use a zigzag or a straight stitch.

2. Cut 10 pieces of ¼-inch ribbon, each 3 inches long.

3. Fold 1 ribbon piece in half and pin it 2 inches from the top on the outer edge of 1 of the end zippers, with the loop pointing toward the middle of the corset, as in the photo.

4. Pin 4 more loops on, spacing them about an inch apart.

5. Repeat steps 3 and 4 on the other end zipper.

6. Stitch the remaining 2 zippers to those you just pinned your ribbons to, sandwiching the ends of the ribbon between layers of zippers. Make sure to backtack over the ribbon ends so they can withstand lacing.

7. Take your 2-yard-long piece of 1-inch ribbon and lace up the loops as you would a shoe (or an awesome corset).

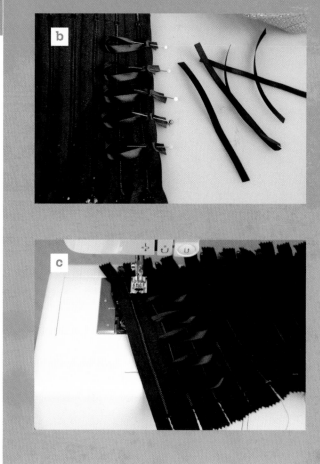

HINT

The trick to putting on a corset is to lace it up in front first, and then twist it around so the laces are in the back before finally tightening it around your waist.

COME OUTSIDE!

Living in big cities sometimes means that you have to share your outdoor space with thousands of people, and for me that can be frustrating. Whenever I visit my family in Colorado I'm always jealous of how big their yards are. I believe there's nothing better than being outside, and so in this section I've offered up a few projects that'll help you maximize your time outdoors. Whether you have an expansive lawn all to yourself or share a public park with a few million neighbors, I hope you'll find something that suits you in the following pages.

"CHECK OUT THAT KITE!" KITE

Have you ever considered how useful a kite can be? Think about it: Say you want to advertise your school car wash. Do it on a kite! Or how about taking your mom on a picnic for Mother's Day and flying kites with photos of your brothers and sisters on them. She would love that! Try this basic kite project and watch how much attention you'll get from your flying creation.

YOU'LL NEED

- X-ACTO knife
- 34-inch dowel for the spine
- 22-inch dowel for the spar
- Thin twine or kite string
- Scissors
- An image you like—photocopy or original art—24 inches by 36 inches
- Pencil
- Elmer's glue
- Clear packing tape
- 6 yards of 1-inch satin or grosgrain ribbon

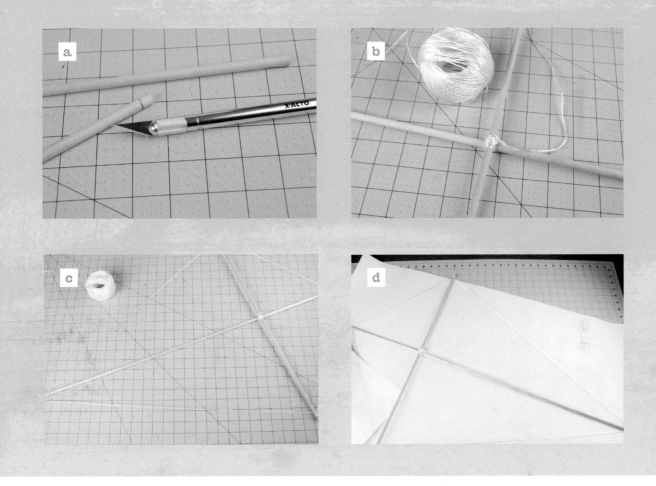

HERE'S HOW

1 With your knife, make a groove ⅜ inch from both ends of each dowel. These will help keep your string in place later.

2 Make a cross with your dowels, placing your spar dowel 9 inches down from the top of the spine dowel. Tie the dowels together with string where they cross.

3 Create your kite skeleton: tie string on one end of one dowel and then connect the ends of each of the dowels with the string. Loop the string around the dowels and in the grooves you cut as you go around. When you reach the first dowel again, cut your string and tie a knot.

4 Lay your image facedown on your workspace, and place your kite skeleton on top of the paper.

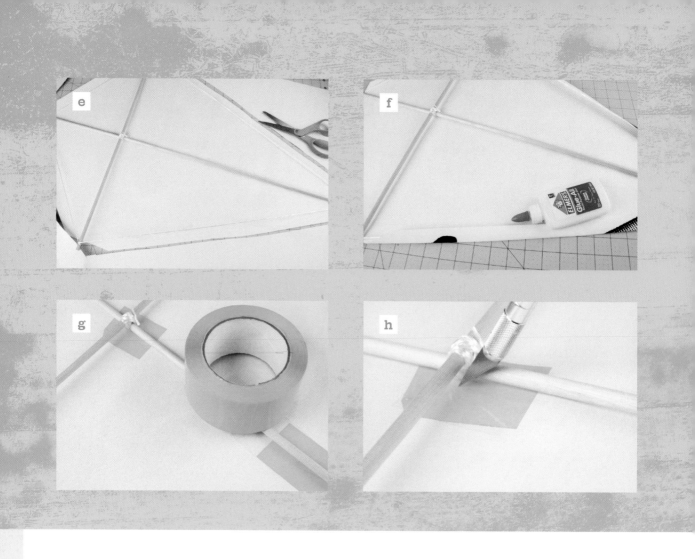

5. Trace your skeleton onto the back of the image, then measure a ½-inch border outside it. Cut out the shape along the borders.

6. Draw a dot on your paper under each groove in the dowels, then cut off the points of your paper diamond where the grooves in the dowel and the paper meet.

7. Fold the paper over the string of your kite skeleton, glue it down, and let dry.

8. Place a piece of clear packing tape on the back of the kite right under where the spine and spar cross. (I used yellow tape to demonstrate where to place it, but you should use clear.)

9. Place another piece of clear tape on the back of the kite just behind the spine, 11 inches down from the top.

10. Using an X-ACTO knife, cut a small hole in both pieces of tape.

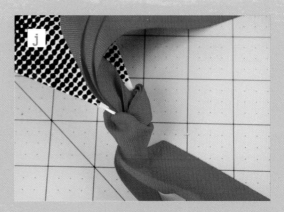

11 Cut a 24-inch piece of string. Push the ends through the holes you just cut through the front of the kite. Tie each end to the spine so it can't move. You've just created your kite's bridle.

12 Cut the ribbon in half, and tie both pieces to the bottom of the spine to form your kite's tail.

13 Tie the end of the kite string around the bridle in a loose loop so it can slide up and down.

14 Head outside and wait for some wind.

NATURE SILHOUETTE

I was recently at the Metropolitan Museum of Art in New York City, and in one of the large halls I noticed a hand-cut silhouette dating from the 1800s. It was of a berry twig, matted on Confederate blue paper, and it was just perfect. Modern technology has given us a distinct advantage over our silhouette-making ancestors in the form of a copy machine: just cut a few sprigs of leaves during your morning walk and you're halfway done!

YOU'LL NEED

- Sprigs of plants, trees, or flowers from your garden
- Copy machine
- Scissors
- X-ACTO knife
- Dark paper (to mat your project)
- Simple frame
- Elmer's glue stick

HERE'S HOW

1 Cut a sprig from a tree, flower, bush, or shrub, bearing in mind you'll want to use something that can be easily flattened in the copy machine.

2 Place your sprig on a copy machine and make a black-and-white copy of it.

3 Carefully cut out the copied image with scissors and an X-ACTO knife, making sure to get as much detail as you possibly can.

4 Cut the dark background paper to fit your frame.

5 Dab the printed side of the silhouette (the black side) with your glue stick, and lay it in place on your dark background.

6 Frame the silhouette and put it somewhere that needs a touch of nature.

CONCRETE PLANTERS

Lately I've been seeing lots of natural concrete everywhere. I like the look of it, so I decided to make some concrete bowls to use as planters. The process ended up being much easier than I anticipated, and I think the results are really chic. In fact, I'm going much bigger next time, now that I feel I've mastered this technique. This makes four small pots.

YOU'LL NEED

- 1 (25-pound) container of mortar (see which brand has the least sand, and get that one)
- Large mixing bowl
- 4 bowls, different sizes, for the molds
- 4 bowls that fit inside the others
- Drill with masonry drill bit about the diameter of a pencil
- Heavy-duty sandpaper or sanding block

HERE'S HOW

1 Make about 3 cups of mortar in a big bowl. Use cold water and follow the directions on the box.

2 As soon as your mix is ready, quickly pour some into the 4 outside bowls until they're about halfway full, and then push down 4 bowls designated to go inside.

HINT

> You might have to put some weights inside the inner bowls to keep them from floating up.

3 Wait about 15 to 20 minutes for the cement to start to set, then remove the molds. Your new concrete pots should feel very warm (but not hot).

4 Turn the pots over, and drill a hole in the base of each one to allow for drainage.

5 Sand off any rough edges before the pots get too hard.

6 Let the pots dry for a few more hours, and your new planters are ready to go!

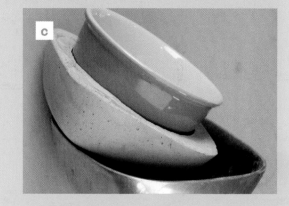

UMBRELLA CABANA

You know how when you're sitting outside on a beautiful day, at some point you realize that the sun is pounding down on you, even though you're under an umbrella? Well, no more! This cabana will keep you covered all day long.

YOU'LL NEED

- Outdoor umbrella stand with an old umbrella cover that needs replacing
- Scissors
- Pencil and craft paper (to make your pattern)
- Straight pins
- 9 yards of heavy-duty or outdoor fabric (3 yards for the umbrella, plus 6 yards for the side panels)
- Sewing machine
- ¼ yard of suedecloth or other heavy-duty fabric that will not fray
- Measuring tape

HERE'S HOW

1 Remove the old fabric from the umbrella, keeping at least 1 triangle piece fully intact for your pattern.

2 To make the pattern, trace 1 triangle, and then add a ½-inch border all the way around the outside (the extra

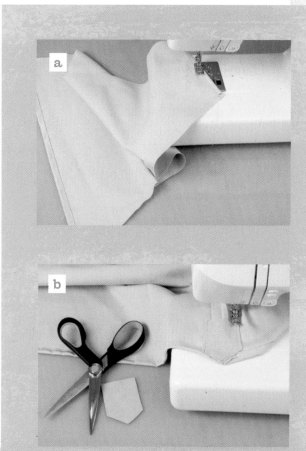

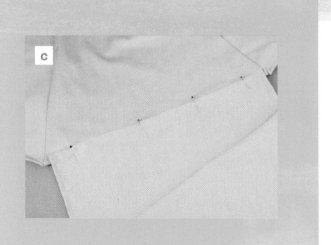

c

¹/₂ inch is for your seam allowance). If your umbrella had a circle at the top, make a pattern for that, too, and also add a ¹/₂-inch seam allowance all the way around it.

3 Pin your patterns on your fabric, and trace and cut out the shapes.

4 Stitch a ¹/₂-inch hem along the top (narrowest end) and bottom of your triangles: fold the ends over ¹/₄ inch and then ¹/₄ inch again and stitch across. Now hem your circle, if you have one, and cut a small hole in the center if your umbrella has a finial.

5 Pin the triangle pieces together side by side. Sew them together with a ¹/₂-inch seam allowance.

6 Cut your suedecloth into 6 pocket shapes, each 2¹/₂ by 3 inches, as shown in photo b on page 57. Sew the pockets on each corner of your umbrella where the triangles meet, leaving the ends that face the center of the umbrella open. The pockets will hold the tips of the umbrella's ribs. (Those are the spokes that extend from the top of the pole to stretch out your umbrella.)

7 Measure the distance from the tip of 1 rib of your umbrella to the ground. Now add 10 inches to that number and call it A.

8 Measure the distance from the end of one rib to the rib next to it. Add 2 inches to that number and call it B.

9 Cut 4 panels of heavy fabric that are the width of B and the length of A. (My panels were 40 inches by 70 inches.)

10 Stitch a ¹/₂-inch hem all the way around each panel.

11 Pin a short end of 1 panel to the end of 1 of the umbrella triangles, then sew it on. Repeat for the 3 remaining panels.

12 With the help of a friend, center the top and stretch your umbrella over the ribs, tucking the ends of the ribs into the pockets. Attach the finial if you have one, and enjoy the sunny day.

PEGASUS WEATHERVANE

I have a clear view of my neighbor's roof, and though it's fairly good-looking, I thought it could be just a little bit more attractive, so I made her this weathervane for Christmas. It looks terrific through my kitchen window!

YOU'LL NEED

- 2 feet of aluminum flashing at least 12 inches wide
- Permanent marker
- Tin shears or heavy-duty scissors
- 24 feet of ⅜-inch dowel
- Awl
- 1 foot medium-gauge wire
- Needle-nose pliers with wire cutter
- Drill with ⅜-inch bit
- 1 yard of 1½-inch dowel
- E-6000 glue
- Two L brackets approximately 10 inches long
- 2 clothespins
- 2 (½-inch-long) wood screws
- Piece of scrap wood
- Gold, brown, and black Krylon spray paint
- Spray bottle
- Two U clamps with screws for 1½-inch dowel or pipe

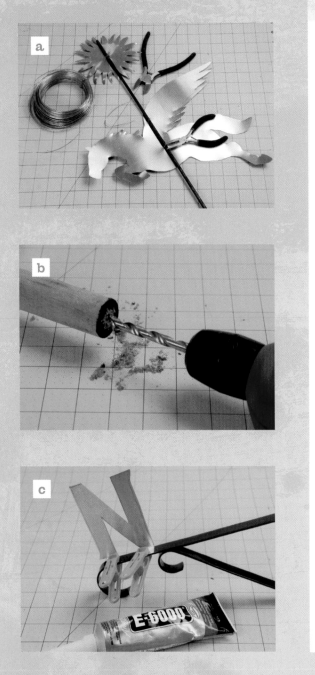

HERE'S HOW

1. Enlarge and trace the patterns provided on page 375 onto the aluminum flashing, then cut the shapes out using your tin shears or heavy-duty scissors.

2. Place the ³⁄₈-inch dowel across the center of the sun and Pegasus, as in the photo, and with your marker, place dots where you will need to poke holes for the wire that will hold the shapes in place.

3. Use the awl to poke holes in the sun and Pegasus.

4. Cut the wire into 3-inch-long pieces and place the dowel on the sun and Pegasus. Using needle-nose pliers, thread the wires through the holes and twist them around the dowel to keep the aluminum pieces in place.

5. Drill a hole with the ³⁄₈-inch bit in one end of the 1½-inch dowel. Drill as far as you can go, and also wiggle the drill so

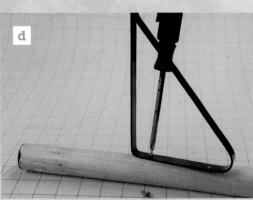

that the hole is just a bit bigger than the drill bit. (This will be where you insert the dowel that's attached to Pegasus.)

6. Bend the bottom ends of the N and S, and glue them on the ends of the L brackets with E-6000. Use clothespins to hold them in place while the glue dries.

7. Screw the L brackets to the large dowel about 5 inches from the top (where you drilled your hole).

8. Insert the dowel with the Pegasus into the hole. Now spray-paint the entire weathervane gold.

9. When the gold paint is dry, spray the weathervane with water, then immediately spray it with brown paint. Spray it again with water, and immediately after, spray it with black paint. Add more gold and brown paint until you're satisfied. This gives it an antique look.

10. Secure the weathervane to your roof or a fencepost or with two U clamps.

FANCY FISHBOWL LANTERN

This project might be a little messy, but don't let that stop you from tackling it. It's a piece of cake, and when you're done, the lanterns look like jewelry for your yard—which is totally worth the cleanup.

YOU'LL NEED

- 280 flat glass chips (this will cover an 8-inch-tall fishbowl)
- Hot glue gun and glue sticks
- Glass fishbowl, 8 inches tall
- Grout
- Plastic container in which to mix grout
- Rubber gloves
- Several sponges

HERE'S HOW

1. Hot-glue glass pieces all over the outside of the fishbowl, forming whatever pattern you choose.

2. Mix up a batch of grout to the consistency of toothpaste. Make about 1 cup, and if you need more you can always make some later.

3. Put on your rubber gloves, scoop out some grout, and start filling in the spaces between the chips, making sure to smooth it out with your fingers while you work. Get it in between every glass marble!

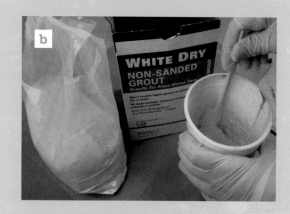

4. Once all the gaps are filled, go over the lantern with a slightly damp sponge to wipe away excess grout and smooth out the spaces between the glass pieces.

5. Rinse out the sponge and repeat step 4 until the gaps are very smooth. (You may need to use a few sponges to get all of the grout smoothed out.)

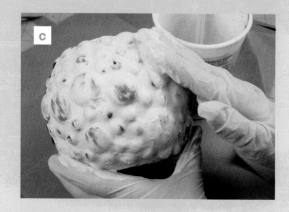

TIP

> Once it's dry, if you realize you missed a spot, just add more grout. Also, don't worry if there is still a film of grout covering your marbles. It will wipe off easily when it's dry.

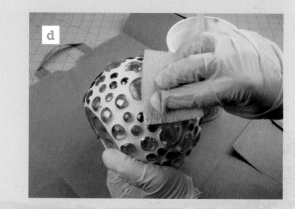

6. When the grout is dry (it should take about 8 hours to set), wipe off the glass chips with a damp sponge.

7. Put a tealight in your lantern and take it outside.

CUTTING BOARD AND TWIG ADDRESS PLAQUE

I really like big wooden cutting boards. They make terrific canvases for all of my crafty mayhem and you can find them anywhere, from thrift stores to dollar stores. As for twigs, well, they're twigs. If you can't find a twig, put down this book and walk away slowly.

YOU'LL NEED

- Wooden cutting board
- High-gloss latex paint in 2 or 3 colors (I chose Benjamin Moore's Monmouth Green, Coral Essence, and Suede Brown)
- Pencil
- Paper
- Twigs
- Heavy-duty scissors
- E-6000 glue
- Painter's tape
- Paintbrushes
- Minwax Polycrylic Protective Finish

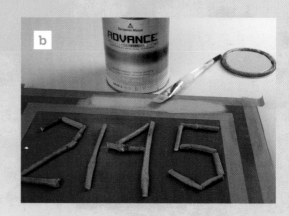

HERE'S HOW

1 Paint your cutting board all over with whatever you choose as your base color.

2 While the paint dries, draw the numbers of your street address on a sheet of paper. This will serve as your template, so make sure your numbers are the size you want them to be on the cutting board.

3 Lay your twigs on top of the numbers. If necessary, cut them to fit using scissors.

4 Transfer the twigs to the board, securely gluing them in place one by one with E-6000.

5 Tape off a border, apply paint, and let it dry. Repeat until you're satisfied.

6 Clear-coat the entire plaque to protect it from the elements, then let dry.

7 Proudly hang your plaque by your front gate and listen to the neighbors ooh and aah!

SIMPLE, SUBTLE HURRICANES

I like to entertain outside. I also like candlelight, so of course I had to make a couple of special hurricane lamps for my back porch. Usually I'm a flashy kind of guy, so it took me a while to get used to how simple and subtle these are, but I love the light they give off and how they make my evening gatherings a little bit classier.

YOU'LL NEED

- Mortar mix (small bag) or Quickrete concrete mix
- Container in which to mix mortar
- Bowl that has an interesting shape to use as your mold (the base of a 2-piece plastic planter would work, too)
- Heavy-duty sandpaper sanding block
- E-6000 glue
- Glass vase

HERE'S HOW

1. Mix enough mortar to fill the mold that you've chosen, following the instructions on the package. (I recommend wearing rubber gloves while you do this.)

2. Fill your mold with mortar and let it set.

3. Remove the hardened shape and sand off any rough edges. You now have the base of your lamp.

4. Apply a generous amount of E-6000 to the top of your lamp base and adhere the glass vase on top.

5. Let the glue dry, then place a candle inside the vase. Voilà!

CRAFTS-MAN

While writing this book and creating things like glitter nail polish and tote bags, I realized there was a need for some "man crafts." You know, stuff that a guy could make and then puff out his chest in pride while biting the cap off of a beer bottle. At least, that's what I did when I finished a few of these projects. (By the way, biting the lid off of a beer bottle is not good for your teeth. I learned that the hard way.) Of course, women can rock these crafts, too, so no one should consider skipping this chapter. Now put that six-pack in the fridge to chill so you can toast yourself after a long day of crafting!

"GOD SAVE THE QUEEN!" BRIEFCASE

I've been finding hard plastic briefcases everywhere lately, particularly at thrift stores and yard sales, and often they don't cost more than a couple of bucks. I bought a few in hopes that one day I'd turn them into a distinctive crafty project, and here you go.

YOU'LL NEED

- 1 hard plastic briefcase
- Damp cloth and dry towel
- Fine sandpaper
- Newspaper
- Masking tape
- White Krylon Fusion for Plastic spray paint
- Image of Union Jack flag
- Ruler
- Pencil
- Scissors
- ¼ yard of blue plaid fabric
- ¼ yard of red plaid fabric
- Elmer's spray adhesive
- 1 small can of Minwax Polycrylic Protective Finish
- Small paintbrush
- *Optional:* Cameo-size picture of the queen of England and E-6000 glue

HERE'S HOW

1 Find an image of the Union Jack flag to use as your guide.

2 Clean and lightly sand your briefcase to prepare it for painting.

3 Cover the parts of your briefcase that you don't want to paint (like the handle and the metal clasps) with newspaper, and use tape to hold the paper in place.

4 Paint your briefcase with white spray paint, and let it dry.

5 Draw the Union Jack pattern on your briefcase using a pencil and ruler.

6 Measure and cut out fabric pieces to make the Union Jack.

7 Spray the backs of the fabric pieces with Elmer's spray adhesive and lay them in place on your briefcase.

8 Once all the fabric is in place, apply clear coat to the fabric and surrounding areas, and let dry.

9 Apply another coat of clear coat to your briefcase so that it will hold up to the elements, and let dry.

OPTIONAL

Add a cameo-size photo of the queen of England in the center of the Union Jack. Follow the instructions on page 343 to make the cameo, and glue it on with a gob of E-6000.

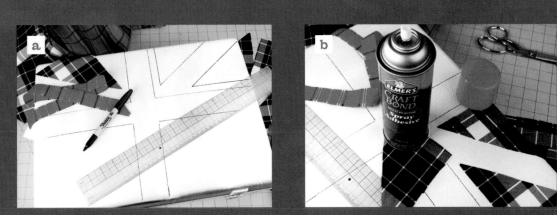

SUPER STRIPED MAILBOX

Why don't people take more pride in their mailboxes? Everyone has one, and they're always so boring! I painted stripes on my box, and though it's nothing fancy, I really like it. So does my mail carrier—she said it made her happy.

YOU'LL NEED

- Plain mailbox
- Krylon primer in white or gray
- Blue painter's masking tape
- Minwax Polycrylic Protective Finish
- Several small paintbrushes
- Latex paint in several colors

HERE'S HOW

1. Spray the exterior of your mailbox with primer and let dry.

2. With blue painter's tape, mark off stripes around the box and across the lid.

3. Paint over the tape with clear coat and let dry. (This will ensure that you will have very clean lines when you remove the tape.)

4. Paint stripes using different colors, and let the paint dry. Use 2 coats if needed.

5. Remove the tape, then tape off the unpainted stripes in between the painted ones and repeat steps 3 and 4.

6. Remove the tape and coat the entire mailbox in clear coat to give it a protective finish.

GET YOUR ROCKS OFF PAPERWEIGHT

Okay, it's not what you think! I just happened to use images of 1950s pinup girls on these smooth river rocks to make paperweights, and the name was a natural progression.

YOU'LL NEED

- A copy of an image that you like, roughly the size of your stone
- Scissors
- A smooth, flat stone that you've cleaned and dried
- Damp cloth and dry towel
- Elmer's glue
- Flat artist's paintbrush
- Minwax Polycrylic Protective Finish

HERE'S HOW

1 Carefully cut out the image, getting as much detail around the edges as possible.

2 Cut several slits along the edges of the image to allow the paper to lie flat on your rock.

3 Spread Elmer's on the back of your image using a small paintbrush, then adhere it to the stone.

4 When the glue is dry, coat the image with at least two coats of protective finish, allowing each coat to dry before adding the next.

OILCLOTH WALLET

I make these wallets to sell at flea markets that I host with friends, and I can usually get at least ten bucks for them. When you master how to make them, consider using them for your own moneymaking project. People love a wallet, and you can earn some cash for craft supplies!

YOU'LL NEED

- 1 yard of oilcloth
  (this makes 5–6 wallets; generally you can only buy this fabric by the yard, so hopefully you have a few friends in need of a new billfold)
- Pencil
- Scissors
- Sewing machine with zigzag stitch
- 1 yard of ¼-inch ribbon (or thinner)

HERE'S HOW

1. Enlarge and trace the pattern provided on page 367 onto the oilcloth, and cut it out with scissors.

2. Zigzag-stitch the ribbon all over the wallet in a swirly pattern, making sure to go around the curves on each side.

3. Lay the wallet facedown, with the curves toward the top, and fold down the top ⅓ of the wallet, as in the photo.

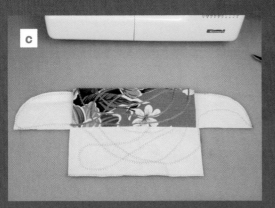

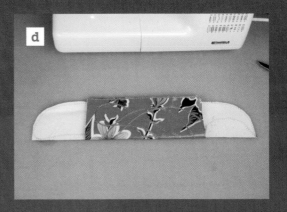

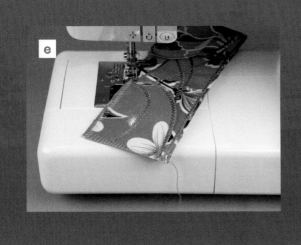

4 Fold up the bottom $1/3$ of the wallet.

5 Fold the curved edges toward the center.

7 Zigzag-stitch along the sides and across the bottom of the wallet, making sure to go through all layers of the fabric and to backtack when you start and finish your stitches.

CARGO PANT CARRY-ALL

Cargo pants have come in and out of fashion more times than Cher has changed hairstyles. I for one have had it with them, and have turned all of my old pairs into Cargo Pant Carry-alls (which, by the way, are perfect for carrying my Cher memorabilia).

YOU'LL NEED

- Pair of old cargo pants
- Scissors
- Sewing machine and thread in a contrasting color
- Iron and ironing board
- 2 D rings, $1^{1}/_{2}$ to 2 inches wide on the straight side of the D
- *Optional:* Cool fabric patch to sew on the flap and 2 inches of Velcro

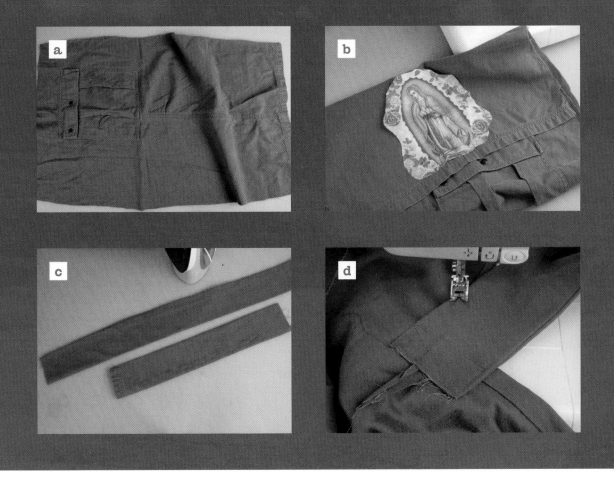

HERE'S HOW

1 Cut off both pant legs just under the bottom of the fly zipper.

2 Cut along the inseam of each leg, then unfold the fabric. Now you have 2 large pieces of fabric to work with.

3 Cut 1 leg into a large rectangle (mine was about 32 inches by 18 inches) so that the pocket on the side seam will be the pocket on the front of your cargo bag, and the bottom hem of the pant will form the edge along the flap.

4 Finish the end opposite the hem by folding the raw edge $1/2$ inch, then folding it $1/2$ inch again. Stitch along the folded fabric $3/8$ inch from the edge.

5 If you're adding a patch, fold the flap over the pocket and pin the patch in place. Sew it on the flap with a zigzag stitch.

6 Fold your bag into the satchel shape with right sides facing and the flap open, and stitch up the sides using a $3/4$-inch seam allowance on both sides. Make sure to backtack on the ends so it's nice and strong!

7 Finish the raw ends of the sides of the flaps by folding them in $1/4$ inch and then $1/4$ inch again and stitching along the folded fabric.

8 Turn the bag right side out.

9 Cut the other pant leg into 2 long strips about 6 inches wide for the shoulder strap (mine ended up 25 inches long by about 4 inches wide). One end of the strips should be the pant hem.

10 Stitch the strips into long tubes: fold right sides together and stitch the long edges together using a $\frac{1}{2}$-inch seam allowance. Turn the tubes right side out and iron them flat.

11 Stitch 1 strap to each side of the bag by stitching the ends across the side seams on the inside of the bag. Use extra stitches to make sure that they're sewn on tight.

12 Thread the end of 1 of the straps through the 2 D rings and sew the loop shut.

13 Put your other strap through both D rings, then back through 1 so you can adjust the strap to the desired length.

OPTIONAL

Stitch some Velcro on the flap and where it meets the bag for a secure closure.

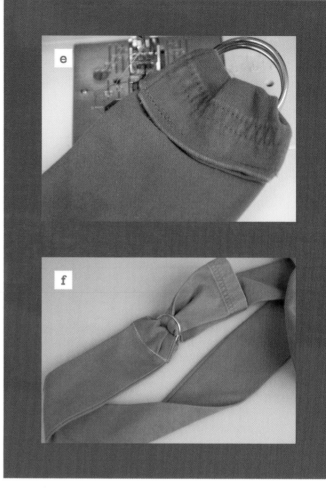

EVERYTHING BUT THE BATHROOM SINK BACKSPLASH

I'm so tired of rules. There comes a point in your life when you say, "I'm going to do this my way and I don't care if anyone else likes it." For me, that point came as I was making this backsplash. I couldn't decide on one theme, color, or tile, so I decided to fly by the seat of my pants. I loved the result.

HERE'S HOW

1 Determine the size and shape you need your backsplash to be.

2 Cut out the shape from your plywood with a jigsaw, and sand the edges.

3 Glue on your decorative items with E-6000. Go nuts! Arrange them into flowers, swirls, whatever. Just cover every bit of wood that you can.

4 Let the glue dry overnight.

5 Mix about 2 cups of plaster of Paris (or more, if the area you're covering is really big), then put on your rubber gloves and smoosh the plaster all over your backsplash, making sure to get it into every crack and crevice.

6 With a damp sponge, wipe as much excess plaster off your decorations as you can, but make sure you leave it in the crevices.

YOU'LL NEED

- Piece of $1/2$-inch-thick plywood big enough to cover the area you're working with
- Jigsaw
- Sandpaper
- Strings of pearls, buttons, rhinestones, large beads, dominoes, flat glass chips
- Plaster of Paris
- Rubber gloves
- Sponge
- Large tub of water
- Double-stick tape
- E-6000 glue

The items you glue on will be covered with a light layer of plaster, but it will wipe off easily when dry.

7 When the plaster has set, wipe off your backsplash with a wet sponge until you can see all of your beautiful little glued-on pieces. Keep wiping until it's perfect!

8 If you notice any holes, add more plaster, then wipe away any excess.

9 Attach your backsplash to the wall with double-stick tape.

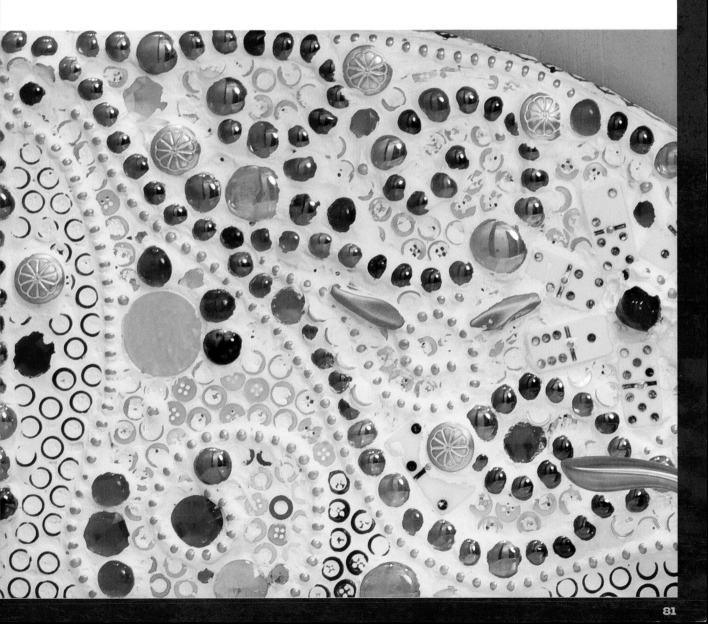

METAL AND WIRE BUGS

I really enjoy making these, but I haven't decided what to do with them yet. I could put a magnet on the back and stick them on the refrigerator, but it seems odd to have bugs on the fridge. I could also put a paper clip on them and use them to help me stay organized, but I'm afraid I'll accidentally give them away with a stack of papers. For now, they are just crawling happily all over my furniture.

YOU'LL NEED

- Aluminum flashing
- Pencil or permanent marker
- Tin shears or heavy-duty scissors
- Awl
- Medium-gauge wire
- Wire cutters
- E-6000 glue
- Needle-nose pliers
- Gold or silver and brown or green Krylon spray paint
- Spray bottle

HERE'S HOW

1. Enlarge and trace the patterns provided on page 362 onto the metal, then cut out the bug shapes with tin shears or heavy-duty scissors.

2. Use the awl to punch 6 holes in the body of the bug just below the head—3 holes on both sides of the spine.

3. Slightly fold the wing piece down the middle on each side to add dimension.

4. Cut 3 pieces of wire, each 4 inches long, and bend them in half. Poke the ends of 1 piece through the top 2 holes you made in the body, then poke your next 2 wires through the second and third row of holes, making sure the wires lie flat across the bug's back (use your pliers if necessary). These are your bug's legs.

5. Bend the legs a bit so your bug stands up. (You may have to cut them a little to make them even.)

6. Squeeze some E-6000 on the bug's spine and attach the wings. Let the glue dry overnight.

7. Curl the ends of each leg up into a tiny circle by wrapping the wire around your needle-nose pliers.

8. Lightly spray the bug with gold or silver spray paint. When the paint is dry, lightly spray with water, and then immediately spray it with brown or green spray paint. This gives it an antique look.

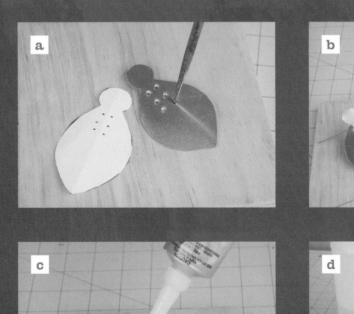

a

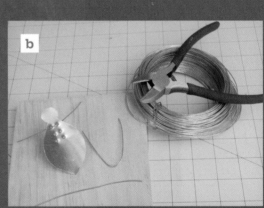

b

c

d

FAST AND FURIOUS FURNITURE

I always feel like I'm in need of more furniture. Whether it's summertime and I have fifteen friends coming over for a barbecue and only six chairs for them to sit on, or I need a tiny table for my guest room and can't seem to find one that fits my taste, I'm constantly trying to stock up. Luckily, I know the way to the lumberyard and enjoy making pieces myself. My handmade furniture is cheaper than the stuff I could find in a store, and the amount of time I spend making it is far less than the amount of time I'd spend searching for the perfect upholstered bench. The next time you need a piece of furniture, try one of the projects in this chapter. I think you'll be glad you did.

MOROCCAN THUMBTACK TABLETOP

This table turned out even better than I expected, and I think this technique would be great for a dresser top or mirror. It's easy to do, and it makes such an impact. I hope you'll be inspired to try it out soon!

YOU'LL NEED

- Tabletop in need of refinishing (I used a 24 inch by 24 inch piece of ¾-inch plywood mounted on a wrought iron table)
- Black Krylon Fusion for Plastic spray paint
- 15 sheets of 7-inch by 5-inch aluminum flashing
- Permanent marker
- Tin shears or heavy-duty scissors
- Pencil
- Ruler
- E-6000 glue
- 900 thumbtacks
- Needle-nose pliers

HERE'S HOW

1 Paint the tabletop black and let it dry.

2 While the paint is drying, enlarge and trace the patterns provided on page 361 onto the aluminum flashing with your permanent marker. To make the design I created, you'll need to trace 8 of each pattern.

3 Using heavy-duty scissors or tin shears, cut out the shapes.

4 With pencil and ruler, divide the table-top into 4 equal sections.

5 Starting in the center, glue down the metal pieces with E-6000, leaving just enough space between each piece for a row of thumbtacks.

6 Gently hammer thumbtacks around each piece of metal, using needle-nose pliers to hold the tacks in place while you work.

DON'T WORRY

The tacks don't have to be perfectly spaced. I think that the irregular spacing contributed to the homemade look of my table.

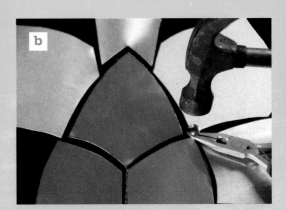

HANGERS ON TABLE BASE

I've always loved how wooden hangers look hanging in my closet, almost like soldiers lined up one after the other. This project is only for experienced crafters who want a challenge. It took me a while to figure out how to make it, but it was well worth the effort.

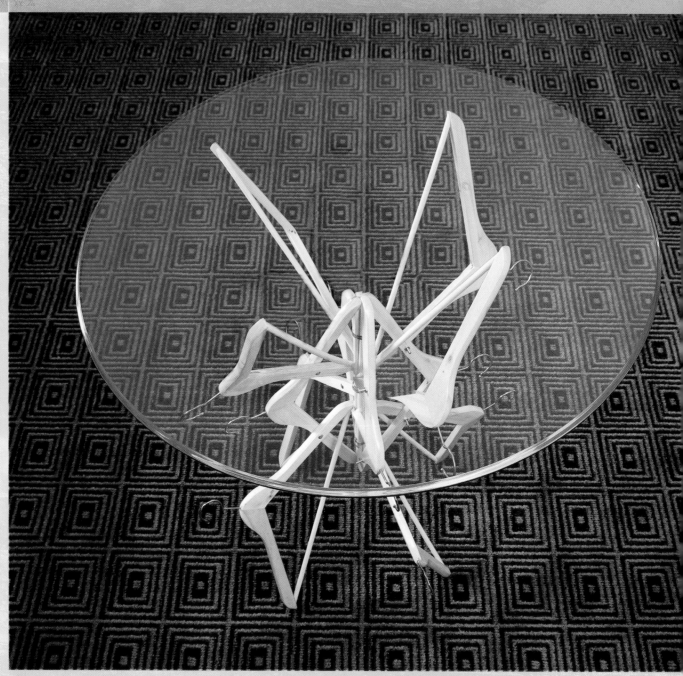

YOU'LL NEED

- 12 sturdy wooden hangers
- Pencil
- Paper
- Scissors
- Drill with $^8/_{32}$-inch bit
- Sandpaper
- Elmer's wood glue
- 8 sets of $^8/_{32}$-inch nuts and $1^1/_2$-inch bolts
- Screwdriver
- 3 hose clamps with a 5-inch circumference
- Pliers
- 24-inch-diameter thin round glass tabletop (make sure it's not too heavy!)

HERE'S HOW

1 Place a hanger on your worktable. This will be one of your 4 center hangers.

2 Place 1 hanger on each shoulder of the center hanger, positioned so a corner of your second and third hangers touch the bar on the first, and an arm of the second and third hangers crosses the first hanger's shoulders about 5 inches from the end of each arm, as shown in the photo.

3 Mark with a pencil where the second and third hangers intersect the first hanger's shoulders so you'll know where to drill and bolt them together.

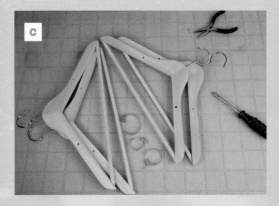

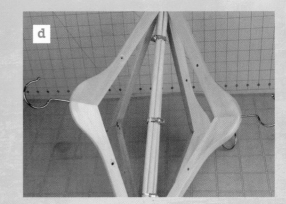

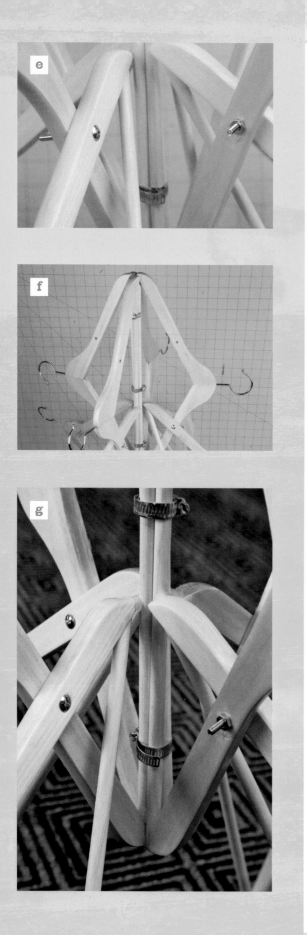

4 Make a paper pattern of the outer half of the first hanger's arms, including the drill targets, that you can use to mark other hangers.

5 Divide your hangers so that you have 4 sets of 3 hangers in each group. One hanger in each group will be a center hanger. Mark a drill hole on both arms of your center hangers, then mark a drill hole on 1 arm of each of the remaining hangers. Drill all the holes.

6 Sand the hangers where they will intersect. (This will give the wood a slightly rough surface, which helps the wood glue form a good bond.)

7 Attach your 4 sets of 3 hangers by applying some wood glue where each hanger intersects. Then screw them together with nuts and bolts, leaving a little wiggle room.

8 Gather the four center hangers together so the bars meet up evenly, and clamp them together with 3 hose clamps.

IMPORTANT

Work quickly so you've completed this step before the wood glue dries.

9 Adjust the hangers so that the top and bottom of the table base are level, then tighten the nuts and bolts so they don't move and the wood glue can form a strong bond. Let the glue dry overnight.

10 Place the glass tabletop on top of the base.

WOVEN RIBBON TABLETOP AND MIRROR

We all have a little side table or mirror that needs a makeover. (I, for one, have oodles of IKEA Lack tables that need some sprucing up so it doesn't look like I live in a catalog!) Here's an easy way to make a table or mirror look like a million bucks.

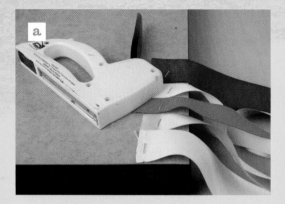

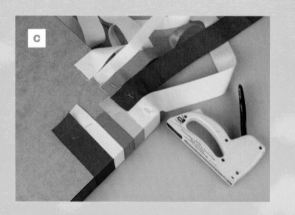

YOU'LL NEED

FOR BOTH
- 36 yards of ribbon (enough for a 22-inch by 22-inch tabletop or mirror)
- Staple gun with ¼-inch staples
- Scissors

FOR THE TABLETOP
- Tabletop that needs sprucing up

FOR THE MIRROR
- Piece of ½-inch plywood large enough for the project (mine was 22 inches by 22 inches, but yours could be any size)
- Mirror that's smaller than your plywood
- E-6000 glue or mirror mounts

HERE'S HOW
FOR THE TABLETOP

1 Take 1 roll of ribbon, and starting at the edge of your table, staple the end of the ribbon right underneath the tabletop.

2 Stretch the ribbon across to the opposite side and hold it just under the edge of the tabletop. Cut the ribbon, pull it taut, and staple the end in place. Continue to staple ribbon stripes to the tabletop until it's fully covered.

3 Weave ribbon in the opposite direction, stapling the ends on both sides (you'll have to cut your ribbon piece off the roll before you start weaving).

HINT

> If you have trouble grabbing the loose
> ribbon end while you weave, use a long
> ball point pin to pick it up in between the
> other ribbons.

HERE'S HOW
FOR THE MIRROR

1 Follow steps 1 through 3 for covering
the tabletop, only you'll be covering the
plywood.

2 Mount your mirror on top of the ribbon,
right in the center, with E-6000 or mirror
mounts. If you use E-6000, make sure to let
the glue dry overnight before hanging.

PYRAMID SIDE TABLE

This table only took a couple of hours to make, and it looks amazing (if I do say so myself). It's a bit heavier than I anticipated, which is an added bonus since I'm a klutz, always knocking over tables and sending crafts flying.

YOU'LL NEED

- 2 pieces of 1-inch-thick birch plywood in each of the following dimensions:
  19" x 19"
  18½" x 18½"
  18" x 18"
  17½" x 17½"
  17" x 17"
  16½" x 16½"
  16" x 16"
  15½" x 15½"
  15" x 15"
  14½" x 14½"
  14" x 14"
  13½" x 13½"
  13" x 13"
  12½" x 12½"
  12" x 12"
  11½" x 11½"
  11" x 11"
  10½" x 10½"
  10" x 10"
  9½" x 9½"
  9" x 9"
  8½" x 8½"
  8" x 8"
  7½" x 7½"
  7" x 7"
  6½" x 6½"
  6" x 6"

- Sanding block
- Elmer's wood glue
- Heavy weights (use free weights or dumbbells if you have them)
- Wood stain (I prefer Minwax)
- Paintbrush

HERE'S HOW

1 Sand all of your pieces, making sure to get the edges nice and smooth.

2 Divide your pieces into 2 piles, with 1 piece in every graduated size in each pile.

3 Starting with the largest piece on the bottom, stack the pieces from 1 pile in order of size, gluing them together with wood glue and making sure they're centered (use a ruler if you have to).

4 When you get to the smallest piece in the first pile, take the smallest piece from the second pile and continue adding and gluing pieces, from smallest to largest.

5 Once all the pieces are in place, put heavy weights on top of the stack to help the glue form a strong bond.

6 When the glue is dry, apply wood stain and let dry.

BAUHAUS STRIPED TABLE BASE AND STOOL

I love how easy this table base and stool are to make. They take only a few pieces of wood, and depending on how you paint them, they can take very little time to create. The point is, whether you go nutty with stripes like I did, or just stain the wood, you don't have to spend a fortune or be a carpenter to make something terrific for yourself.

YOU'LL NEED

FOR BOTH

- Ruler
- Pencil
- Elmer's wood glue
- Hammer
- Blue painter's tape
- Paint or wood stain, any color (I used white paint for my base coat)
- Minwax Polycrylic Protective Finish
- Paintbrushes

FOR THE TABLE BASE

- 2 pine boards, 26 inches (1" x 6")
- 1 pine board, 26 inches long (1" x 12")
- 6 (2-inch) finishing nails
- 24-inch-diameter (or smaller) round glass tabletop

FOR THE STOOL

- 2 (1" x 12") pine boards, 17 inches long
- 1 (1" x 12") pine board, 13 inches long
- 1 (1" x 12") pine board, 18 inches long
- 12 (2-inch) finishing nails

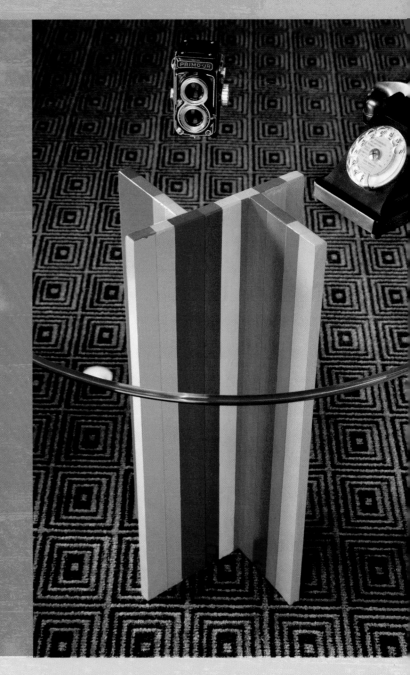

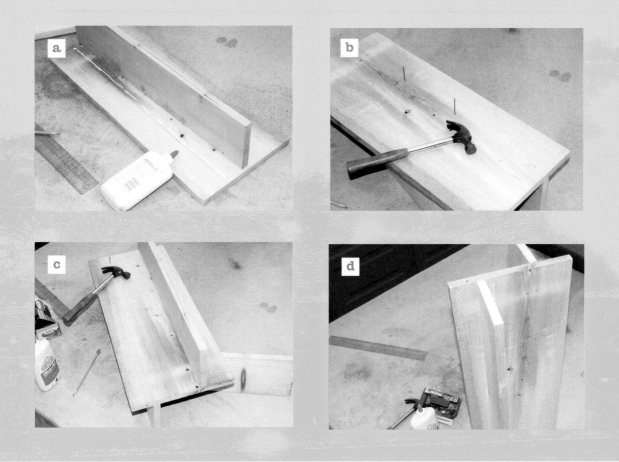

HERE'S HOW
FOR THE TABLE BASE

1 Using pencil and ruler, draw lines 3 inches from each 26-inch-long edge of the 1" × 12" pine board, from top to bottom. These will indicate where to place your 1" × 6" pieces and serve as your nail guides.

2 Spread wood glue down one of the lines. Center the 1-inch side of one of your 1" × 6" pieces of wood along the line.

3 Once the glue has set, turn the 1" × 12" board over and nail the 1" × 6" piece to the 1" × 12" piece with 3 finishing nails.

4 Glue the other 1" × 6" piece of wood to the 1" × 12" board on the same side where you just hammered your nails. Once the glue has dried, turn the 1" × 12" board over and nail it in place.

5 Paint the entire bench white and let it dry.

6 Using blue painter's tape, mark off your stripes on the white base.

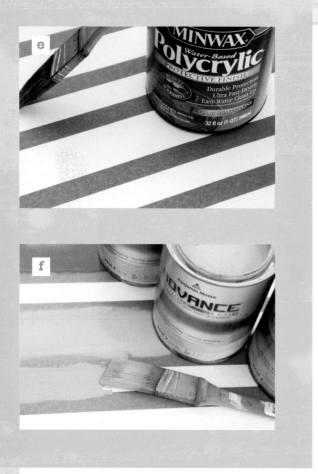

10 Top off your masterpiece with the glass tabletop.

HERE'S HOW
FOR THE STOOL

1 Using pencil and ruler, draw a line from 12-inch side to 12-inch side down the exact center of all of the pineboards. Do the same on the other side of each board.

2 Spread wood glue on 1 of the 12-inch edges of your 13-inch-long board. Align the glue-covered edge along the center line of 1 of your 17-inch-long boards, right where the line begins on 1 of the 12-inch sides of your 12" × 17" board, so the pieces are flush.

3 Apply glue to the other 12-inch side of your 13-inch-long board and place your other 17-inch-long board opposite the first. Nail the pieces together with 3 nails on each side. This is the base for your stool.

4 Using your drawn lines as a guide, center the 18-inch board on top of the base, apply wood glue, then nail it in place.

5 Follow steps 5 through 9 for painting the table, then take a seat on your sweet new stool.

7 When all the tape is in place, paint clear coat over the tape pieces and let dry. (This will prevent the colored paint from bleeding under the tape so you'll have a perfect stripe when you remove the tape later.)

8 Paint on your colors.

9 Once the paint has dried completely, remove the tape.

OPTIONAL

> If you want to paint over the white stripes, tape them off, apply clear coat to protect the surrounding stripes, then add your colors.

BEAUTIFUL UPHOLSTERED BENCH

This impressive-looking piece is super-easy to construct. Just have your local lumberyard or home improvement store cut the boards in the dimensions listed below, apply a little bit of wood glue, tack on some fabric, and in no time you'll have something terrific to show off to your friends.

YOU'LL NEED

- 2 (1" x 12") pine boards, 17 inches
- 1 (1" x 12") pine board, 40 inches
- 1 (1" x 12") pine board, 48 inches
- Pencil
- Elmer's wood glue
- 7 (2-inch) finishing nails

- 2 hammers (1 large, and 1 small)
- 1 yard of batting
- Staple gun with $1/2$-inch staples
- 2 yards of fabric
- 90 silver thumbtacks or upholstery nails
- Needle-nose pliers

HERE'S HOW

1 Follow the instructions for making the Bauhaus Striped Stool on page 98, substituting your 40-inch board for the 13-inch board and the 48-inch board for the 18-inch board. Use additional nails to nail the top piece in place.

2 Cut the batting into a rectangle 12 inches by 48 inches.

3 Cut the fabric into a rectangle 15 inches by 52 inches.

4 Attach batting to the top of the bench by stapling it in place along the edges.

5 Center the fabric on top of the bench. Starting in the center of 1 of the long sides of your bench, fold the fabric under 1 1/2 inches, hold a tack in place over the folded fabric on the edge of the bench with needle-nose pliers, and tap the tack into the bench with the small hammer.

6 Hammer a tack into each end of the same side while pulling the fabric taut.

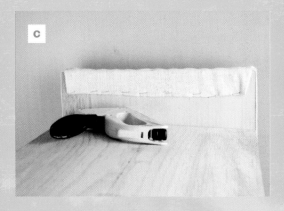

7 Repeat steps 5 and 6 on the other side of the bench.

8 Fill in the spaces in between the tacks on the long sides of your bench with more tacks.

9 When you're done adding tacks to the long sides, pull a short end of the fabric under the bench, fold the edges as if you were wrapping a present, and staple the fabric in place under the bench.

10 Hammer tacks along the short edges.

WHEEL OF FORTUNE THUMBTACK TABLE

Last summer I was at a carnival where there was a prize wheel just like on *Wheel of Fortune*. I became obsessed with it and wanted to make one of my own. Halfway through the project I came to my senses. Why was I making it? I mean, did I really need a wheel of fortune in my house? No! I stopped making a wheel and decided to make a side table of fortune instead. Much better!

YOU'LL NEED

- 24-inch-diameter table round (this is a great size for making tables of all kinds)
- Pencil
- Ruler
- High-gloss latex paint in 2 colors
- Paintbrushes
- 2 boxes of brass thumbtacks (you'll need about 400 total)
- Needle-nose pliers
- Small hammer
- Dinner plate to use as stencil

HERE'S HOW

1 With a pencil and ruler, divide your table round into a pie with 8 equal "slices."

2 Paint every other slice the lighter of the two colors.

DON'T WORRY

> If the edges aren't perfect, they will be covered by the thumbtacks.

3 When the first-color paint is dry, paint the remaining segments in the second color.

4 Starting in the center, hold a thumbtack in place with your needle-nose pliers, and gently tap it in with your hammer. Keep adding thumbtacks between each slice, working your way out toward the edge of the tabletop, then add a thumbtack border all the way around the perimeter of the tabletop.

5 Using the dinner plate as a stencil, trace an arc in each pie slice with your pencil to create a reverse scallop border, as shown in the photo.

6 Hammer thumbtacks along the scallop border all the way around the table.

PAPIER-MÂCHÉ HEAD TABLE

My intention when I began making this table was to give it to my niece when I was finished. That idea went out the window when I saw how totally adorable it is. My niece is going to have to make her own!

YOU'LL NEED

- 2 large plastic bowls with wide, flat bottoms for the head
- Heavy-duty scissors
- Small trash can for the neck
- Hot glue gun and glue sticks
- Large mixing bowl
- 3 cups warm water
- 1 tablespoon cornstarch
- ½ cup Elmer's glue
- 2 cups white flour
- Hand mixer
- Newspaper or phone book pages torn into 2-inch by 8-inch strips
- Sandpaper or sanding block
- Flesh-colored spray paint
- Pencil
- Black, red, pink, brown, and blue latex paint
- Paintbrushes
- Minwax Polycrylic Protective Finish
- Round piece of glass for tabletop

HERE'S HOW

1 If the bowls you're using for the head have rims with a lip, cut the lip off using heavy-duty scissors.

2 To create the head, glue the bowls together mouth-to-mouth with hot glue.

3 Place the trash can mouth side down. Glue the head on the bottom of the trash can to form the base of your table.

4 Make papier-mâché paste: put 3 cups warm water in a large mixing bowl, then add the cornstarch, then the glue, then the flour. Mix the ingredients with a hand mixer, and let the mixture cool. Once mixed it should have the consistency of glue.

5 Dip the strips of paper in the paste and cover the head and neck evenly.

6 When the structure is fully covered, let it dry overnight.

IMPORTANT

> Keep the papier-mâché paste covered in the refrigerator when you're not using it.

7 Add a layer of paper to the structure every day over the next three days, letting it dry overnight, until the structure is hard as a rock.

8 Sand off any rough edges with your sandpaper or sanding block.

9 Spray-paint the entire structure in flesh color, and let the paint dry.

10 Draw on hair and facial features, then paint over them with latex paints. Let the paint dry.

11 Cover the entire structure with protective clear coat and let dry.

12 Put the glass tabletop on and marvel at your creation.

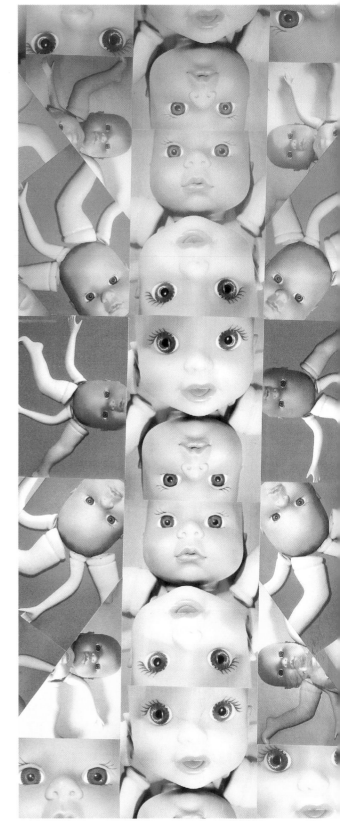

HEADY STUFF

I'm obsessed with doll heads, particularly porcelain ones; I have one sitting on my desk that I turned into a pencil holder, and she stares at me all day long with her glass eyes that seem to say, "Stop eating those chocolate turtles, you fatty!" For that reason I will soon have to turn her into a doorknob or a garden ornament.

If you're intrigued by heady crafts, this is the chapter for you. But don't feel like you have to decapitate your antique doll collection for your craft session—just head to a thrift store or yard sale. I always find tons of dolls at these places. Take them home, remove the heads, wash them, and turn them into something creepy and cool. Sure, you might give your kids nightmares or make your friends wonder if you're a psychopath, but it'll be so much fun!

AUXY McMOUSY BABY HEAD SALT AND PEPPER SHAKERS

I'm sure you're wondering about the name of this project. Well, Auxy, which rhymes with "Mousy," was shooting photos for this book, saw my stash of baby doll heads, and came up with the idea for these shakers, so I had to name them after her (and her nickname is McMousy). I love you, Auxy!

YOU'LL NEED

- 2 baby doll heads
- Bucket of soap and water mixed with a capful of bleach
- Drill with a bit the size of a salt/pepper shaker hole
- 2 rubber plugs or large corks that fit snugly inside the dolls' neck holes
- *Optional:* Latex clear coat and paintbrush

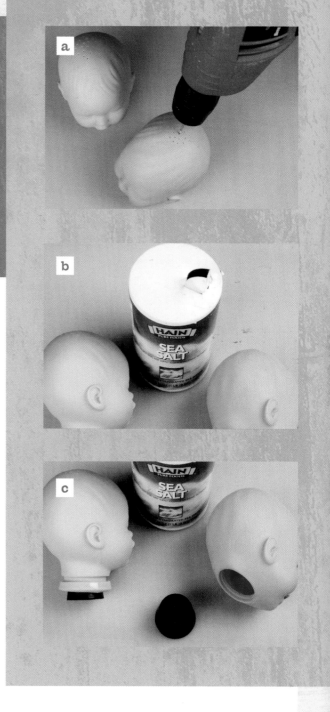

NOTE

Please make sure there are no children around when you're making this project. I made the mistake of crafting these in front of kids and it wasn't a good scene. If you email me I'll tell you what happened.

HERE'S HOW

1 Remove the doll heads from the bodies.

2 Soak the heads in a bucket of soap and water and a little bleach to make sure they're super-duper clean. Rinse and dry.

3 Drill 10 to 15 holes on the top of each head.

4 Fill 1 with salt and the other with pepper.

5 Plug the neck holes with rubber or cork plugs.

SUGGESTION

Coating the heads with latex clear coat gives them a nice finish. Apply the clear coat and let dry before you drill holes.

BABY HEAD NIGHT-LIGHT

This totally freaked out my houseguests, and I have to admit, sometimes it freaks me out, too. The other night I walked into the bathroom while still half asleep and it gave me a small heart attack. So, consider yourself warned: this night-light is not for the faint of heart!

YOU'LL NEED

- Porcelain doll head
  (press the top to make sure there is a
  hole on top of the head where you can
  insert the lightbulb. There usually is.)
- Craft knife
- Night-light with small bulb
- Safety goggles
- Dremel tool with grinding attachment
- E-6000 glue

HERE'S HOW

1 Remove the doll head from the body, then remove the hair and scrape off any leftover glue with a craft knife or Dremel.

2 Unscrew the bulb from the night-light. If you can fit the night-light base inside the head through the neck hole, go to step 3. If you can't, put on your safety goggles, and with the Dremel and grinding attachment, enlarge the neck hole until it's big enough for the light base to fit through.

3 Slip the bulb inside the head through the hole at the top and screw it onto the night-light. The bulb should keep the head in place on the night-light, but if the head wiggles a bit, secure it with a little E-6000 around the neck hole where it touches the night-light base.

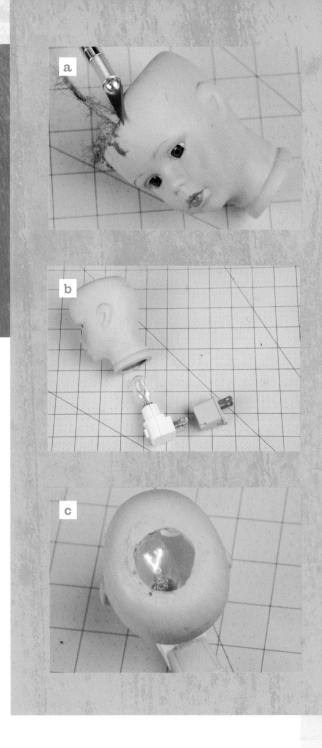

A PICTURE WORTH 1,000 WORDS

I have a few friends in show business, and they all have a huge photo or painting of themselves hanging in their living rooms. I thought, Why shouldn't I have a little something to commemorate how well I can Photoshop out my zits? So I framed a portrait of myself. Then I felt really uncomfortable looking at a huge image of myself, so I turned it into an art piece. I feel much better about it now.

It's All About Me!

YOU'LL NEED

- 2 copies of a large photo of yourself (or of a friend who thinks very highly of him- or herself)
- Scissors
- Large frame
- Poster board in a color you like (I chose black)
- Double-stick tape
- Enough book pages copied onto acetate to cover your photos (make these at Staples; I used 4 8½" x 11" copies)

HERE'S HOW

1. Cut your photos so that you can fit 2 heads into the frame, positioned neck-to-neck.

2. Cut your poster board the same size as the back of the frame.

3. Mount your photos on the poster board with double-stick tape.

4. Apply tiny bits of double-stick tape around the edges of the poster board where the frame will cover your work, then cover the photos with acetate sheets, lightly pressing around the edges so the tape holds them in place.

5. Frame your artwork and show off your beautiful face.

BABY HEAD PHOTO COLLAGE

One day I started playing around with my digital camera in my workroom and snapped a few photos of my collection of doll parts, and this is what happened. Pretty cool, right?

YOU'LL NEED

- Digital camera
- Cool photos printed out on a home printer, then copied (at Staples) onto 20 ($8^1/_2$" x 11") sheets of glossy card stock
- Swing-arm paper cutter or craft knife
- Magazine with large pages
- Elmer's spray adhesive
- Large poster frame
- Sick appreciation of all things weird

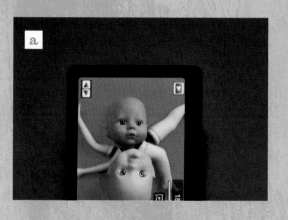

HERE'S HOW

1 Take photos of doll heads and doll parts, bugs, candy wrappers, or anything else you find interesting.

2 Print out your photos on your home printer, getting at least 2 photos on each sheet.

3 Take the printouts to Staples, and get color copies on glossy card stock. (This will save you money on printer ink and paper.)

4 Cut out your photos and decide how you want to arrange them in the poster frame. There is no right or wrong way!

5 Now you'll be working outside. Take your photos, the cardboard from your poster frame, spray adhesive, and a large magazine. Starting with the photo that will go in the center, place your images facedown on a magazine page, apply spray mount, and stick them to the cardboard, working your way out to the edges of the cardboard.

6 Frame and hang, baby!

IMPORTANT

Make sure to spray each photo on a separate page of the magazine or you might accidentally mount a photo to a sticky page.

FABRIC-COVERED MASQUERADE MASK

I was fortunate enough to be in Italy during Carnival one year, and I will never forget the beautiful costumes I saw in San Marco Square. The experience has influenced everything, from my home décor to what I choose to wear on Halloween each year to this fun project. My brother Phillip helped me figure out how to make this mask years ago for a party, and I hope it inspires you as much as it has me.

YOU'LL NEED

- Cardboard
- Pencil
- Scissors
- X-ACTO knife
- ¼ yard of fabric (I like brocade for this)
- 4 feet of ¼-inch satin ribbon
- Hot glue gun and glue sticks
- 1 yard of matching woven trim
- 2 yards of plastic pearl trim
- 4 rhinestones, ½ inch to 1 inch in diameter

HERE'S HOW

1 Enlarge and trace the mask pattern provided on page 376 onto cardboard and cut it out. Slightly bend it so it curves around your face, and try it on to make sure it's comfortable. Trim it down if necessary.

2 Enlarge and trace the fleur-de-lis pattern onto cardboard and cut it out.

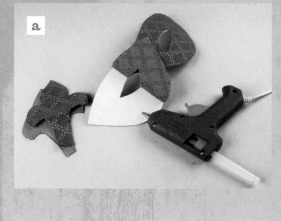

3 Using your cardboard shapes as guides, trace 2 masks and 2 fleurs-de-lis onto the fabric and cut them out.

4 Using the hot glue gun, adhere the fabric pieces to both sides of the cardboard mask and the cardboard fleur-de-lis. (You'll only decorate the front with trim and rhinestones, but adding fabric to the back will make your mask more comfortable to wear.)

5 Hot-glue the woven trim all the way around the mask, starting from the center of the top of the mask and working your way out.

6 Hot-glue the pearl trim all the way around the fabric-covered fleur-de-lis, and then glue pearls around the mask's eyeholes. Then add a row of pearls to the mask right inside the woven trim.

7 Cut the ribbon in half and hot-glue a piece to each side of your mask. Cover the ribbon ends by gluing rhinestones on top.

8 Glue a couple of rhinestones to the fleur-de-lis, then glue the fleur-de-lis to the mask and let dry.

9 Put on your mask and paint the town red!

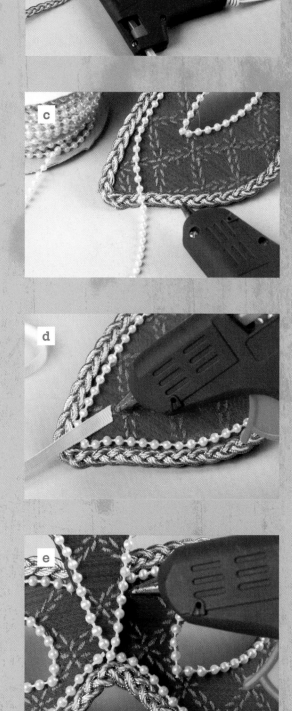

...NG OUT WIG

...igs. Just the word *wig* makes me laugh! However, I have a tough time finding wigs I'm willing to shell out money for. Last Halloween I finally realized that if I can sew an entire costume from scratch, I can make a wig, so I picked some colors that matched my outfit and rocked out on this project. Pretty soon Dolly Parton herself will be calling me for help!

YOU'LL NEED

- Wig head or balled-up news-paper to fill the cap while you work
- Knit hat that fits snugly on your head
  (try to find one that matches the color of your ribbon)
- 2 large spools of curling ribbon
  (I used 2 different colors)
- Scissors
- Hot glue gun and glue sticks

HERE'S HOW

1 Set up your wig head or make one out of newspapers, and fit the cap over it to work on.

2 Cut about 30 strands of curling ribbon, each 15 inches long, apply about 1½ inches of hot glue to the end of each ribbon, and glue the strands across the cap to make a row of very long bangs.

3 Cut 3 strands of curling ribbon, each 20 inches long. Fold the strands in half, dot a bit of hot glue at the crease, and stick the strands horizontally onto the cap, just above the row of bangs.

4 Cut 15 strands of curling ribbon, each 45 inches long. Gather them together, tie a knot in the middle, then curl the ends with your scissors.

5 Glue the knot onto the knit cap above the row of 20-inch strands.

6 Repeat steps 4 and 5 until you get the desired fullness for the wig.

7 Put your cap on, frame your face with the bangs, and add more curl to the ribbon "hair" with your scissors if necessary.

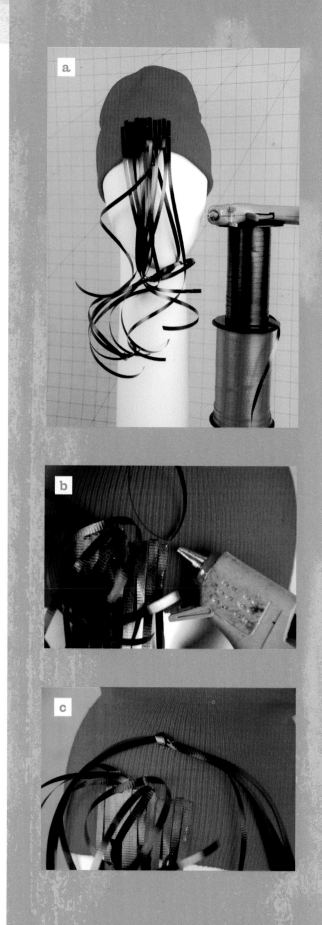

HEY, I COULD USE THAT!

I find it's the little things that make my life more enjoyable. Whether it's a favorite nail polish, a fresh pair of socks, new seat covers for my car, or a sharp pair of scissors, small things that I can use every day make me happy. In the following pages, I've included a few of my favorite little things. Try them out and make your life a little happier too, or make some as gifts and spread the joy around.

LICENSE PLATE BLING

I have always wanted a personalized license plate, but I'm just too lazy to figure out how to get one. So when I bought my new car, I decided to craft myself
a license plate frame to beat all. I now have several, and they all say different
things, like "Get Off of Your Phone!" or "Stop Texting and Watch the Road!"

YOU'LL NEED

- Enough magnet letters to make your statement
- License plate frame
- E-6000 glue
- Krylon Metallics spray paint in gold
- *Optional:* Rhinestones

HERE'S HOW

1 Decide what you are going to spell out, then arrange the letters around the license plate frame.

IMPORTANT

> Make sure you don't cover the holes for the screws, or you won't be able to attach the frame to the car!

2 Using E-6000, glue on 1 letter at a time. Let the glue dry.

3 Spray the entire frame with gold spray paint, and let the paint dry for 10 minutes.

4 Spray on 2 more coats of paint, letting dry between applications.

SUGGESTION

> When the paint is completely dry, add rhinestones with E-6000 for some extra bling.

5 Screw your new frame onto your car and get your message out!

COOLING MINT BODY SPRAY

During summers in New York City, one of the things that saved me from feeling like I was going to melt into a pool of sticky ick was my cooling mint body spray. Mint is a natural coolant, and when I spray this on, it's like I have my own air conditioner in my underwear. Wherever you choose to spray it, I promise you'll feel wonderful. (This one is for adults only, kids.)

YOU'LL NEED

- ¼ cup of vodka
- 20 drops of peppermint oil
- 5 drops of lemon extract
- Liquid measuring cup with a pour spout
- Perfume bottle

HERE'S HOW

1. Combine all of the ingredients in the measuring cup and stir with a spoon.

2. Pour the mixture into a small perfume bottle.

3. Spray the cooling mist all over after you've showered and toweled off, or whenever you feel the need to cool down.

STRIPED COMFORTER COVER

Need a comforter cover to match your décor? Well, then, hit the white sales, honey, because sewing two flat sheets together can do the trick for not a lot of money, and it's a piece of cake.

NOTE

I made a comforter cover for a full-size, but you should buy 2 sheets the size of your own bed. Here are the standard measurements of sheets and comforters to help you get started:

Sheet sizes: Twin 66" x 96", Full 81" x 96", Queen 90" x 102"

Comforter sizes: Twin: 68" x 86", Full: 76" x 86", Queen: 86" x 90"

HERE'S HOW

HINT

> The key to sewing a comforter cover out of 2 flat sheets is to scale the sheets down to the size of the comforter. (Otherwise it will be like your comforter is wearing a huge pair of panties, and we don't want that!) Since flat sheets are approximately 10 inches longer than comforters for the same size bed, I used a $^3/_4$-inch seam allowance across the width of the comforter and a 2-inch seam allowance down each side of the comforter to make mine the right size.

1 Cut both sheets from side to side into strips, each 16 inches long. For a full-size comforter you will have 6 (16" × 81") strips of each color.

2 Divide the strips into 2 piles of 6 strips, each consisting of 3 strips of 1 color and 3 strips of the other color.

3 Sew together the strips from 1 pile using long stitches and a $^3/_4$-inch seam allowance. When you alternate the colors, use the top of the sheet for the top stripe and the bottom of the sheet for the bottom stripe, so your comforter will have nice finished edges.

4 When you finish with the first pile of strips, repeat step 3 to form the other side of your comforter cover.

5 Place the 2 sewed pieces together face-to-face, and pin all the way around the edges.

6 Starting at the top, sew down one side using a 2-inch seam allowance.

7 Sew across the bottom using a $^3/_4$-inch seam allowance.

8 Sew up the remaining side using a 2-inch seam allowance.

9 When you get to the top, sew 25 inches across from 1 corner with a $^3/_4$-inch seam allowance and then stop.

10 Sew 25 inches across the top from the opposite corner and then stop.

11 Turn the comforter cover inside out through the opening in the top. You're almost done!

12 Arrange three small pieces of Velcro across the opening of your comforter cover so they are evenly spaced, then stitch them on. (Or sew buttons and button holes—a classy touch.)

13 Slip your comforter inside your new cover, close it up, and tuck yourself in!

MAGNET VINE

For some reason my fridge ended up covered in ugly magnets. One day I couldn't stand it anymore, so I made this magnet vine. Now, every time I go to sneak a spoonful of Cool Whip, I smile.

YOU'LL NEED

- 12 faux flowers and a few faux leaves
- 6 plain round magnets
- Hot glue gun and glue sticks
- 1 yard of green satin cord or ribbon

HERE'S HOW

1. Glue a flower and a couple of leaves to each magnet with your hot glue gun.

2. Apply a dab of glue to the side of each magnet flower and attach them to the satin cord, spreading them about 8 inches apart.

3. Add a few more flowers and leaves along the cord to make it look like a vine.

4. Have fun decorating your fridge!

GLITTER GLAM NAIL POLISH

I love nail polish. When I was little I would sit at the kitchen table and hang out with my mom while she painted her nails. To me, it was like she was making art. Recently I was out to dinner with my friend Kelly, and she started capital-*B* capital-*itching* about how she couldn't find nail polish with enough glitter in it to really complete her trampy look. I skipped dessert and went straight to the 99-cent store to grab some clear nail polish. That gleam in my eye became this project.

YOU'LL NEED

- Small piece of paper
- Bottle of clear nail polish
- Loose glitter

HERE'S HOW

1 Roll the piece of paper into a cone-shaped funnel.

2 Take the top off your polish, place the funnel in the mouth of the bottle, and pour in as much glitter as you can.

3 Shake it until you bake it, baby, then tramp it up!

FAUX FLOWER KEY HOOK

I'm always losing my keys. If I set them down for even a second they disappear! It's like I have a magic evil elf in my house who hides them to torture me. When I find that elf, he's going down, but I'm hoping this flower key hook will help in the meantime.

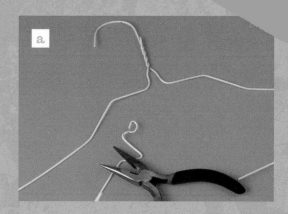

YOU'LL NEED

- Small piece of cardboard
- Scissors or X-ACTO knife
- Needle-nose pliers with wire cutter
- Wire hanger
- Hot glue gun and glue sticks
- 1 large faux flower
- Stapler
- 1 large round rhinestone

HERE'S HOW

1 Cut out a cardboard circle approximately 2 inches in diameter.

2 Using wire cutter, cut a 10-inch-long section from the hanger.

3 Bend the wire piece with pliers to resemble the pieces in the photo. It should have a hook and an area where you can glue it down to your flat circle of cardboard, and each end of your wire should have a tiny loop (the loop at the top is for the nail; the loop at the bottom is just to give it a finished look).

4 Hot-glue the wire to the cardboard circle with a generous amount of glue.

5 Remove all the plastic pieces that hold your faux flower together, but keep the shape of the flower intact.

6 Staple the layers of petals together with a single staple in the middle.

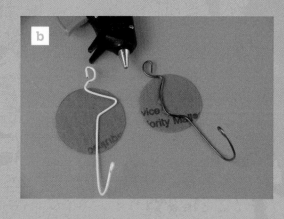

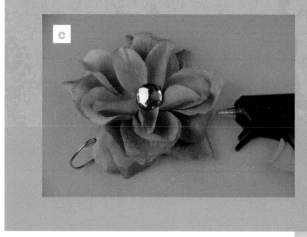

7 Hot-glue the flower to the cardboard and put the rhinestone in the center.

8 Nail your beautiful hook to a wall near your door and your keys will naturally gravitate to it!

TWISTY FABRIC TWINE

I like to take my time wrapping gifts and make them look really special. Last year I decided to be eco-friendly and use all of the scraps of fabric I had lying around the craft room to make my own twine. I think it's just beautiful, and it was a hit with the recipients.

YOU'LL NEED

- Strips of fabric, $\frac{1}{2}$ inch wide, in various colors (it's okay if they're different lengths)
- Hot glue gun and glue sticks

HERE'S HOW

1. Hot-glue 2 different-colored strips of fabric together on 1 end with a tiny dot of glue.

2. Trap the glued end in a drawer or under something heavy, then twist the fabric strips clockwise while simultaneously wrapping them together counterclockwise, until you reach the end of your fabric strip.

3. If you want to create a longer piece of twine, glue strips to the bottoms of the strips you were twisting, and continue twisting and adding strips until your twine is the desired length.

4. Glue the loose ends of your strips together with a dot of hot glue to finish your length of twine.

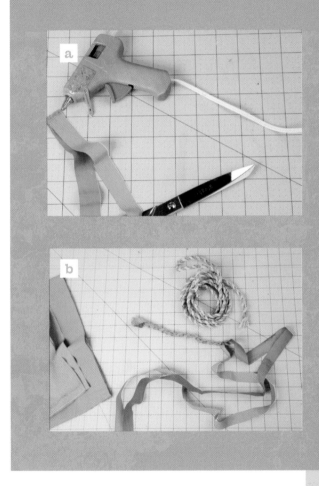

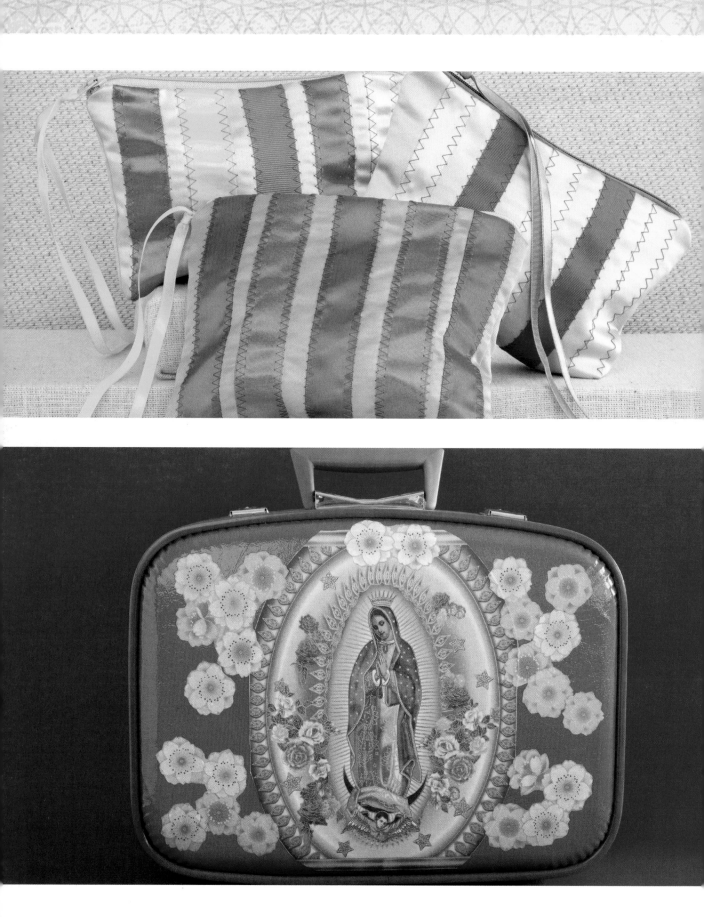

Almost every girl I know is obsessed with staying abreast of the latest "it" bag from the designer du jour. I think that's great if you can actually afford to be walking around with two months' rent on your shoulder, but if you can't (and I'm guessing this group includes most of us), then why not make your own stylish handbag that reflects your needs and personal tastes? In this chapter, I've provided instructions for many types of bags, from small clutches to large carryalls, and I urge you to personalize them in any way you see fit. Who knows, you just might invent the new "it" accessory yourself!

BEADED EYEGLASS CASE CLUTCH

If you want to cover something in beads, don't bother with a sewing needle. Just glue them on! It's just as effective when you add some clear coat on top, and it'll spare you a lot of eyestrain. Use this technique to make yourself an evening bag that no one else will have, and everyone will want.

YOU'LL NEED

- Plastic eyeglass case
- Drill with a small drill bit, so the hole is just large enough to slip your ribbon through
- Laser-copied image (see note page 249)
- Scissors
- Elmer's glue
- Cup of water
- Paintbrushes
- Enough black beads to cover your case
- Minwax Polycrylic Protective Finish
- 14 inches of ¼- to ½-inch ribbon
- 1 tassel

HERE'S HOW

1 Open the eyeglass case. Drill a hole in the center of both sides of the bottom of your case, as shown in the photo. The holes should be just big enough for a ribbon to fit through.

2 Cut your copied image so it fits nicely in the center of the top of the case. Add a few drops of water to some Elmer's glue so it's easy to spread, and use it to glue the image in place.

3 Cover the rest of the top of the eyeglass case with Elmer's glue—full strength, not diluted!—and carefully dip it into a pile of beads. Sprinkle more beads on top to cover any empty spots, and let the glue dry.

4 Turn the case over and cover the other side in glue, then dip it in beads, sprinkling more beads on where necessary. Let the glue dry.

5 Cover the entire case with clear coat and let dry, then add at least one more layer of clear coat to make sure that the beads are going to stay in place, and let dry.

6 Poke both ends of the ribbon through the hole at the top of your clutch so the ends are inside the case. Tie the ribbon ends in a double knot so they can't slip through the hole.

7 Poke the loop of the tassel through the bottom hole into the clutch and tie a knot in the loop big enough so that it can't slip through the hole.

VINYL COMPUTER ENVELOPE

I travel constantly, and carrying a computer bag in addition to my backpack and carry-on just wasn't working for me, so I decided to make a cover for my computer that would allow me to stow it safely in my backpack. I quickly stitched one up out of vinyl and I've been happily flying the friendly skies with it ever since.

YOU'LL NEED

- Ruler
- Pen
- ½ yard of vinyl
- Pinking shears
- Scissors
- Cool image from a printed fabric that'll fit on the case as a patch
- Sewing machine with zigzag stitch
- Stick-on Velcro dots

HERE'S HOW

1 To make your pattern, measure the width of your laptop and add 2 inches to that measurement (so if your laptop is 14 inches wide, your pattern would be 16 inches wide).

2 Measure the depth of your laptop, double that number, and add 6 inches (so if your laptop is 10 inches deep, your pattern would be 26 inches deep).

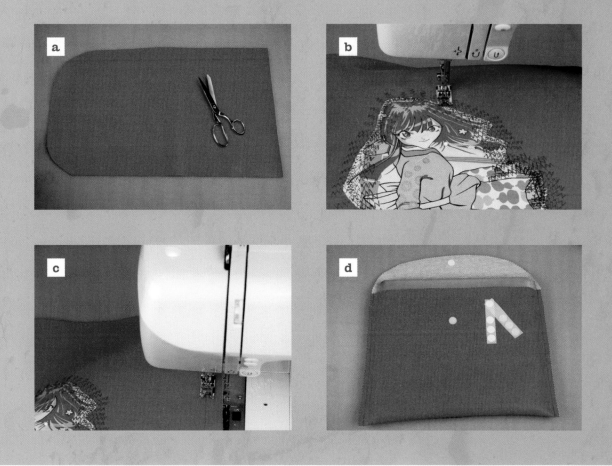

3 Draw a slight curve on one of the short ends of the pattern for the flap. (Try using a dinner plate as a stencil.)

4 Trace your pattern onto the fabric and cut it out.

5 Cut across the noncurved short end with pinking shears to give it a cool edge.

6 Cut out the image you plan to use as a patch from the fabric. Be sure to give the outline a fun shape.

7 Center your image 6½ inches from the edge of the curved flap. Or, if you're unsure about the placement, wrap the vinyl around your laptop to see how the finished envelope will look and mark with a pen where you want the patch to go.

8 Pin the patch in place, and zigzag-stitch all the way around it. Make it look funky!

9 Fold your vinyl to create the envelope shape, leaving the 6-inch flap open. Stitch up the sides with a straight stitch, using a ½-inch seam allowance and making sure to backtack.

10 With pinking shears, cut around the raw edges of your case outside the stitches.

11 Slip your computer into the case and figure out where to put your Velcro dots on the inside of the flap and where it folds over. Stick your Velcro on, and you're ready to go!

ARTIST'S CLUTCH

If Jackson Pollock or Andy Warhol had been women, I figure this is the bag they would have carried. I had a blast making these with those avant-garde artists in mind, and I think Jackson and Andy would be very proud.

YOU'LL NEED

- 1 yard of heavy-duty canvas
- Pencil
- Scissors
- Sewing machine with zig-zag stitch (or a serger) and thread in a bold color
- 2 inches of Velcro
- Masking tape
- Krylon spray paint in 2 colors
- Latex paints in several colors
- Artist's brushes
- Plastic bottle (I like to use Ocean Spray bottles because they're thick)
- Pliers
- Lighter
- Needle and thread
- 1 cool button
- E-6000 glue

HERE'S HOW

1 Enlarge and trace the pattern provided on page 378 onto the heavy-duty canvas twice. Cut out the shapes.

2 Put one piece on top of the other, and with your sewing machine, zigzag-stitch all the way around the pieces.

3 Fold the bottom of the piece toward the pointy top to form the clutch shape.

4 Figure out where you need to place the Velcro closure, then peel and stick the Velcro pieces on the bag and stitch them in place.

5 Stitch the sides of the bag together about ³⁄₈ inch from each edge.

OPTIONAL

> To make a thinner clutch, fold up the clutch 1 more time and stitch the sides again. This will also give you more pockets.

6 Place masking tape over the Velcro to protect it from the paint.

7 Go outside, set the clutch on some newspaper, and spray-paint both sides with your 2 colors, creating a funky, swirly pattern.

8 Get a big blob of latex paint on a paintbrush and splatter it on the clutch. Keep splattering and dripping different paint colors until you're satisfied, then let dry overnight.

9 Cut out 2 or 3 flower shapes from your plastic bottle, 1 about 3 inches in diameter and the other about 2¹⁄₂ inches in diameter.

10 Holding a flower with your pliers, melt the edges of the plastic with the lighter to give the petals a cool, wavy shape. Repeat for the remaining flowers.

11 Spray-paint the flowers and let dry.

12 Put the smaller flower on top of the bigger flowers, and then stitch them all to the flap of the bag with needle and thread.

13 Glue the button in the middle of your flower with E-6000.

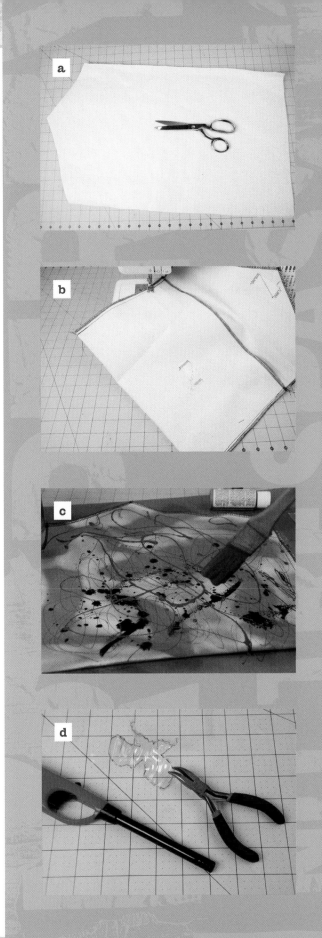

VIRGIN MARY SUITCASE

I grew up with images of the Virgin Mary all over my house, and I felt this was the perfect way to honor that part of my upbringing. My grandmother is either going to slap me silly for making this or she'll insist I send it to her immediately, but one way or another I know she's going to have something to say about it. (By the way, she won't even utter the name of my book. That woman is bound for sainthood, I'm sure of it!)

YOU'LL NEED

- 1 hard suitcase
  (check local thrift stores)
- Damp cloth and dry towel
- Newspaper
- Masking tape
- Krylon Fusion for Plastic spray paint
  in any color
- Scissors
- Fabric with a couple of large images
- Fabric with small matching flowers or
  shapes that complement your images
- Elmer's spray adhesive
- Minwax Polycrylic Protective Finish
- 1-inch paintbrush

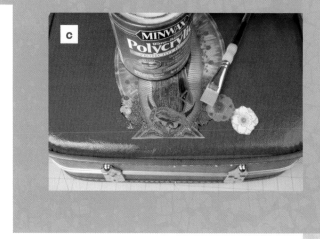

HERE'S HOW

1 Prep your case for action by wiping off
any dirt and grime and toweling it dry.
Then, cover the parts of your case that
you don't want painted with newspaper,
and tape the paper in place.

2 Take the case outside, spray-paint it
thoroughly, and let dry.

3 Cut out the fabric images and figure out
how you want to arrange them.

4 Apply Elmer's spray adhesive to the back
of each fabric piece and stick them to the
suitcase.

5 When the entire case is decorated, gen-
erously apply 2 coats of clear coat, letting
the first coat dry before adding the next.

LEATHER PANT SATCHEL

How many times do you see leather pants at a yard sale and think to yourself, "How in the name of Pat Benatar did that hefty man squeeze into these?" Recently I found the most amazing pair of bronze leather pants at a tag sale and I bought them knowing there were at least twenty different craft projects I could make with the leather. Here's one.

YOU'LL NEED

- 1 pair of leather pants in pretty good condition
- Scissors
- Ruler
- Sewing machine
- Matching thread
- Pinking shears
- Heavy-duty needle
- 1 large button

HERE'S HOW

1. Cut a 23-inch-long tube from 1 pant leg and remove the lining if there is one.

2. Stitch across the leg 7 inches from 1 end of the tube. This will be the base of your satchel.

3. Cut the material below the satchel base into ¼-inch-wide strips for a fringe.

4. Measure 5 inches down from the top of your bag, then cut off the 5-inch section from 1 side of the tube, leaving the other side intact to turn into your flap.

5. Cut the remaining 5-inch section into a semicircle with pinking shears.

6. Cut a buttonhole in the flap, fold the flap down, position the button on the bag, and stitch the button in place.

7. With pinking shears, cut a long 1½-inch-wide strip from the remnants of your leather pants for your strap. Determine how long you want your strap to be and trim the strip accordingly.

8. Insert the ends of your strap into the mouth of the satchel and stitch them in place with your sewing machine, making sure to backtack.

SUPER-SIMPLE SHOE BAG

I always like to give someone a very simple gift that they can actually use. Something that says, "Hey, this isn't a ceramic figurine of a dog that somewhat looks like your dog. It's a shoe bag that might come in handy on your next trip. I made it with you in mind and I hope you like it." Now, that's a gift that tells it like it is!

YOU'LL NEED

- ¹/₂ yard of fabric
- Scissors
- Iron and ironing board
- Sewing machine
- Matching thread
- 1 yard of matching ribbon
- Safety pin

HERE'S HOW

1 Cut your fabric into a rectangle 16 inches by 21 inches.

2 With fabric right side down, fold over one of the 21-inch sides ½ inch and press with your iron.

3 With the ½-inch fold still in place, fold over again 1 inch and press. You're creating a tunnel for your ribbon, which is in the mouth of your bag.

4 With the pressed side unfolded, fold right sides together widthwise along a 16-inch side, and using a ½-inch seam allowance, stitch down ¾ inch from the top (where the mouth of your bag will be), and backtack. Leave a ½-inch gap—this will be the opening for your ribbon—then resume sewing, making sure to backtack, all the way down the side and across the bottom of the bag.

5 Turn the bag right side out and fold down where you pressed your bag to form your tunnel.

6 Stitch all the way around the mouth of the bag.

7 Put your safety pin on one end of the ribbon and push it through the tunnel.

8 Cut your ribbon at a slant, tie a knot at each end, and press the bag flat.

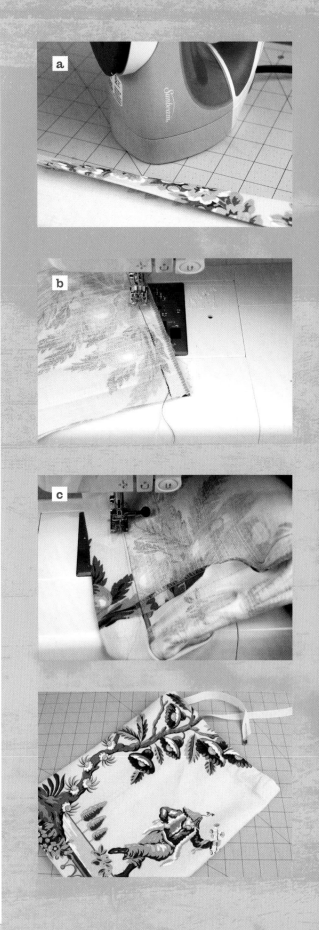

ZIGZAG RIBBON MAKEUP BAG

I sold hundreds of these in my boutique in the East Village of New York, and to this day my friends call me and ask if I still make them. (I do, occasionally.) Well, now you and my pals can make them, too, and I can take a rest!

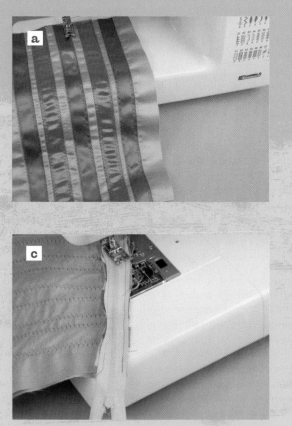

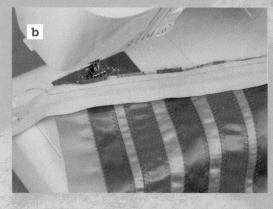

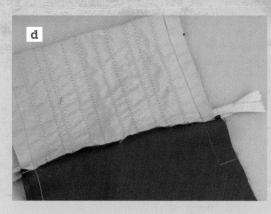

YOU'LL NEED

- 5 pieces of 1-inch ribbon that matches your satin, each 12 inches
- 1 piece of satin fabric, 9 inches by 12 inches
- 1 piece of lining fabric, 9 inches by 12 inches
- Sewing machine with zigzag stitch
- Colorful matching thread
- 1 (10-inch) zipper
- 12 inches of ¼-inch ribbon (for the zipper pull)

HERE'S HOW

1 In even zigzag stitches, sew the 1-inch ribbon side by side onto the satin rectangle.

2 Lay your zipper facedown on the ribbons, so the zipper pull is against the ribbons, and stitch 1 side of the zipper to a 9-inch edge of ribbons.

3 Fold the piece in half, with right sides together, so the 9-inch edges meet, and stitch the other side of the zipper to the other 9-inch side of the ribbon piece.

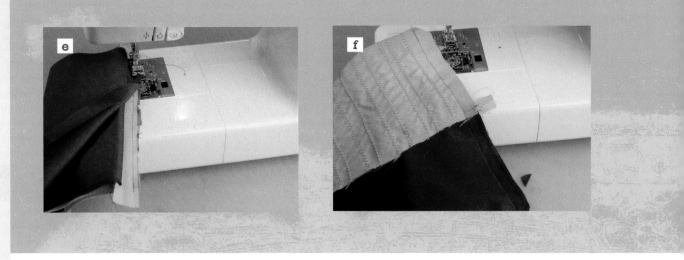

4 Lay your ribbon piece on your sewing machine so both sides of the zipper are visible. Place your lining piece on top so that one 9-inch edge matches up with one of the zipper's edges, and stitch along the edge.

5 Repeat on the other side, sandwiching the zipper between the 9-inch edges of the lining, as shown in the photo.

6 Unzip your zipper halfway.

7 Spread lining and ribbon pieces out on either side of the zipper so they lie flat. Stitch along one side using a $1/2$-inch seam allowance, and then clip the corners outside the seams so that when you turn the bag right side out there's no bulk in the corners.

8 Stitch along the other side, using a $1/2$-inch seam allowance and leaving 3 inches of the lining open. Clip the corners.

9 Clip the excess zipper on each end of the bag.

10 Pull the bag through the opening you left in the lining, then stitch closed and push the lining inside the bag.

11 Put your $1/4$-inch ribbon through the hole in the zipper, pull it through halfway, and tie a knot so it stays in place.

CHIC RAG RUG BAG

My friend Esther needed a cool bag for a black outfit she was wearing to an art opening but she had no time to shop, so I whipped this up for her in about an hour. The one I made is simple, but there are all kinds of things you can do to embellish it—try gluing on flowers or buttons, or you could add funky fabric patches.

YOU'LL NEED

- Rag rug
  (mine was 30 inches by 18 inches; sizes vary)
- Piece of thick fabric the same size as your rug
- Scissors
- 1½ yards of ½-inch grosgrain ribbon
- 2 chain dog collars
- Straight pins
- Sewing machine with thread to match fabric

HERE'S HOW

1 Cut the fabric into a rectangle that's just a bit smaller than the rug.

SUGGESTION

> Zigzag-stitch around the piece of fabric (or use a serger, if you have one), to give it a nice, finished edge.

2 Cut 2 pieces of ribbon that are about 4 inches longer than the dog chains, and weave 1 through each chain, letting a couple inches of ribbon hang through each loop at the ends of the chains.

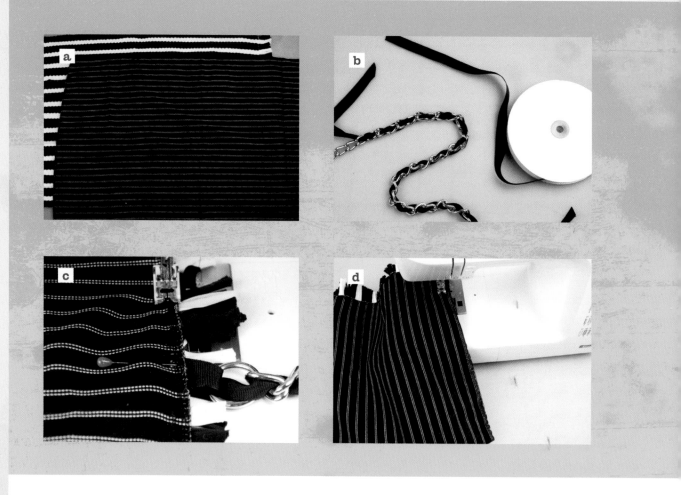

3 Cut 4 pieces of ribbon, each 3 inches long, and pin 2 to each fringed side of the rug where you want your handles positioned. (I placed mine by finding the center of each side of the rug, then pinning a ribbon piece $3^{1}/_{2}$ inches left of center and another piece $3^{1}/_{2}$ inches right of center.)

4 Attach a handle to each side by folding the ribbon tabs over the end loops on the dog chains and pinning the excess ribbon hanging from the dog chains to the ends of the loops of ribbon.

5 Place the fabric on top of the rug, sandwiching the ribbon loops and the excess ribbon from the chains between the fabric and the rug. Pin the fabric in place.

6 Stitch all the way around the edges of the fabric, zigzagging over the ribbons twice so the handles are secure.

7 Fold up the bag with right sides facing, and sew up the sides using a $^{1}/_{2}$-inch seam allowance.

8 Turn the bag right side out and you're done!

BACKPACK PILLOWCASE

There are two things that drive me nuts (okay, there are more like five hundred things that drive me nuts, but I'm only listing two here). 1. People who travel in their pajamas. 2. Having to carry my full-size pillow around the airport like a hobo. So you can see why this project was a must. Make one for yourself, and stop traveling in those hideous pajamas!

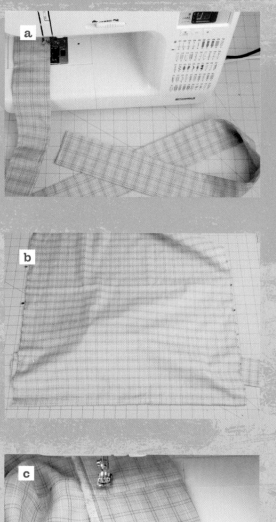

YOU'LL NEED

- 1 yard of 60-inch cotton fabric
- Scissors
- Iron
- Sewing machine
- Matching thread
- Straight pins
- 2-inch Velcro strip
- Pillow

HERE'S HOW

1 Cut out a rectangle from your fabric, 20 inches by 60 inches.

2 Cut out a strip from your fabric, 10 inches wide and 60 inches long.

3 Fold the 10-inch strip in half down the length and press the fold with your iron.

4 Fold the now 5-inch-wide strip in half down the length again and press. You have an ironed and folded piece of fabric $2\frac{1}{2}$ inches wide and 60 inches long for your strap.

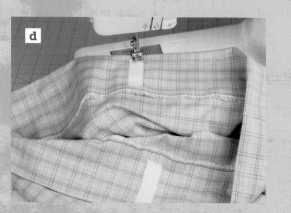

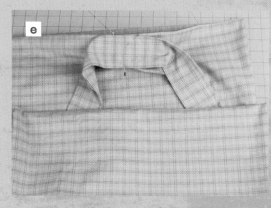

5 Stitch along all sides of the strap, about ¼ inch from the edges.

6 Fold the 20-inch by 60-inch piece of fabric in half lengthwise to form a rectangle 20 inches by 30 inches.

7 Sandwich each end of the strap between the layers of folded fabric 3½ inches from the fold and pin in place. (In the photo, I left an end peeking out a bit so you can see where the strap goes, but you should make sure to match up the edges of fabric before you pin.)

8 Fold down 3½ inches of both layers of fabric at the mouth of the case, and pin all the way up the sides of your case.

9 Stitch up the sides, using a ½-inch seam allowance.

10 Turn the case inside out. You'll notice that by sewing your case this way you have finished the inside side edges of the pillowcase around the mouth.

11 Stitch all the way around the mouth of the pillowcase 3 inches from the edge to finish it.

12 Find the center of each side of the case right inside the mouth, and apply Velcro strips. Stitch the Velcro in place.

13 Pin the center of the strap to the exact center of one side of the mouth on the outside of your pillowcase.

14 Carefully try your backpack pillowcase on for size and make sure the strap is pinned on correctly before you sew it. (It can easily get twisted leading up to this step.)

15 Stitch the center of your strap in place, put a pillow in your backpack pillowcase, and you're off!

SUGGESTION

If you don't want to make an entire pillowcase from scratch, consider just making the straps by following the instructions provided and adding them to an existing pillowcase to save time. You might also want to consider adding a pocket to your Backpack Pillowcase so that you can stash a book in it to read during your journey.

IT'S NOT PIFFLE, IT'S WIFFLE!

Piffle" means nonsense, and wiffle balls are anything but that. I happen to think that wiffle balls will make their way into every crafty person's arsenal very soon. They are just too cool to overlook, and their uses are many. For instance, I very much enjoy tossing them at my assistant to get her attention. But back to crafts. In this chapter, you'll find a few fun projects to get you on your wiffley way. However, I know deep in my glitter-covered soul that there are tons of other wiffle ball projects to be done, so if you think of a fantastic project for me using some wonderful wiffles, whip one at the back of my head and get my attention. I'd love to hear from you.

WIFFLE BALL DNA LAMP

When I first saw wiffle balls in the dollar store I was so excited I bought fifty of them. Every once in a while the balls would spill on the floor in my craft room, so I decided to string them on a piece of heavy nylon string, and lo and behold, this lamp was born.

YOU'LL NEED

- 1 white cord and socket set
- Ruler
- Pencil
- Dremel tool
- 12 large wiffle balls
- 12 small wiffle balls
- Small piece of heavy-duty sandpaper or sanding block
- 1 small, low-wattage lightbulb
- 3 yards white nylon heavy-duty string, plus extra for hanging lamp
- Small wall hook, for hanging finished lamp

HERE'S HOW

1. Measure the circumference of the socket in your cord and socket set.

2. Draw a hole the size of your socket on 1 of the large wiffle balls, and cut it out with the Dremel.

3. Sand off the rough edges with the sandpaper or sanding block.

4. Attach the bulb to the socket and insert it into the wiffle ball, making sure that it fits in the ball properly.

5. String the remaining wiffle balls on the nylon string as if you were making a big wiffle ball necklace.

6. Tie the ends of the string together tightly. You don't want to lose any balls!

7. Now tangle the "necklace" so that it looks like DNA gone wild.

8. Add the wiffle ball that is connected to the cord and socket by stringing the cord through the wiffle jumble and wrapping the cord around the string so that it stays in place.

9. Hang the lamp, plug it in, and enjoy the wiffley glow.

BOOK PAGE-COVERED WIFFLE BALLS

I can't resist playing with decorative balls if I see them sitting in a bowl on top of a coffee table. I can't help it—hearing people tell me to stop touching their balls makes me laugh! These book page-covered balls are quite beautiful in their simplicity, so get some balls and make these fantastic tabletop accessories!

YOU'LL NEED

- Pages from an old book
- Scissors
- Wiffle balls
- Elmer's glue
- Cup of water
- 1-inch paintbrush
- Minwax Polycrylic Protective Finish

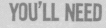

HERE'S HOW

1. Cut book pages into strips about $\frac{3}{8}$ inch wide by 4 inches long. You can make them longer if you want, but I find the shorter strips are easier to work with.

2. Water down your Elmer's glue just a tiny bit so it's easy to spread, then paint it on a section of the wiffle ball and lay down a strip of book page.

3. Continue gluing strips on until the entire ball is covered, then add some more for a pretty overlapping effect.

4. When the glue is dry, clear-coat the ball for a nice glaze.

WIFFLE BALL PENCIL HOLDER

I lose pencils all the time, so I appreciate a good pencil holder. This one currently resides on my desk and I love it. It's playful and keeps me organized—two excellent qualities in a desk accessory.

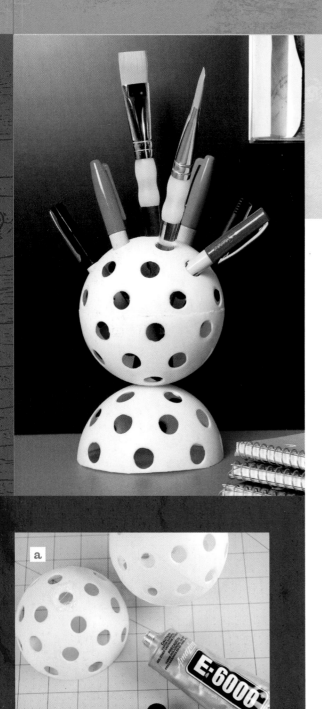

YOU'LL NEED

- 2 large wiffle balls
- Dremel tool with cutting wheel
- Sandpaper
- E-6000 glue

HERE'S HOW

1 With the Dremel, carefully cut 1 of the wiffle balls in half to form the base of your pencil holder. (Most wiffle balls have a seam that runs through the middle; try to use that as a guide.)

2 Sand off the rough parts from the edge so that it's smooth and even.

3 Sand the top of your half–wiffle ball and a small section of the full ball.

4 Put a gob of E-6000 on the sanded area of your half wiffle and place the full wiffle on top, matching up the sanded areas. Let the glue dry.

WIFFLE BALL NIGHT-LIGHT TOWER

At night when this night-light is lit up, I feel like I'm looking up at the stars in the comfort of my own bed. While you might think it is more suitable for a kid's room, I promise that after you make it and try it out just once, you'll want one in every room.

YOU'LL NEED

- 1 battery-operated disk light
- Ruler
- Pencil
- 3 large wiffle balls
- Dremel with cutting wheel attachment
- Sanding block or sandpaper
- E-6000 glue

HERE'S HOW

1. Measure the top of your disk light.

2. With a pencil, draw a circle the size of the disk light on one wiffle ball, then carefully cut it out with the Dremel.

3. Sand off any rough edges.

4. Trace a circle approximately the size of a quarter on the opposite side of the wiffle ball, cut it out, and sand the edges. This will be the base of your tower.

5. Cut 2 quarter-size holes on opposite sides of another wiffle ball to create the middle piece.

6. On your last wiffle ball, cut 1 quarter-size hole. This will be the top piece of the tower.

7. Glue the 3 balls together where the holes meet, with the hole for the disk light on the very bottom.

8. Glue the tower to the disk light and get ready to see the stars!

a

Adults are always saying that they wish they could be kids again. Whenever I hear this, I always ask, "Why can't you?" I mean, it's pretty easy—just go have some fun for a little while partaking in something simple. Dig a hole, bust out the finger paints, get on a swing set, or read a children's book, and you'll soon remember that life's not about paying bills or trading stock tips, it's about enjoying every day to the fullest. So go get out a box of crayons and draw a picture of your mom. You remember how to do that, right? Start with a stick figure with curly brown hair and then fill in the rest. Once you're done you'll be ready to fully appreciate the projects in the following section.

STUFFED ALLIGATOR

I'm extremely scared of getting eaten alive by an alligator, and I thought a fun way to conquer my gator phobia would be to make one that I could either sleep with or step on. So I did!

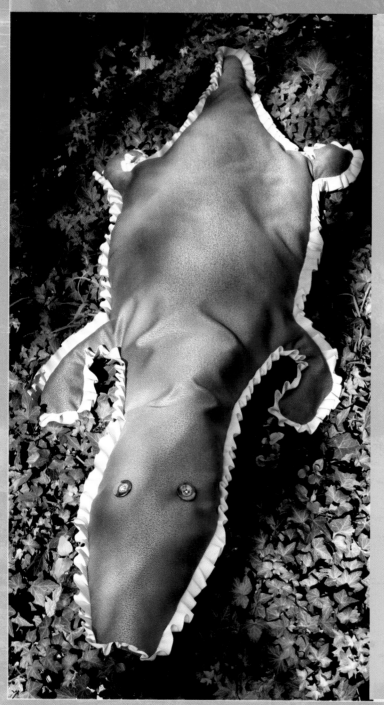

YOU'LL NEED

- 2 yards of 60-inch heavy-duty fabric
- Pencil and paper for pattern
- Straight pins
- Scissors
- 2 large buttons for the eyes
- Needle and thread
- Sewing machine with matching thread
- 6 yards of pleated ribbon, rickrack, or some other type of trim
- 2 large bags of pillow stuffing

HERE'S HOW

1 Fold your fabric in half widthwise so you have a folded piece 60 inches long and 36 inches wide.

2 Enlarge and trace the pattern provided on page 368 (or sketch out your alligator freehand if you're brave), then pin your pattern on the folded fabric and cut out two layers of your alligator.

3 Sew the eyes on one of the alligator layers. This will be the top layer.

4 Stitch trim around the top layer, making sure the trim points toward the inside of the gator and using a little less than a ½-inch seam allowance.

5 Put the second layer of your gator on top of the decorated gator layer so the pieces are face-to-face. Pin the pieces together, leaving a 6-inch-long opening in one side, and stitch the layers together around the edges, trapping an edge of the trim inside the alligator. Don't stitch up the 6-inch opening.

6 Clip the curved edges of your gator, making sure not to clip any stitching, to ensure that when you turn your alligator right side out it will keep its true shape.

7 Turn the alligator right side out through the opening, fill it with pillow stuffing, then stitch closed with needle and thread.

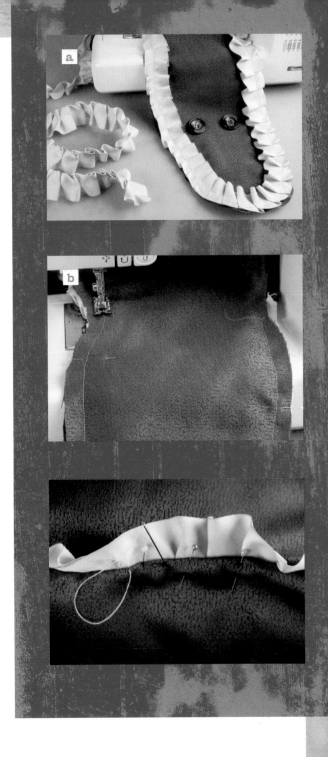

ALPHABET LAMPSHADE

This lampshade is so cheerful, don't you think? Whether you see it decorating a child's room or envision it livening up your home office, have fun making it and be sure to use a cool, energy-efficient bulb.

YOU'LL NEED

- Small white plastic trash can or small paper lampshade
- Plastic alphabet magnets
- E-6000 glue
- Clear tape
- Drill with ¼-inch drill bit (if you're using a small plastic trash can)
- Energy-efficient cool lightbulb (see page 307—this is the only type of bulb you should use here!)

HERE'S HOW

1 If you're using a small trash can, turn it over and drill a small hole in the center of the bottom, just big enough for the screw at the top of the harp. (The bottom of your trash can is now the top of the lamp.)

HINT

> The harp is the curved metal wire that goes around the lightbulb. It has a screw at the top that pokes through the shade and then gets topped with a little knob called a finial.

2 Using E-6000, glue your letters all the way around the lampshade or trash can. Arrange them in different positions and try to fit on as many as you can.

3 Hold the letters in place with clear tape while the glue dries.

4 When the glue has set, remove the tape, install your energy-efficient bulb, and screw your new shade on top of your lamp.

JUMBLED ALPHABET ART

Usually when I need a specific item to make something, I can never find it. This piece of art requires the perfect piece of Plexiglass for the inside of the frame, and I thought for sure I would have to get it custom cut and it would be a big pain in my big-ass book of crafts. However, when I went to the Home Depot, there was a stack of Plexiglas pieces the exact size that I needed. I almost fainted! Maybe it's due to that rare experience, but this is one of my favorite art projects in the book.

YOU'LL NEED

- 1 (18" x 24") plastic box frame
- Enough plastic magnet letters to fill up the frame
- 1 (18" x 24") piece of Plexiglas (make sure it fits inside the frame perfectly)
- E-6000 glue

HERE'S HOW

1 Lay your plastic frame facedown and remove the cardboard box from inside.

2 Fill the frame with letters, making sure they're all facedown inside the frame. Arrange them in a random pattern, and include as many as possible.

3 Place the Plexiglas sheet down on the letters.

4 Dot E-6000 all the way around the inside of the frame where it touches the Plexiglas to help keep it in place. Let the glue dry overnight.

FRILLY FLOWERY PRINCESS TENT

I currently have this tent hanging over my bed, and I feel like a princess every morning when I wake up to the shimmery fabrics and faux flowers. I'm sure the minute my niece sees it I'll have to give it to her (that's the cost of being an uncle who knows how to sew), but in the meantime, I'm going to enjoy every minute I have with it.

YOU'LL NEED

- 2 yards of 60-inch pink satin
- Scissors
- 1½ yards of yellow satin or cotton
- Sewing machine
- Straight pins
- 1 Hula-Hoop that can be cut down to 24 inches in diameter
- Heavy-duty craft knife
- 5 yards of yellow organza
- 5 yards of green organza
- Sewing needle and thread
- 24 large faux flowers
- 20 yards of 1-inch satin ribbon
- *Optional:* Iron and ironing board; hot glue gun and glue sticks

SUGGESTION

> Create your own color scheme to match your room!

HERE'S HOW

1. Fold the pink satin in half and cut out 8 double-layer flower petals, each approximately 18 inches long and 15 inches at the base.

2. Fold the yellow satin in half and cut out 2 circles 25 inches in diameter.

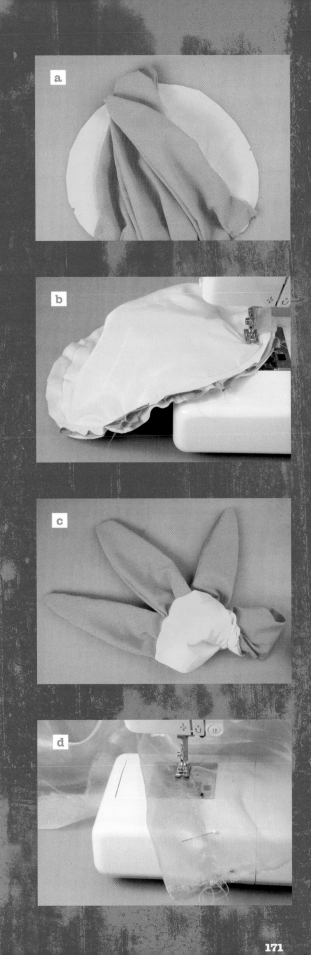

3 With right sides facing, sew the 2 layers of satin petals together around the long edges, leaving the bases of the petals open.

4 Turn the 8 petals right side out and pin the base of each to the edge of 1 of the yellow circles, with the points of the petals pointing toward the center of the circle.

5 Put the other yellow circle on top of the first, sandwiching the petals between the 2 yellow pieces. Sew around the edge of the circles, catching the ends of the petals and leaving a 5-inch opening in the circle.

6 Pull the petals out through the opening.

HINT

> If you want your petals to be perfectly flat and smooth, press them with an iron. (I didn't press my petals because I wanted them to have more dimension.)

7 Fold the seam allowance that sticks out from the opening inside the yellow circle, and sew the opening shut on the sewing machine.

8 Cut a rectangle 18 inches by 3 inches from your leftover yellow fabric. Fold it in half widthwise with right sides facing, then sew it into a long tube along the long edges and turn it right side out.

9 Fold the tube in half to create a loop and stitch both ends onto the center of 1 side of the yellow circle so that you can hang your tent later.

10 Pull the Hula-Hoop apart at the joiner and cut it down with a heavy-duty craft knife until you have a 24-inch-diameter hoop. Save the joiner because you will use it later.

11 Cut the yellow and green organza rectangles in half so you have 4 pieces that are $2\frac{1}{2}$ yards long.

12 Create a tunnel along one end of each panel by folding the end over $2\frac{1}{2}$ inches, pinning the folds in place and stitching along the edge of the folded fabric.

13 Run the hoop through the tunnels of the 4 panels, and close the hoop with the joiner.

14 Using needle and thread, attach your flower to the hoop by stitching around the hoop and through the flower in at least 8 places.

DON'T WORRY

> Your yellow center should slightly overlap the hoop, but if you have to attach the petals to the hoop instead, it will still work.

15 Cut the ribbon into 4 pieces, each 5 yards long.

16 Stitch or hot-glue the faux flowers to the ribbon pieces, then drape the ribbons over the hoop, between the panels.

17 Hang your tent above your bed or, on a nice day, from a tree in the backyard.

SNAPPY THE SNAIL PILLOW

Who doesn't want a pillow that looks like a snail? My niece and nephew love this guy. In fact, I was barely done stitching him before he disappeared, and when I found him he was being ridden like a horse and had nearly fallen apart. I doubled up on my stitches before I let him out of my sight again.

YOU'LL NEED

- 2 yards of 54-inch green fabric
- Scissors
- Sewing machine with matching thread
- Enough pillow stuffing to fill 3 large bed pillows (approximately 3 large bags)
- Needle and thread
- 1 yard of 54-inch or 60-inch yellow fabric
- 8-inch by 8-inch piece of black felt

HERE'S HOW

1 Cut the green fabric in half lengthwise so that you have 2 long strips of fabric, each 27 inches wide by 2 yards long.

2 Sew the 2 pieces together along a 27-inch side of each piece so you have 1 piece of fabric that is 27 inches wide by 4 yards long.

3 Fold the piece in half lengthwise and with a $\frac{1}{2}$-inch seam allowance, sew it into a 4-yard-long tube. Sew across 1 short end to form a long sock.

4 Turn the long sock inside out and stuff it with pillow stuffing. When it's full, stitch the open end of the tube closed on the sewing machine.

5 Roll the tube into a spiral, hand-stitching the fabric in place as you go. Use lots and lots of stitches. I mean really sew it together here!

6 Enlarge and trace the pattern provided on page 368 onto the yellow fabric two times, and cut out the shapes.

7 Cut out 2 big circles and 1 smaller circle from your black felt to use as your snail's eyes and nose, and zigzag stitch them on 1 of the yellow pieces.

8 Place the plain snail body on top of the snail body with a face. Stitch the fabric pieces together face-to-face, using a $\frac{1}{4}$-inch seam allowance and leaving a 5-inch opening on 1 side.

9 Turn your snail's body inside out and fill it with pillow stuffing. Make sure to really stuff the antennae so they stick straight up! When you're done, stitch the opening closed.

10 Hand-stitch the snail body to the shell, making sure to use tons of stitches.

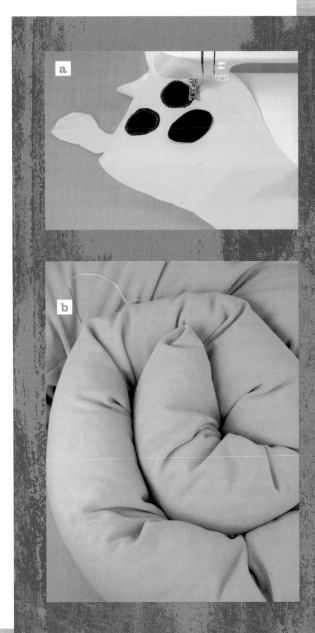

LETTER PERFECT

I never take the postal service for granted. It's really the coolest thing when you actually think about it: You put a letter in your mailbox and magically it finds its way across the world. That is fantastic. I take advantage of this awesome service by writing a letter every day. When I find that my daily routine is becoming a bit overwhelming, I stop what I'm doing and write a note to someone I love. It helps me put things in perspective. I also devote one day a year to really flexing my letter-writing muscles. Each January, I pick a day in the beginning of the month to write all of the birthday cards I plan to send to friends for the entire year while I transfer my date book from one year to the next, and then I file the cards by the day I need to send them. It takes about an afternoon, but let me tell you, what a relief when it's done!

Whether you're a letter-writing fanatic like me or just enjoy sending the occasional postcard, I hope this chapter will inspire you to send some love.

MASQUERADE MASK GREETING CARD

I made this card in honor of one of my favorite movies, *The Count of Monte Cristo.* I just love how the main character invites everyone to the ball so he can introduce himself as the count and seek revenge on his ex–best friend who schemed to get him tossed into the Château d'If!

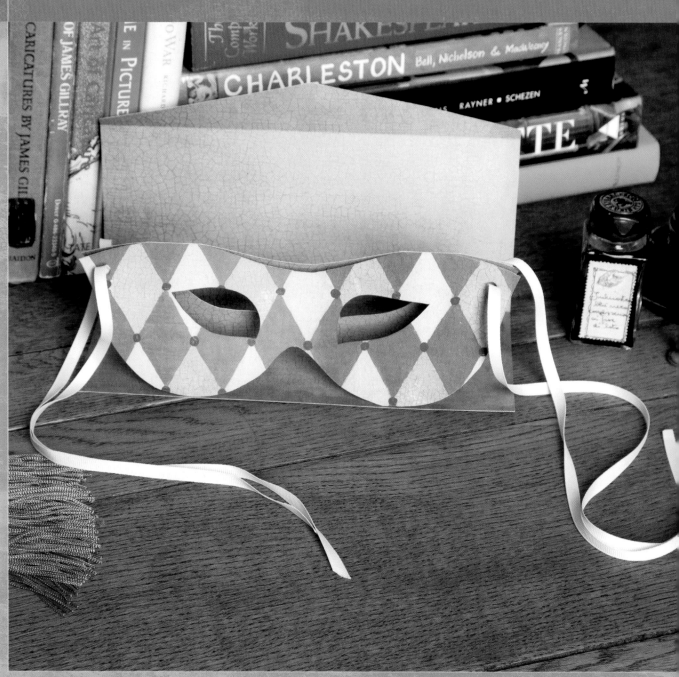

YOU'LL NEED

- Pencil
- 1 sheet of scrapbook paper that you like
- Scissors
- Cutting knife
- Hole punch
- 1 yard of ¼-inch ribbon
- Clear tape

HERE'S HOW

1. Enlarge and trace the patterns provided on page 376 onto your scrapbook paper and cut out the shapes.

2. Carefully score the envelope and where the 2 masks meet so that they will fold together easily, making sure not to cut all the way through the paper.

3. Tape the bottom edge of 1 of the masks to the end of the envelope.

4. Fold the 2 masks into 1, and punch a hole on each side.

5. Cut your ribbon in half and string a piece through each of the holes.

6. Write your note on the inside of the envelope, fold the masks and tuck them inside, and send.

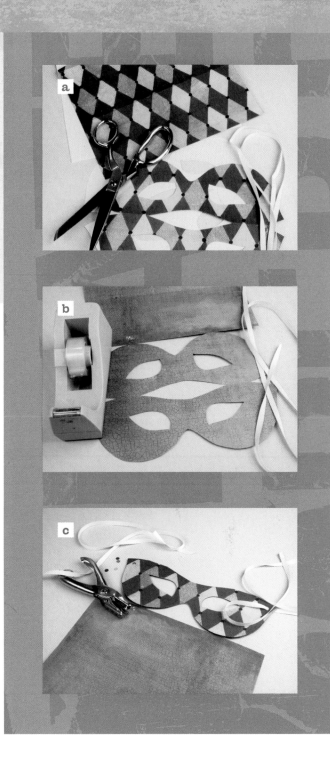

STENCILICIOUS NOTECARDS AND ENVELOPE LINERS

I was browsing through the stationery section of my local 99-cent store and found these super-cool alphabet stencils. A few weeks later, almost everything I owned was covered with letters. These stencils are available pretty much everywhere, so pick some up, grab some spray paint, and lock up anything you don't want decorated!

YOU'LL NEED
FOR BOTH

- Plastic alphabet stencils
- Krylon spray paint, (a color you like for the notecards and metallic gold for the envelope liners)
- Scissors

YOU'LL NEED
FOR THE NOTECARDS

- Poster board in different colors or cardboard and book pages
- Elmer's spray adhesive (for the book page–covered cards)
- Newspaper
- *Optional:* A second can of spray paint in a contrasting color (if you plan on creating a shadow effect for your lettering)

YOU'LL NEED
FOR THE ENVELOPE LINERS

- Colorful paper (the heavier the better)
- Envelopes
- Pencil
- Elmer's glue stick

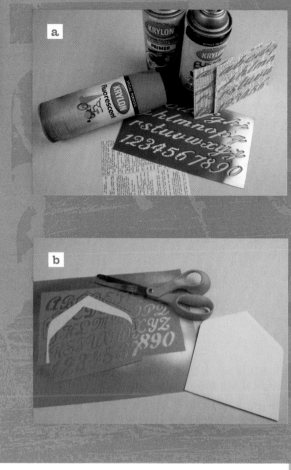

HERE'S HOW
FOR THE NOTECARDS

1. Cut your poster board down to the size you want your notecard to be (I usually make mine 4 inches by 6 inches). If you're using book pages as a background, spray-mount the page to your cardboard first, then cut your notecard to size.

2. Position the stencil on top of your poster board or book page–covered card, spray-paint it, and let dry.

HINT

> If you're going for the shadow effect, spray the stencil with your lighter color first and let dry. Then, move the stencil just a tiny bit to the right, spray it with the darker color, and let dry.

HERE'S HOW
FOR THE ENVELOPE LINERS

1. Place your stencil sheet on top of your colored paper, and spray-paint it with metallic gold. Let dry.

2. With the flap open, lay your envelope flat on the stenciled paper and trace around the flap and halfway down the body.

3. Cut out the shape, shaving off ¼ inch all the way around the edges.

4. Apply glue to the back of the liner with your glue stick, then carefully tuck it inside the envelope.

CEREAL BOX POSTCARDS

I have to admit, I can never toss out a cereal box, because I love the cardboard. The weight is perfect for all kinds of projects, especially postcards. I also collect cool images, which I photocopy and use over and over, so it was only a matter of time before I came up with this project.

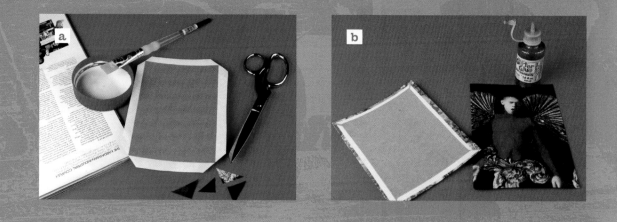

YOU'LL NEED

- **Cereal boxes**
- **Photocopied images** (images cut out of an old magazine will work too)
- **Ruler**
- **Pencil**
- **Scissors**
- **Elmer's glue**
- **Cup of water**
- **1-inch paintbrush**
- **Glitter glue** (the most important ingredient in any project!)

HERE'S HOW

1 Decide how big you want your postcard to be (I send all different sizes), and cut up your cereal box accordingly.

2 Copy your original image on an $8\frac{1}{2}" \times 11"$ sheet of paper, then reduce it to fit your postcard size.

3 Using your pencil and ruler, draw a $\frac{1}{2}$-inch border all the way around your image, then cut out your image along these lines.

4 Water down some glue just a tiny bit so that it spreads easily but is not watery.

5 Paint the glue on the colorful side of the cardboard, not on your copied image.

6 Lay the cardboard plain side up in the center of the back of your copied image.

7 Cut the corners off the borders of the copied image.

8 Paint glue on the back of the $\frac{1}{2}$-inch border and fold over.

9 Embellish with glitter glue and whatever else you want.

BOOK PAGE–LINED ENVELOPES

Megan Mullally has always been one of my favorite actors. I went on her talk show a while ago, and as we were making a project together she screamed out, "Easy squeezy!" and the phrase has stuck with me ever since. These book page–lined envelopes are not only beautiful but truly easy squeezy to make. Maybe I'll send Megan a fan letter in one someday!

YOU'LL NEED

- Envelopes
- Pencil
- Ruler
- Scissors
- Pages from an old book
- Elmer's glue stick

HERE'S HOW

1 Lay your envelope flat on a book page with the flap open. Trace around the flap and halfway down the body using your pencil.

2 Cut out the shape, shaving off ¼ inch all the way around the edges.

3 Apply glue to the back of the liner with the glue stick, then carefully tuck it inside the envelope.

FRIENDLY FURRY HELLO

I know, you're probably thinking, What in the name of pink poodles is this guy talking about? Trust me, this postcard was a hoot to make and really fun to send. These have made it through the mail, but just in case, be sure to put your return address on them, and put them in a post office drop-off box (rather than in your own mailbox for the mailman to pick up).

YOU'LL NEED

- Cardboard
  (use your cereal boxes, people!)
- ¼ yard of faux fur
  (this is enough to make about 20 postcards)
- Scissors
- Hot glue gun and glue sticks

HERE'S HOW

1. Cut your cardboard into 4" × 6" rectangles.
2. Cut your faux fur into an equal number of 4" × 6" rectangles.
3. Apply hot glue to the back of your fur pieces, then stick them to the cardboard.
4. Write a note, add a stamp, and drop it in a mailbox.

SUGGESTION

Cut the fur outside, because it's a flurry of fur fury when your start snipping!

Can't wait until you're here. I have tons planned us to do!
♥ Mark

Kelly Jones
2417 Diablo Rd
Lawrence, KS
36126

WALLET LETTER

I was so excited when I came up with these wallet letters. I make tons of them in one sitting, using the extra paper I have lying around my craft room. The coolest thing about them is that they are beautiful envelopes and paper all in one little package—just glue the flap shut, add a stamp, and send 'em on their way!

YOU'LL NEED

- Scrapbook paper
- Lined paper
- Scissors
- Sewing machine
- Matching thread
- Elmer's glue stick
- *Optional:* Swing-arm paper cutter (If you have one it'll save you time. Otherwise scissors will do.)

HERE'S HOW

1. Cut your scrapbook paper into a 4-inch by 12-inch rectangle.

2. Cut 5 to 6 sheets of lined paper to 4 inches by $10^{1/2}$ inches.

3. Fold the lined paper in half widthwise. This fold line will be where you sew the papers together and where your wallet letter will fold.

4. Lay the lined paper on top of the scrapbook paper, with the 4-inch edges flush on one end of the stack so you have $1^{1/2}$ inches of excess scrapbook paper at the other end.

5. Stitch along the fold line, making sure to keep your line very straight. (The lines on the paper work very well as a guideline, too.)

6. Fold the wallet at the stitch line.

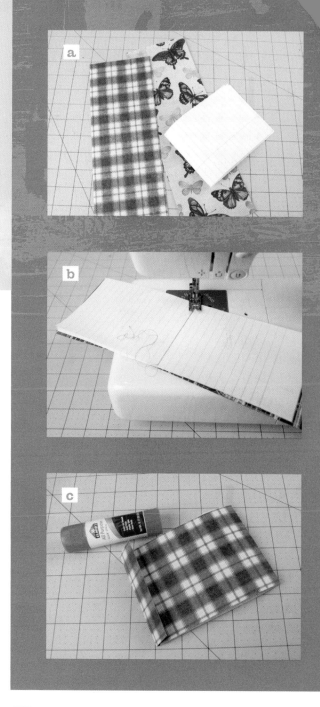

7. Fold over the excess scrapbook paper to create your flap.

8. When you're done writing your letter, glue the flap shut with a glue stick.

BLOOMING ENVELOPES

Have you seen the price of greeting cards lately? It costs *six dollars* to tell someone they're getting old! Luckily, these blooming greetings look like they cost a fortune and are guaranteed to brighten anyone's day, so try the classic onion dome or the pretty-petaled flower for your next card-giving occasion.

YOU'LL NEED

- 5 sheets of paper, each a different color

- Pencil
- Scissors (basic Fiskars work well on all types of paper)
- X-ACTO knife
- 1 office brad fastener
- Elmer's glue stick (for the flower)
- Sticker address label (for the onion)

HERE'S HOW

1. Using the patterns provided on pages 370–73, trace and cut out your pieces. If you're making the flower envelope, make sure to cut out 2 of the center disks; 1 will serve as your address label on the outside of the envelope, and the other will form the center of your envelope.

2. Arrange your pieces so that they fit one inside the other, and fold the petals inward to create a 3-D blooming effect. If you're making a flower, place 1 of your disks in the center of your stacked pieces.

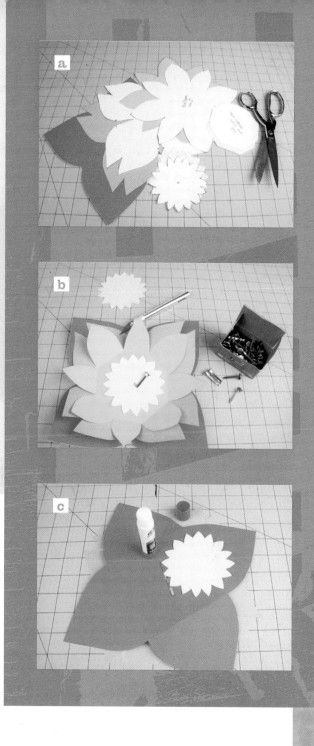

3 Using an X-ACTO knife, cut a hole through all of the layers in the center of your flower or onion that's just big enough for the fastener to go through.

4 Push the fastener through the hole on the front and unfold the ends on the back of the envelope.

5 For the flower envelope, glue the second disk on the outside of the envelope to cover the ends of the fastener and create your address label. For the onion envelope, use a sticker address label to cover the ends of the fastener.

6 Using the paper left over from your petals, create a card to enclose in your flower envelope.

7 Fold your greeting into the center of your bloom, and seal the outer petals with a dab of glue.

8 Spend the six dollars you just saved on a snack.

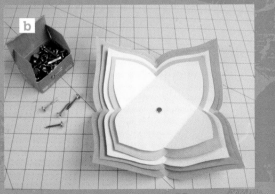

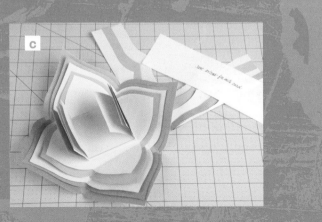

GLUE GUN SEAL

Did you know that hot-glue sticks come in different colors? I'd see them when I was out shopping for craft supplies, and I always wondered what to do with them. Finally I figured it out: a faux wax seal for the back of an envelope!

YOU'LL NEED

- Small dish with ice cubes
- Seal (for sealing wax)
- Envelope with your letter inside
- Hot glue gun and colored glue sticks
- Kitchen towel

HERE'S HOW

1. Place your seal on an ice cube.

2. With your glue gun, squeeze a blob of colored glue onto your envelope.

3. Quickly blot the seal dry with your towel and smoosh it on the hot glue.

4. After 2 or 3 seconds, remove the seal. Fun, right?

ride a scooter, and even in the summer my hands get cold while I ride, so I'm always buying knit gloves from the 99-cent store to keep in my seat compartment. Now, since we all know that accessorizing is more fun than eating in bed while watching a movie, I thought I would take my simple, inexpensive gloves and spruce them up a bit. Give them some "glove love," so to speak. I had a blast dreaming up ways to turn my cheap hand warmers into attention-grabbing accessories, and I'm sure you'll come up with tons more ways to make your gloves special. And if you ever see me scooting down the street with argyle arms, please wave hello!

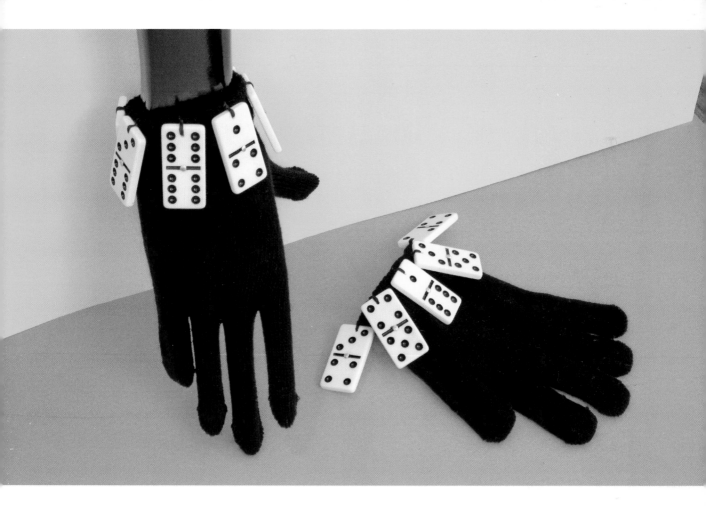

FANCY BIAS CUFF KNIT GLOVES

To make these gloves, I recommend using a fabric that contrasts with your winter coat so you'll really wow passersby with your haute hands.

YOU'LL NEED

- ¹/₂ yard of fabric (I like to use plaid)
- Scissors
- Sewing machine
- Matching thread
- Iron and ironing board
- Pair of knit gloves
- Straight pins

HERE'S HOW

1 Cut a 12-inch by 12-inch square of the fabric you've chosen on the bias.

HINT

> Cutting on the bias is when you place your fabric at a 45-degree angle instead of straight up and down, and then cut out your shape.

2 Sew 2 ends of the fabric square together to create a tube.

3 Press the seam open. People won't see the seam, but pressing it will make it a little more comfortable.

4 Fold the tube in half inside of itself, matching the raw ends, seams on the inside.

5 Place the glove inside the tube, with the opening of the glove and the raw ends of the tube at the same end.

6 Pin the glove and raw ends together with 2 straight pins.

7 Stitch your cuff to the glove, stretching the opening of the glove so that you can fit your hand inside.

8 Flip the cuff right side out.

BUTTON CLUSTER GLOVES

You know how every time you buy a new shirt it comes with a couple of extra buttons? Well, I can't ever seem to throw them out, so I'm always on the lookout for ways to put them to use. This is one of my favorites, and I think the results are glovely.

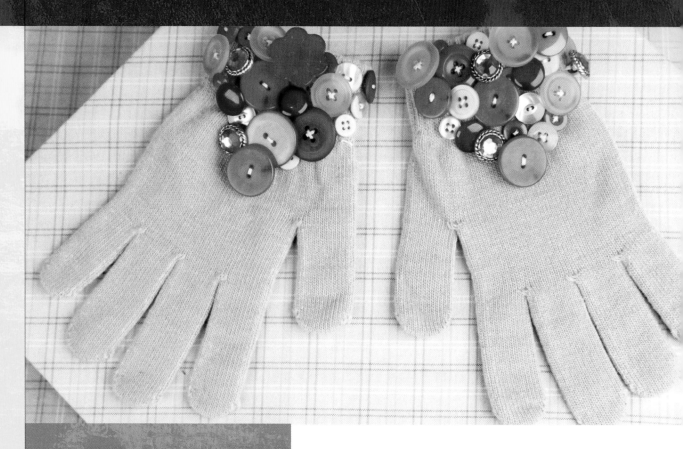

YOU'LL NEED

- 1 pair of knit gloves in a color you like
- Buttons in colors that match the gloves
- Needle and thread in a color that matches the gloves

HERE'S HOW

1 Arrange half of your buttons in a pattern you like on the top of one of your gloves.

2 Re-create the pattern on your other glove, then sew the buttons in place.

3 Use the finished glove as a template to sew the buttons on your first glove. Enjoy!

WINNING HAND DOMINO GLOVES

One day I found a pair of old gloves in a drawer and thought, Why not dress them up with some dominoes? Then I started wondering what else I might want to sew some dominoes onto. A scarf? The end of a curtain? A sweater for my friend's cat?

YOU'LL NEED

- 16 dominoes (8 per glove)
- Drill with ¹⁄₁₆" drill bit
- Small piece of scrap wood
- Pair of black knit gloves
- Needle
- Black thread

HERE'S HOW

1. Drill a small hole at 1 end of each domino. Use the scrap wood to protect your work surface.

2. Sew the dominoes onto the opening of your gloves individually, tying off each as you go around the mouth of the glove. This way there won't be thread connecting the dominos, so your gloves will easily stretch over your hand.

3. Have fun looking like a dominotrix!

SWEETER SWEATER GLOVES

How many sweaters do you have in your drawer that you really should toss, but don't because you think you might wear them again? My guess is at least three. Well, I've got a way to make more room in your dresser *and* put those sweaters to use!

YOU'LL NEED

- Sweater you really should toss
- Scissors
- One pair of knit gloves
- Straight pins
- Sewing machine with matching thread

HERE'S HOW

1 Cut off the sleeves of the sweater in a length you like.

2 Pull the cut-off sleeves up your arms by the cuffs. The cuffs should be tight enough to keep in place on your upper arms, but if they're not, pinch them and see how much you will need to take them in. Also see how much, if any, you will have to take in the sweater sleeves at the wrist (you don't want them too baggy).

3 If you need to take in the sleeves, gather the extra material along the seam of the sweater and stitch, then cut off the excess.

4 Turn the sleeves inside out and place the gloves in the end that you cut off, matching up the openings. (The fingers of the gloves should be pointed toward the sweater cuff end.)

5 Place a couple of straight pins in the openings to hold the gloves in place.

6 Sew the raw edge of the sleeve to the opening of the glove using a $^1/_2$-inch seam allowance. Make sure to stretch the fabric while you're sewing so that the glove opening will stretch when you put it on.

7 Turn the sleeves right side out.

ARGYLE SOCK GLOVES

I dig kneesocks! I like the length, the colors, and the argyle patterns, and I often wear them to bed on cold nights so my toes, feet, and calves stay toasty. One night I thought, If these superlong socks can keep me warm up to my knees, then why not sew them to some gloves that'll keep me warm up to my elbows? I whipped these up the very next day.

YOU'LL NEED

- 1 pair of long argyle socks
- Scissors
- 1 pair of knit gloves
- Straight pins
- Sewing machine with matching thread

HERE'S HOW

1 Cut off the foot of the socks and trim the remaining tubes to a length you like. I wanted my gloves to end at the elbow, so I measured up to my elbow and cut the socks accordingly.

2 Turn the socks inside out and place the gloves in the end that you cut off, matching up the openings. The fingers of the gloves should be pointing toward the part of the sock that will meet your elbow.

3 Place a couple of straight pins around the openings to hold the gloves in place.

4 Using a $\frac{1}{2}$-inch seam allowance, sew the opening of the sock to the opening of the glove, stretching the fabric of your glove opening as you work.

5 Turn the sock right side out and start warming up immediately.

NEVER BORED WITH CARDBOARD

When I was a kid we didn't have tons of money for art supplies, but my parents showed genius in utilizing whatever we had around the house for fun projects. One of my favorite things to use was cardboard. I'd repurpose a shoe box for an art project or make a cool fort out of several huge boxes with my five younger brothers (this was a daily event in my house). There wasn't enough cardboard to go around!

To this day, cardboard remains a staple in my crafty house. I encourage you to save your boxes and make something wonderful out of them the next time you're feeling inspired. Because, trust me, you're never bored with cardboard.

CARDBOARD CREATURE BOWL AND VASE

Lately I've been putting different cardboard shapes together just to see what happens, and, well, these just sort of happened. Give these projects a try using whatever image you like—the octopus I provided, a picture you drew, a photo of your pet, whatever!

YOU'LL NEED

FOR BOTH

- Pencil
- Cardboard
- X-ACTO knife
- Tape
- Elmer's glue
- Pages from an old phone book
- Cup of water
- 1-inch paintbrush
- 11" x 17" black-and-white image of your choice (*Optional:* Turn to page 366 to find the octopus image shown in the photos.)
- Mod Podge or Minwax Polycrylic Protective Finish

HERE'S HOW

FOR THE BOWL

1. Using the patterns provided on page 367, trace and cut out the hexagonal base and 6 side pieces from the cardboard.

2. Tape the pieces together so they create the shape of the bowl.

3. Apply Elmer's glue where the edges of your sides meet so that the bowl is nice and sturdy.

4. Cut phone book pages into 3-inch-wide strips.

5. Using Elmer's glue that has been watered down just a tiny bit so it's easy to spread with the paintbrush, adhere the strips to the entire bowl. Apply several layers of strips to give the vessel strength, then let the glue dry. (See photo on page 206.)

6. Cut out the cool image you chose.

7. Using your paintbrush, apply glue to the back of the image, and then position it in the center of your bowl.

8. Coat the entire bowl in the Mod Podge or clear coat to make it even more sturdy and give it a nice finish.

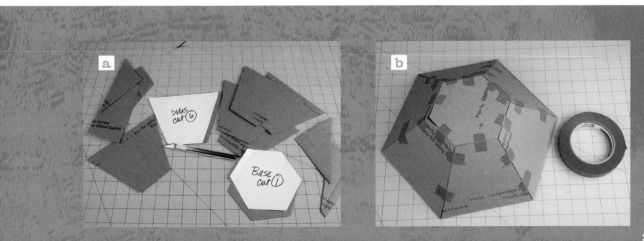

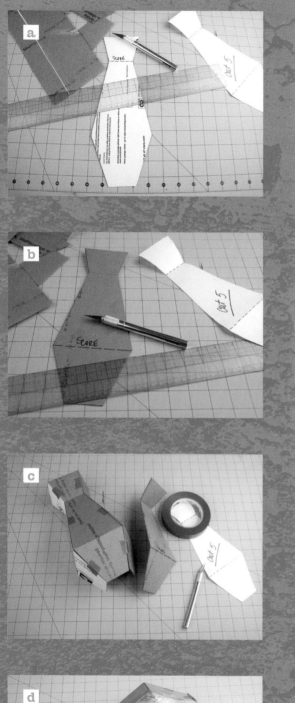

HERE'S HOW
FOR THE VASE

1 Using the patterns provided on page 365, trace and cut out the pentagonal base pattern and 5 side pieces from your cardboard.

2 Lightly score a line where the top of each vase piece tapers in. Turn the pieces over and score a line where the bottom of each vase piece is at its widest. This will make it easy to bend the pieces to form the vase shape.

3 Follow steps 3 through 8 for making the Cardboard Creature Bowl.

TIP

> Since this cardboard vase is light, you might want to put something heavy (like some marbles) in the bottom to keep it from toppling over.

MONEY OBELISK AND BUILDING BLOCKS

Anything covered with money looks interesting to me. In fact, if I could cover myself with money I would. However, I don't have money to burn or a desire to get thrown in jail for counterfeiting. Luckily, a little research yielded a solution that eased my mind: Turns out it's not illegal to copy currency as long as you change the size and color of the bills a little bit. So that's what I did, and these are what I made.

YOU'LL NEED

- Cardboard
- X-ACTO knife
- Ruler
- Pencil
- Elmer's glue
- Cup of water
- 1-inch paintbrush
- Tape
- Mod Podge or Minwax Polycrylic Protective Finish
- Photocopies of currency, or real currency if you're terribly rich

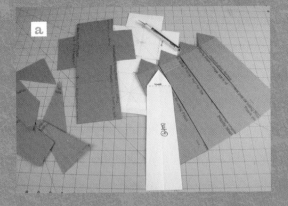

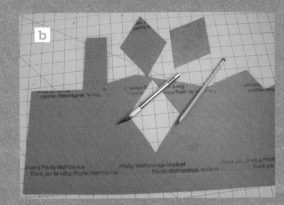

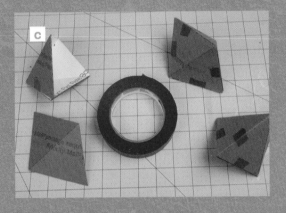

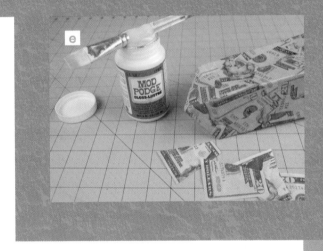

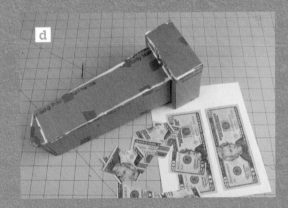

HERE'S HOW

1 Enlarge and trace the patterns provided on pages 363–64 onto the cardboard, and then cut them out. You can make them any size you want. As long as you enlarge the patterns all at the same percentage, the pieces will fit together perfectly.

2 With your X-ACTO knife, score along the dotted lines so that you can easily bend your pieces. Make sure not to cut all the way through the cardboard.

3 Tape the pieces together to make your obelisk or block shape.

4 Add Elmer's glue where the cardboard edges meet.

5 Cut the copied currency into small pieces, and start adhering them with slightly watered-down Elmer's glue.

6 When the object is covered and the glue has dried, coat it with Mod Podge or clear coat to give it a nice sheen.

CARDBOARD ART–HEAD HAT STAND

Usually I use photos of my friends in my craft projects, but no one I know is pretty enough for something this size. Just kidding! I love using photos of my friends as well as vintage images, and for this project I decided to use an image of Lina Cavalieri, a famous opera singer from the early 1900s. Lina's image was made iconic by Piero Fornasetti, who used it for his art and furniture, but you should feel free to substitute your own face or the face of an attractive friend for this project.

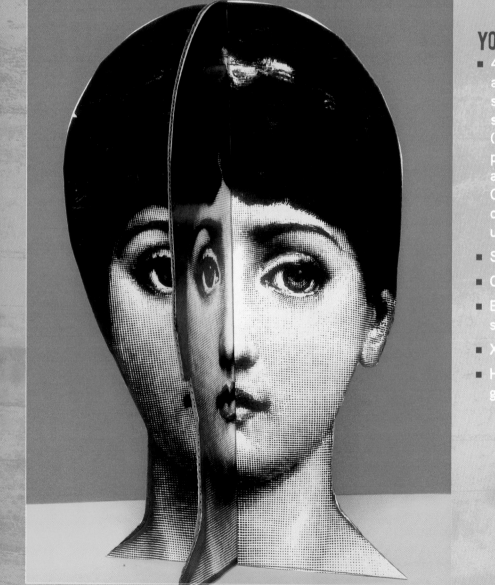

YOU'LL NEED

- 4 photocopies of a face that fills a standard 8¹/₂" x 11" sheet of paper (*Optional:* Turn to page 377 to find an image of Lina Cavalieri that you can enlarge and use.)

- Scissors

- Cardboard

- Elmer's spray adhesive

- X-ACTO knife

- Hot glue gun and glue sticks

HERE'S HOW

1 Cut out 1 of your copied faces.

2 Lay a piece of paper with a copied image facedown on your workspace, then lay your cutout face faceup on top, so that the faces are back to back. Trace around your copied image.

3 Cut out the shape that you just traced.

4 Spray Elmer's adhesive on the back of one of the images you just cut out, then glue it to a piece of cardboard.

5 Carefully cut out the cardboard-backed face with an X-ACTO knife.

6 Spray the second image with adhesive and glue it to the back of your cardboard head.

7 Repeat steps 2 through 6, using the cardboard head you just made as a pattern to trace.

8 Cut one of your cardboard heads in half.

9 Apply hot glue to the center edges of your split face, and glue 1 to each side of the full cardboard head.

ASTRO BRIGHT CANDLE TOWER

If, like me, you're often scrambling to find a centerpiece at the last minute, try whipping up this simple cardboard candle tower for your next dinner party. If time permits, make some in different sizes and use different images to match your décor, then give them to the guest who makes the biggest fuss over them!

YOU'LL NEED

- Cardboard
- Pencil
- X-ACTO knife
- Tape
- Elmer's glue
- Cup of water
- Scissors
- 1-inch paintbrush
- Pages from an old phone book
- Copy paper in bright colors
- Bold, interesting images you can copy and cut out
  (I used illustrations from an old book on butterflies)
- Mod Podge
- Glass saucer/plate/cup
- Votive candle

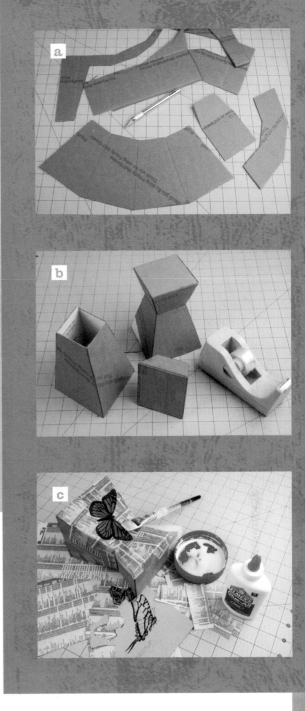

HERE'S HOW

1. Follow steps 1 through 4 for making the Money Obelisk on page 209, substituting the candleholder pattern provided on page 374 for the obelisk pattern.

2. Cut some phone book pages into thin strips. Apply them to the outside of your holders with watered-down glue using the paintbrush and let dry.

3. Copy your images onto bright paper and cut them out.

4. Adhere the images to the candleholder with Elmer's glue.

5. Cover the candleholder with Mod Podge for a nice finish, then let dry.

6. Put your glass plate, saucer, or cup on top, add your candle, and you're done.

6-POINT CARDBOARD STAR

These are really fun to make and you can decorate them with almost any kind of material you have around the house. I opted for paper, but you can come up with something even more fantastic to cover your stars with, I'm sure of it!

YOU'LL NEED

- Pencil
- Cardboard
- X-ACTO knife
- Hot glue gun and glue sticks
- 5 (8$\frac{1}{2}$" x 11") decorative sheets of paper
- Scissors
- Elmer's glue
- Cup of water
- 1-inch paintbrush
- Double-stick tape

HERE'S HOW

1. Enlarge and trace the diamond-shaped pattern provided on page 369 onto cardboard 6 times, then cut the shapes out and lightly score down the center of each (as shown on the pattern) using a ruler and X-ACTO knife.

2. Enlarge, trace onto cardboard, and cut out the backing pattern.

3. Bend your diamond pieces along the scored lines.

4. Apply hot glue to the edges of the cardboard backing and glue the diamonds to the backing, adding hot glue to the short sides of the diamonds to help the star keep its shape.

5. Cut your decorative paper into approximately 50 strips, each 4 inches long and 1 inch across.

6. Slightly water down some glue, then spread glue on the star with a paintbrush and apply your paper strips until the entire front of the star is covered. Let the glue dry.

7. Hang your star using double-stick tape.

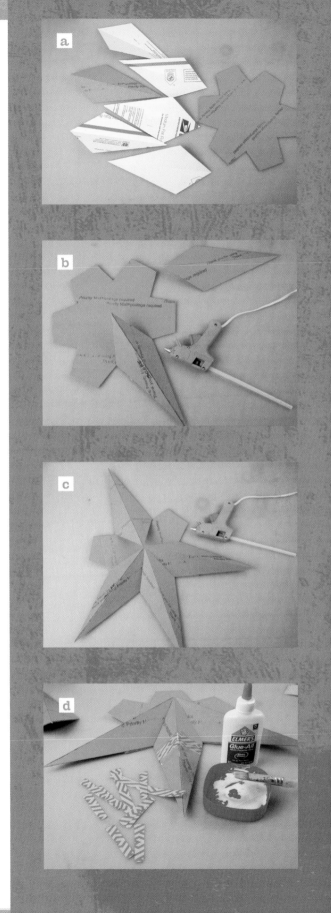

WOVEN CARDBOARD VASEBOXCONTAINER

I love how sturdy cardboard gets when you weave it together and add some glue. You can make any size and shape of container that you want using this technique, but my personal favorite is the tall vase because I think my twigs-and-paper flower arrangement looks amazing in it. Don't you agree?

YOU'LL NEED

- Cardboard
- Heavy scissors or X-ACTO knife
- Stapler
- Elmer's glue
- Hot glue gun and glue sticks

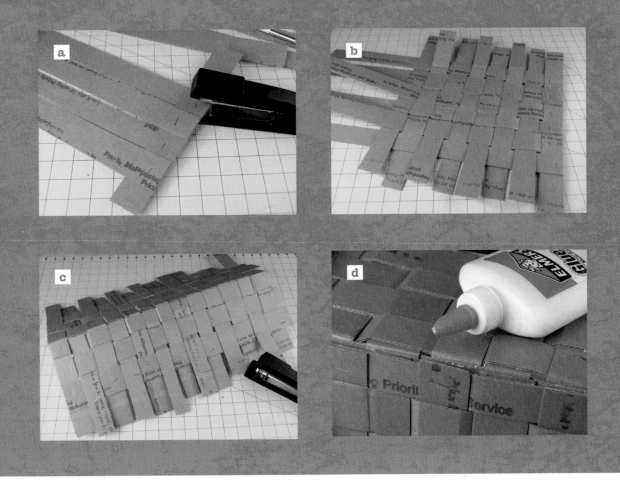

HERE'S HOW

1. Cut 12 cardboard strips, each 23 inches long by 1½ inches wide, but don't worry if they aren't perfectly straight. I actually like them to be imperfect.

2. Cut 26 cardboard strips, each 1 inch to 1½ inches wide by 13 inches long.

3. Start by working with 6 long strips and 13 shorter strips. Line up your 6 long strips, then, beginning at one end of the long strips, weave a short strip in and out of the long strips. Staple the woven row in place.

4. Continue weaving the remaining 12 rows.

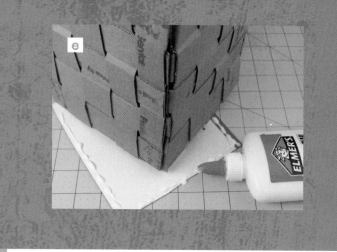

5 Staple all around the sides of your woven piece where the 2 long outer strips overlap short strips.

6 Repeat steps 3 through 5 with the remaining strips to make the other half of the vase.

7 Bend your 2 woven pieces in half to create two 5-inch-long sides from each piece.

8 Trim the ends of the short strips off one side of each of your woven pieces along the outer edge of the long strip.

9 Bend the ends of the short pieces hanging off the other side of each of your woven pieces along the outer edge of the outer long strip.

10 Join the pieces together by hot-gluing the bent ends to the inside of each piece.

11 Add a line of glue along all of the edges where the woven pieces meet and let dry.

12 Place the woven tube on a piece of flat cardboard and trace around the bottom.

13 Cut the shape out and apply a line of glue around the edges. Set the bottom of the woven tube on top and let dry.

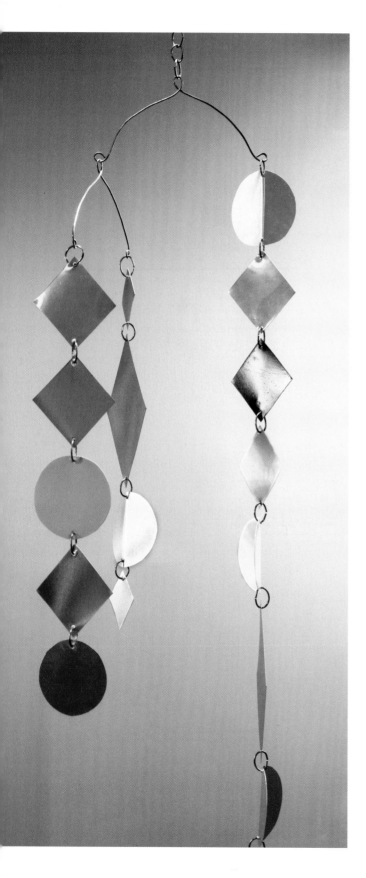

OOPS, I ARTED

Stop laughing for a minute and consider how many times you've accidentally made something really interesting. When I do that I always say to myself, Oops, I arted! Hence, the name of this chapter. Some of my best work comes from spilling and squishing and dropping things, and I urge you to let go of your inhibitions and just start a project without an end goal in mind and see what happens. I can't promise the results will end up in a fancy art gallery, but I can guarantee that you'll have a great time crafting. Oh, and don't attempt these projects without plenty of newspaper on hand to protect your workspace! You don't want to have to explain to your significant other how you accidentally arted all over the dining room table.

DOUBLE VISION ART PIECE

Every time I pass a billboard with a double image I almost get into a car wreck trying to catch the image that's visible from the other side of the road. Look, I'm not a great driver anyway, and these are truly distracting! The concept—squeezing two advertisements in the space of one—is brilliant, and it inspired this very fun craft project. I used vintage images, but you can try using photos of your mom and dad, or photos of you and your best friend.

YOU'LL NEED

- 1 legal size (8½" x 14") manila folder
- Pencil
- Ruler
- X-ACTO knife
- Two 8-inch by 10-inch images
- Spray mount
- 1 piece of cardboard (at least 8 inches by 10 inches)
- Elmer's glue
- 8-inch by 10-inch clear box frame

HERE'S HOW

1 Open the manila folder and cut it into a rectangle 14 inches by 10 inches.

2 With your ruler and pencil, divide the rectangle into 14 sections, each 1 inch by 10 inches.

3 Using your X-ACTO knife, gently score along the lines you've drawn.

4 Fold your large rectangle along the lines like an accordion, and then smooth it out again.

5 Cut your images into 1-inch by 10-inch strips and keep the strips in order as you go.

6 Spray the manila accordion with spray mount.

7 Working from left to right, apply your strips, alternating between images every other inch.

8 Using the back of the frame as your guide, cut your cardboard to fit the frame. Be sure to cut a small hole in the center so that you can hang your artwork later.

9 With your ruler and pencil, divide the cardboard into 8 sections, each 1 inch by 10 inches.

10 Apply tiny dots of Elmer's glue along the lines you drew on the cardboard, then glue the accordion to the cardboard, making sure to leave a tiny bit of room on each side so it will easily slide in the frame.

11 Adhere the cardboard to the back of your clear box frame with Elmer's glue.

12 Have fun watching your friends do a double take when they notice your new art piece.

CRYSTAL KALEIDO–PHOTO POSTCARD

I like weird photos! If you don't believe me, take a look at the doll head photo project on page 114. Thanks to my digital camera's mini lens, I find it's easier than ever to manipulate images into odd photos. One of my favorite techniques is to shoot pictures through a crystal to create a prism effect, and this project grew out of that technique.

YOU'LL NEED

- Cardboard
- 2 images copied onto paper
- Ruler
- Pencil
- Scissors
- 1 large chandelier crystal
- X-ACTO knife
- Elmer's glue
- Cup of water
- 1-inch paintbrush
- E-6000 glue
- Hole punch
- 24 inches of ¼-inch ribbon
- Digital camera

HERE'S HOW

1 Follow steps 1 through 8 for making the Cereal Box Postcards on page 183, using cardboard.

2 Trace the crystal on the center of the postcard, then cut out a hole just a tiny bit smaller than the shape you just traced.

3 With the X-ACTO knife, cut out the crystal shape from your paper.

4 Cover the back of your postcard with your second image, and cut out the crystal-shaped hole.

5 Add a small amount of E-6000 around the hole, and place your crystal inside. Let the glue dry.

6 Punch a hole in the center of the top of the postcard, thread ribbon through the hole, and tie the ends in a knot so you can wear it as you're taking photos.

7 Hold your camera lens up to the crystal and snap a photo of something weird!

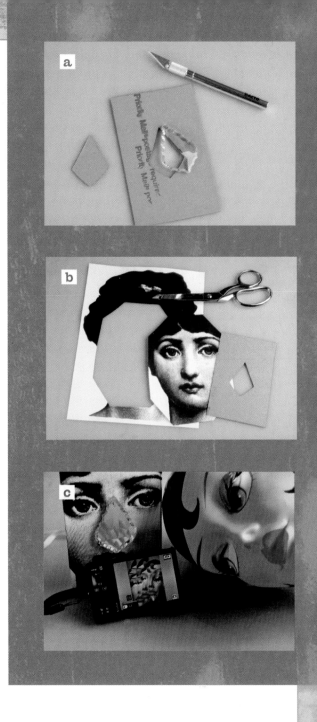

CHILDREN'S BOOK SILHOUETTE

My BFF Shaye recently had a beautiful baby girl named Georgia June. I often think newborns are a little funny-looking, but I have to say, GJ was stunning from day one. I mean, this little girl made the Gerber baby look like a toad. I wanted to make little GJ something special, meaningful, and from my heart, and this is what I created.

YOU'LL NEED

- Children's book with pretty images (I used illustrations from a copy of *Mother Goose*)
- Copy machine
- Scissors
- X-ACTO knife
- Krylon Fusion for Plastic spray paint (I used pale pink)
- Dark paper that contrasts the spray paint (to mat your project)
- Frame
- Elmer's glue stick

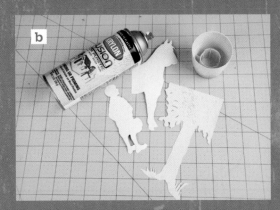

HERE'S HOW

1 Make a black-and-white photocopy of the image you want to turn into a silhouette.

2 Carefully cut out the copy with scissors and the knife, making sure to get as much detail as you possibly can.

3 Lightly spray-paint the back of the copied images. Apply several coats, and let the coats dry in between each application.

4 Cut your dark background paper to fit inside your frame.

5 Dab the printed side (not the painted side) of the silhouette with glue stick, and place your image on the dark background.

6 Frame your artwork and enjoy.

PAINT CHIP ART 3

In almost every book I write I try to include a project that uses some of the mounds of paint swatches I collect during my frequent trips to the hardware store. This time I decided to create something geometric with them, and I really dig the result.

YOU'LL NEED

- 25 (4" x 5") paint swatches
- Swing-arm paper cutter
- Clear tape
- Ruler
- Frame
- Colored poster board
- Elmer's glue

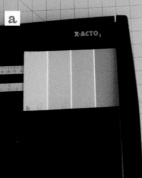

HERE'S HOW

1 Cut the paint swatches into $\frac{3}{8}$-inch to $\frac{1}{2}$-inch-wide strips using a swing-arm cutter so they are perfectly straight.

2 Place 8 or 9 strips facedown in a row. Make sure they are positioned right next to each other, with no space in between. Repeat until all the strips are used.

3 Tape the strips together with transparent tape, making sure to include the corners.

4 With your paper cutter, cut the blocks of strips into $3\frac{1}{2}$-inch by $3\frac{1}{2}$-inch squares.

5 Cut the squares on the diagonal to form a striped triangle.

6 Measure the size of your frame and decide how large you want your design to be to fill it.

7 Cut the colored poster board so it fits perfectly inside your frame.

8 Arrange the striped triangles on top of the poster board, carefully glue them in place, and let dry.

9 Frame your artwork and enjoy the view!

TIN SHELF ART PIECE

When I lived in NYC, nearly once a week I would pass a discarded industrial-looking shelf system on the street waiting for a ride to the landfill. They were almost always gray, and in my opinion, looked perfect for an art project. I think everything can have another use if you take the time to figure it out!

YOU'LL NEED

- Enough photocopied, enlarged images to cover your item
- Scissors
- Elmer's glue
- Cup of water
- 1-inch paintbrush
- Tin shelf rack or other discarded item with flat surfaces, like a large board, old tabletop, chair back, or closet door
- Minwax Polycrylic Protective Finish

HERE'S HOW

1. Carefully cut out your images, getting as much detail around the edges as possible. If your images are very big, cut them into smaller, more manageable pieces.

2. With watered-down Elmer's and your paint-brush, glue your images to the item you're covering, 1 section at a time.

3. When the glue is dry, apply clear coat to the entire piece.

CALDER-INSPIRED MOBILE

Alexander Calder was an American artist known for his mobile sculptures (look up him and his work on the Internet when you get a chance!) and this project was inspired by him. It may look complicated, but don't worry, it was actually very simple to make.

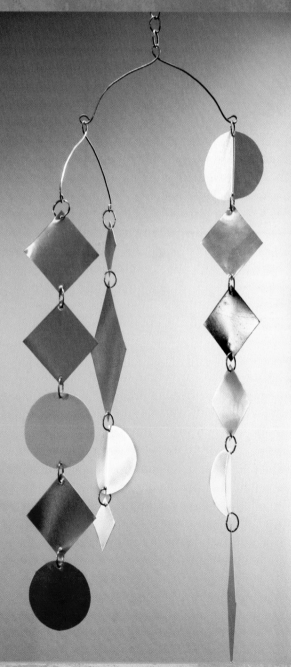

YOU'LL NEED

- 4 sheets of 4-inch by 6-inch steel or aluminum flashing
- Permanent marker
- Red, black, and yellow Krylon spray paint
- Tin snips or heavy-duty scissors
- Awl or large nail
- Small hammer
- Piece of scrap wood
- Needle-nose pliers with wire cutter
- 4 feet of rebar wire tie or heavy-gauge wire (should feel like a very cheap, flimsy wire hanger)

HERE'S HOW

1 Enlarge and trace the patterns provided on page 363 onto the flashing with marker. Cut out your shapes with heavy-duty scissors or snips.

2 Figure out the order in which you want to link your shapes, and decide which pieces you are going to spray-paint.

> You don't have to spray-paint your pieces.
> The mobile looks just as pretty in all silver.

3 Spray-paint your pieces and let them dry.

4 Using a hammer and an awl or large nail, tap a hole on the top and bottom of each shape, *except* for the shapes that will go on the bottom of each strand, which should only have 1 hole at the top.

5 Cut 2 pieces of wire, each 10 inches, and bend a loop in the center of each. Then, with your needle-nose pliers, bend a small loop at each end, leaving a tiny opening, as shown in the photo.

6 Attach the 2 wire pieces by hooking 1 piece's center loop through an end loop on the other piece.

7 Cut 17 pieces of wire, each 1¹⁄₂ inches long, and bend them into rings, leaving a small opening so you can link them through the holes of your shapes.

8 Attach a shape to the end loops on your large wire pieces, then continue connecting shapes, closing the rings as you go using your needle-nose pliers.

IMPORTANT

> While you're working, hang up your mobile from time to time to make sure that it's balanced. Make any necessary adjustments by adding or subtracting a piece here and there.

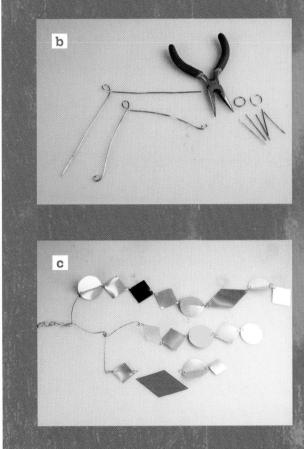

9 Hang your mobile from a chain or make some more loops with extra wire and turn them into a chain for a completely home-made creation.

KALEIDO—PHOTO TUBE

I'm not the greatest photographer, so I kind of shy away from taking pictures. However, since I've been experimenting with my kaleido-photo tube, I've started to enjoy the art form much more. Try it out the next time you want to turn a really simple subject into something amazing.

YOU'LL NEED

- 8 inches of 3-inch metal duct tube
- 63 mirror tile squares, each 1 inch by 1 inch
- E-6000 glue

HERE'S HOW

1 Starting at 1 end of the tube, glue a horizontal row of 4 mirror tiles to the inside of the tube with E-6000. Let dry for about half an hour.

IMPORTANT

> Don't glue in more than 4 tiles at a time because they will slip.

2 Keep adding rows of 4 mirror tiles, one on top of the next, and allow each row to dry for half an hour, until you reach the other end of the tube.

3 Rotate the tube and add more rows of mirrors until the inside of your tube is covered, and let the glue dry.

DON'T WORRY

> The goal here is to cover the entire inside of the tube with mirrors without leaving any empty spots, but it won't be perfect and it doesn't have to be. One mirror may slightly overlap with another mirror but it's not a big deal. It'll just add to the cool effect you'll get when you take your photograph!

4 Put your camera lens up to one end of the tube and start taking photos.

ORNA–MENTAL

There is a reason I've separated these words: the holidays make me mental. I love being with family and participating in all the festivities, but decking my halls is so much work that it gives me panic attacks and leads me to wonder why we can't just leave decorations up all year-round. I mean, wouldn't it be so nice to have glitter and lights everywhere twelve months a year? I think so. The ornaments in this chapter make great gifts, are easy to create, and they're superinexpensive and can be altered in any way you want—which means you can create a color scheme that you'll enjoy in any season. So put on some Bing Crosby (even if you're reading this in July) and take these ideas and run with them.

DISCO ORNAMENTS

We could all use a little disco ball to remind us that life should be a party, right?

These are perfect little ornaments for every occasion.

YOU'LL NEED

- Cardboard
- Pencil
- Large drinking glass to use as a stencil
- X-ACTO knife
- Hot glue gun and glue sticks
- Elmer's glue
- Small paintbrush
- Black Krylon spray paint
- Silver glitter
- 7 inches of ¼-inch ribbon in black, gray, or silver

HERE'S HOW

1 Using the mouth of a large drinking glass as a stencil, trace 4 circles (or more, if you want a denser ornament) onto your cardboard and cut them out with your X-ACTO knife.

2 Leave 1 circle intact, and cut the rest in half.

3 Hot-glue 2 half-circles crosswise onto the whole circle.

4 Hot-glue a half-circle (or more, if desired) between each section.

5 Paint Elmer's glue in each crevice where the halves meet the circle base, to give your ornament a little more support. Let the glue dry.

6 Spray the cardboard with the black Krylon spray paint.

7 When the paint is dry, put a thin line of Elmer's glue on each edge of the ornament, and dip the edges in loose silver glitter.

8 Hot-glue both ends of the ribbon to the top of the ball to form a loop. This will be your hanger.

9 Cover the hot glue on your ribbon ends in glitter to disguise it.

10 Let your ornament dry, then hang it in a place that needs a little disco dazzle.

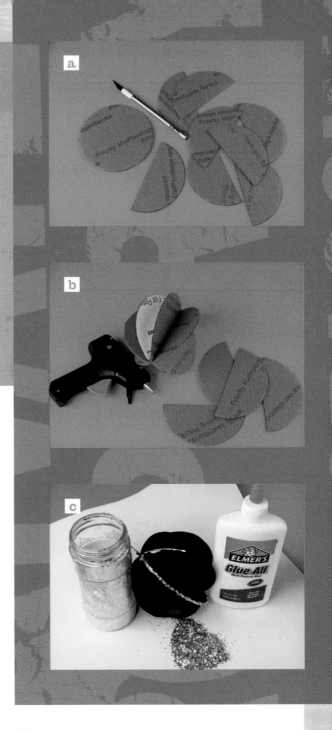

CLOTHESPIN ORNAMENTS

These sparkly ornaments catch the light and are superfun to make. Whip up some black and orange ones for Halloween or yellow and lavender ones for Easter. Heck, I don't care what colors you choose, just make them—and have a good time while you're at it!

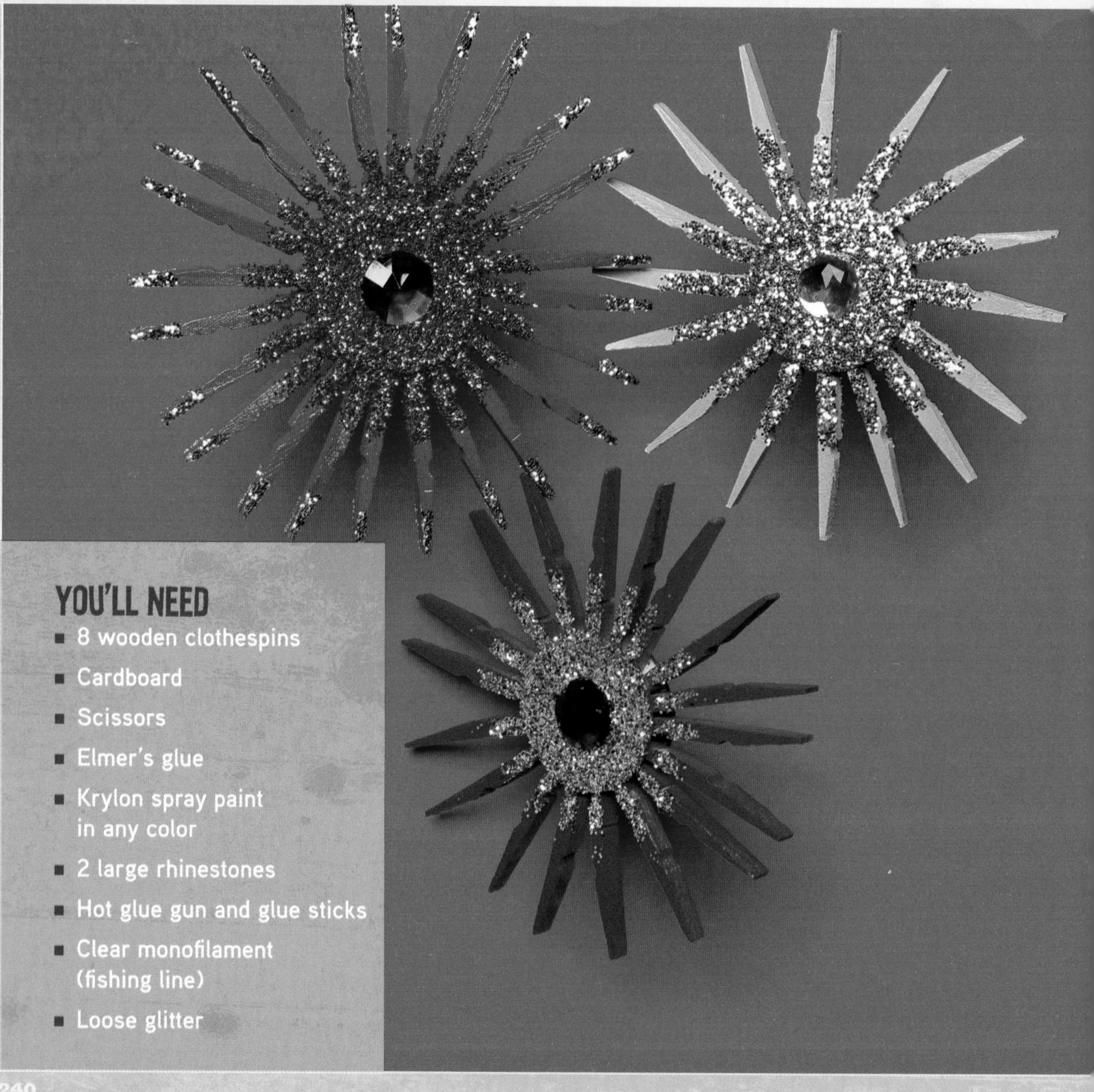

YOU'LL NEED

- 8 wooden clothespins
- Cardboard
- Scissors
- Elmer's glue
- Krylon spray paint in any color
- 2 large rhinestones
- Hot glue gun and glue sticks
- Clear monofilament (fishing line)
- Loose glitter

HERE'S HOW

1 Take the clothespin apart by bending the wood pieces outward and loosening the metal spring until it falls off.

2 Arrange the wood pieces in a starburst pattern, with the fat ends touching in the center and the skinny ends forming the points.

3 Cut out 2 cardboard circles, each about 2½ inches in diameter.

HINT

Use a small drinking glass to trace perfect circles.

4 Glue a cardboard circle in the center of the clothespin starburst and let dry.

5 Flip your starburst over, glue the other cardboard circle in the center, and let dry.

6 Spray-paint the entire ornament. Make sure to paint every angle!

7 When the paint is dry, hot-glue a rhinestone in the center of both sides of the ornament.

8 Cut a 10-inch piece of clear monofilament, fold it in half, and hot-glue the ends to one of the clothespins for the hanger.

9 Cover the rest of the cardboard and about ½ inch of the surrounding clothespins with Elmer's glue and sprinkle glitter on top. Flip the starburst over and repeat.

10 Hang and admire your ornament while the glue dries.

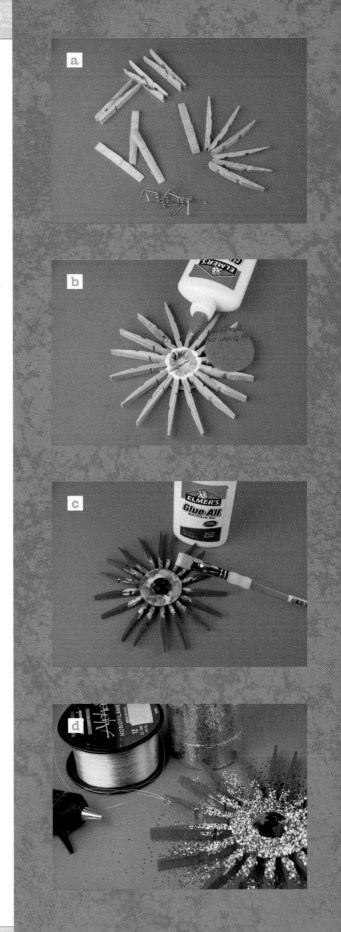

CLEAR PLASTIC PLATE ORNAMENTS

I really like hanging these around the house year-round. I believe that ornaments don't have to be for just the holidays—it all depends on how you decorate them—so choose a theme you like, make a few of these, and hang them in a window or on a wall to enjoy through every season.

YOU'LL NEED

- 2 clear plastic plates per ornament, each 6 inches in diameter
- Photocopied image 6 inches long or wide, printed on card stock
- X-ACTO knife
- Elmer's glue
- Glitter
- 8 inches of ¼-inch ribbon

HERE'S HOW

1 Place a plate on top of your image and trace around it with a pencil.

2 Cut out the circle. Trim some of the background from your image, getting as much detail in the outline as you can.

3 Embellish a few areas of the image with glitter by dabbing the areas with Elmer's glue and sprinkling glitter on top. Let the glue dry.

4 Lay the image on top of one of the plates, noting where the edges of the image touch the plate (since most plates are concave, the whole image probably won't touch the center of the plate). Apply glue to the back of the image where it will touch the plate, and glue the image in place.

5 Make a loop with your ribbon by folding it in half, and glue the ends to the top of the plate, hiding them behind the image if you can.

6 Line the edge of the plate with your image on it with glue, and place the second plate facedown on top.

7 Let the glue dry, then hang your ornament.

COLORFUL CARDBOARD ORNAMENTS

I think these would be great for a kid's birthday party. You could use them as decorations, and at the end, hand them out as favors!

YOU'LL NEED

- Cardboard
- X-ACTO knife
- Masking tape
- Colorful card stock or poster board
- Elmer's glue
- 1-inch paintbrush
- Loose glitter
- 8 inches of ¼-inch satin ribbon per ornament
- Hot glue gun and glue sticks

HERE'S HOW

1 Enlarge and trace the Money Building Blocks pattern provided on page 363 and cut out 3 diamonds, all exactly the same size, from your cardboard. (Mine were 5 inches by 4 inches.)

2 Carefully score across the shorter axis on each diamond so that you can easily fold them. Be careful not to cut all the way through the cardboard!

3 Tape the 3 pieces together with small pieces of masking tape to make a three-dimensional diamond block.

4 Cut out your colorful card stock or poster board pieces the same size as your diamond pieces, and cut them in half along the shorter axis.

5 Brush glue on the back of your card stock pieces, and glue the colorful card stock to the diamond blocks.

6 Squeeze a line of Elmer's glue along the folded edges of your diamond pieces and where the edges of the pieces meet, then dip the edges in glitter and let the glue dry.

7 Add a dot of hot glue to the top of your blocks and attach the ends of your ribbon to make a loop for hanging your ornament.

have a favorite pillow that I hang out with like a friend almost every day, either for a nap or to watch the boob tube. In fact, I happen to love all my pillows. Each one has its own personality. Some are regal and dare me to do anything but just look at them; some are like puppies, begging me to snuggle up with them; still others are part of the family because they've been in the same place for as long as I can remember and my chair or bed just wouldn't look the same without them. You might be staring at this page and thinking I'm crazy, but I suspect you know what I mean.

The pillows in this section are an experiment in fun. Change my ideas to suit your own style and see what happens. I think you'll like the results.

ANTIQUED IMAGE TRANSFER PILLOW

You can use any image for this project. I happen to be a huge fan of Frida Kahlo, so I chose to put her on my pillow. Find a pillow-worthy image you like, then go forth and transfer!

YOU'LL NEED

- Laser copy of an image you want to transfer onto a pillow (see note below)
- 1 yard of smooth fabric in a light color (cotton works very well)
- Scissors
- White gesso or white latex paint
- 1-inch paintbrush
- Spray bottle or sponge
- Straight pins
- Sewing machine
- Pillow stuffing
- *Optional:* 1¹/₂ yards of matching fringe, sewing needle, and matching thread

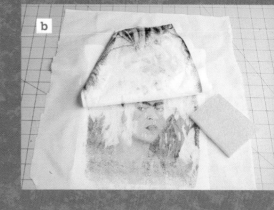

NOTE

The key to making this project a success is using a laser-print color copy rather than a copy from an inkjet printer. Staples generally uses laser printers, while most home printers are inkjets. However, even though laser copies are more colorful and detailed than an inkjet print, it's still not a perfect transfer—not that you want one. This project is designed to look worn and antiqued.

HERE'S HOW

1 Cut out 2 rectangles from your fabric, each 11 inches by 14 inches.

2 On 1 of the pieces, apply white gesso or latex paint with a paintbrush to an area a little smaller than the image you're transferring. (For example, if your image is $8\frac{1}{2}$ inches by 11 inches, paint an area approximately $7\frac{1}{2}$ inches by 10 inches.)

3 Place your image facedown on the treated surface. Make sure that the whole image is pressed firmly against the gesso or paint.

4 Leave to dry overnight. (I know, I know, this takes a while. But it's well worth it!)

5 When your image is dry, carefully peel the paper off the fabric.

WARNING!

> It's going to look like a mess when you peel the paper off, and there will be lots left sticking to the fabric.

6 Lightly wet the fabric with a spray bottle or damp sponge, and carefully roll off the paper bits with your fingertips. As you remove the paper, you will start to see the image sticking to the gesso.

SUGGESTION

> If you want to add fringe to the pillow as I did, on the fabric with the image on it, stitch the woven end of the fringe $\frac{3}{8}$ inch from the edge, with the loose fringe pointing toward the inside of the pillow. Then proceed to step 7.

7 Place your fabric pieces face-to-face with the image on the inside, and pin the edges every few inches to hold them together.

8 Using a $\frac{1}{2}$-inch seam allowance, sew around the edges of your fabric with a sewing machine, leaving a 5-inch opening on 1 side.

9 Clip the corners of your seams at a 45-degree angle near the corner stitches.

10 Turn the pillowcase right side out through the opening.

11 Fill the case with pillow stuffing.

12 Stitch up the opening either by hand or on the sewing machine, and admire your work.

ROCK ON RIBBON PILLOW

There are several fantastic artists who only paint stripes, and Gene Davis is one of my all-time favorites. I kept thinking of him as I was making this pillow.

YOU'LL NEED

- Sewing machine with zigzag stitch
- Thread in a color that matches 1 of your ribbon colors
- 20 pieces of 1-inch to 2-inch satin or grosgrain ribbon, each 20 inches long
- 20 pieces of 1-inch to 2-inch satin or grosgrain ribbon, each 28 inches long
- Scissors
- Fabric square, 20 inches by 20 inches
- Pillow stuffing
- Sewing needle

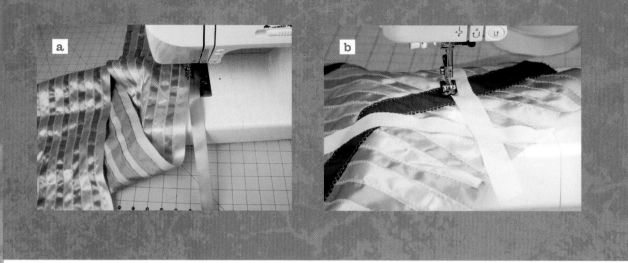

HERE'S HOW

1 Zigzag-stitch the 20-inch ribbons together, side by side and overlapping just a bit.

2 Once you've created a ribbon piece that is about 20 inches by 20 inches, start zigzagging the 28-inch ribbons on top in a random fashion. Cut off any excess ribbon and use to decorate the corners of your pillow.

3 Continue sewing on ribbons until you are satisfied with your design.

4 Place your ribbon piece facedown on top of your fabric. With right sides together, sew your fabric to your ribbon fabric, using a ½-inch seam allowance and leaving a 5-inch opening in 1 side.

5 Clip the corners at a 45-degree angle inside the seam allowance and turn the pillowcase right side out through the opening.

6 Stuff the case with pillow stuffing, sew the hole closed, and rock on with your new pillow!

MILLIONS OF BUTTONS PILLOW

Okay, "millions" is an exaggeration, but this project requires tons of buttons for sure. If, like me, you hoard buttons for some button-popping emergency that never actually occurs, this is the project for you.

YOU'LL NEED

- ¹/₂ yard of fabric
- Scissors
- Ruler
- White pencil
- Sewing machine
- Tons of buttons that match the color of your fabric (I used approximately 400)
- Pillow stuffing
- Needle and thread

HERE'S HOW

1. Cut out 2 rectangles from your fabric, each 16 inches by 22 inches.

2. Draw a line in white pencil all the way around one of the pieces of fabric ¹/₂ inch from the edges to mark your seam allowance.

3. Put your sewing machine on the button setting.

HINT

> If your machine doesn't have a button setting, just drop the feed dog (the teeth that drag the fabric through the machine) and use the zigzag setting to sew on your buttons.

4 Stitch on buttons until you've covered the entire rectangle that you marked off with the white lines, making sure to not stitch any in the seam allowance. This is going to take a while, so be patient and listen to some good music while you work.

5 When you're done sewing on the buttons, clip any loose threads so that your button rectangle looks nice and neat.

6 Pin the pillow pieces together with right sides facing, and stitch around the edges using a 1/2-inch seam allowance and leaving a 4-inch-long opening in one side.

7 Flip your pillowcase right side out through the opening and fill with pillow stuffing.

8 Sew the opening closed with needle and thread.

UNION JACK PILLOW

I dig the Union Jack because it makes me want to scream "God save the Queen!" and then rock out to the Sex Pistols, so I tend to use it in a lot of projects. You can use any three-color combination for this pillow—whatever you choose, it will give your décor a distinctively hip flavor faster than you can say "anarchy."

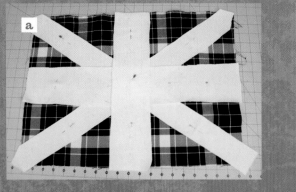

YOU'LL NEED

- ¼ yard of white cotton fabric
- ¼ yard of red plaid fabric
- 2 pieces of blue plaid fabric, each 15 inches by 20 inches
- Straight pins
- Sewing machine with zigzag stitch
- Red and white thread
- Pillow stuffing
- Sewing needle and matching thread

HERE'S HOW

1. Cut the white fabric into strips, as follows: One 20" × 3½", one 15" × 3½", and two 25" × 2½".

2. Cut out your red plaid fabric strips, as follows: One 20" × 2½", one 15" × 2½", and two 25" × 1½".

3. Lay your 25-inch white fabric strips in a big X on top of 1 of your pieces of blue fabric. Trim the ends of the strips into points at the corners, as in the photo.

4. Lay your 20-inch white strip horizontally across the middle of the pillow.

5. Lay your 15-inch white strip vertically down the center of the pillow.

6. Carefully pin the strips in place. With white thread, zigzag-stitch over all of the edges.

7. Lay your 15-inch strip of red plaid vertically down the center of the pillow, centering it on the white strip.

8. Lay your 20-inch strip of red plaid horizontally across the center of the pillow, centering it on the white strip.

9. Cut both of your 25-inch pieces of red plaid in half.

10. Lay a strip in the center of one leg of the white X, and trim the end where it meets the center of the cross at an angle, as shown in the photo. Repeat for the other 3 legs of the X.

11. Pin the red plaid pieces in place. With red thread, zigzag-stitch over all of the edges.

12. Clip excess threads.

13. Place your other piece of blue plaid fabric facedown on top of your design, so right sides are together.

14. Sew the pieces together all the way around the edges, using a $1/2$-inch seam allowance and leaving a 5-inch opening in one side.

15. Clip the corners at an angle inside the seam so that you won't have any excess fabric in the corners of your pillow.

16. Turn the pillowcase right side out through the opening.

17. Stuff the case with pillow stuffing and sew the opening closed with needle and matching thread.

PILLOW PERSON

Sometimes I get lonely while enjoying some downtime in front of the TV, and I figured that hanging out with a pillow person would be a good way to have someone around who wouldn't ask me to share my Fiddle Faddle. Here's how to make your own stuffed companion.

YOU'LL NEED

- ½ yard of fabric for the face
- Pencil
- Scissors
- Small piece of white fabric for eyes
- Small piece of pink fabric for lips
- Sewing machine with zigzag stitch
- Black thread
- Sewing needle
- 2 large buttons (for the eyes)
- Pillow stuffing
- Pink latex paint (for the cheeks)
- Small paintbrush
- ½ yard of fabric for hair
- Yarn in different bright colors
- Several faux flowers
- 10 decorative buttons to make earrings (or you could use an old pair you have lying around)
- Fine-gauge wire
- Wire cutters
- Iron

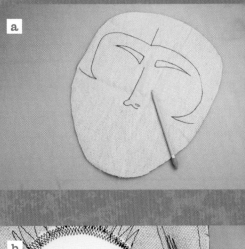

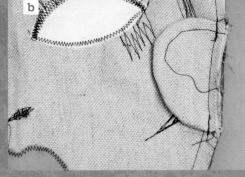

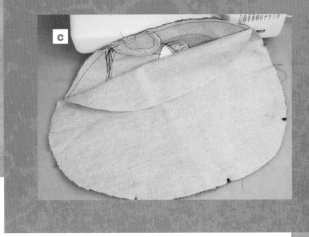

HERE'S HOW

1. Cut out 2 layers of a large head shape from your fabric. Mine were about 18 inches high and about 12 inches wide.

2. With a pencil, draw hair, eyebrows, and a nose onto 1 of the head shapes.

3. Cut out 4 identical ear shapes from the fabric left over from the heads, 2 eyes from the white fabric, and 1 lip shape from the pink fabric.

4. Sew 2 layers of ear shapes together to form each ear, leaving a small opening in each where you'll sew them onto the head. Turn them inside out through the opening and iron them flat.

5. Sew on the ear details with your sewing machine.

6 Stitch over the hair, eyebrows, and nose you drew on your pillow with the sewing machine.

HINT

> Pretend your sewing machine is a pencil and you're sketching with it.

7 Place the eyes and lips on the pillow face, pin them down, then zigzag-stitch around the edges. Stitch on some eyelashes for good measure.

8 Stitch on the ears so they are pointing toward the inside of the face, as shown in the photo on the previous page.

9 Stitch buttons on the whites of the eyes with needle and thread.

10 Place the plain fabric head on top of the face, pin the pieces together, and stitch around the fabric pieces using a $1/2$-inch seam allowance and leaving a 4-inch opening in 1 side.

11 Turn the pillowcase inside out through the hole, and fill with stuffing.

12 Water down some pink paint so it's not too dark, and paint cheeks on your pillow face.

13 Cut the fabric you chose for the hair into 3 strips about 6 inches long and the same width as your fabric.

14 Cut 21 pieces of yarn the same length as your fabric strips.

15 Line up your fabric strips and the yarn, gather them together, and sew across 1 end of the bunch.

16 Divide the fabric strips and yarn into 3 sections, and braid them together. When you get to the end, gather the sections together and stitch across the bunch.

17 Hand-sew the braid onto the head of the pillow. Give your people pillow some nice waves and use lots of stitches.

18 Stitch some faux flowers (or hot-glue them if you get lazy!) on the pillow person's hair.

19 String some buttons together on a couple of wire pieces to form your pillow's earrings, and stitch 1 to each earlobe.

SHRINE ON

Whatever you might think of shrines, which have often been unfairly associated with creepy obsessions or silly voodoo fantasies, toss those ideas out—we're starting over right here and now. I think shrines are about being hopeful and positive. I also believe that making a shrine promotes those ideas. You're creating a specific place where you can make wishes and think positively about something, and at the same time crafting a beautiful reminder that you want some light in your life and for the people around you. Oh, and I also like to have a place to put my favorite fortune cookie fortunes and lucky pennies. I get tired of them falling out of my wallet!

WISH SHRINE

I wish for things all the time, and I created this shrine in order to keep track of my long list of wishes. Now I have a place to put all of those thoughts and forget about them while the universe takes care of it for me. Make this shrine out of everything you have left over from all of your other craft projects. I mean that. The more stuff you add, the better it looks.

YOU'LL NEED

- Pencil
- Scraps of ½-inch plywood
- Jigsaw
- Sandpaper or sanding block
- Elmer's wood glue
- Hot glue gun and glue sticks
- Buttons, colorful twine, strings of faux pearls, glass floral marbles, pieces of cheap or broken jewelry, shiny kids' toys, rhinestones
- Glitter glue
- Elmer's glue
- Loose glitter
- Latex paint in any color
- 15 to 20 paper clips
- Small votive candle

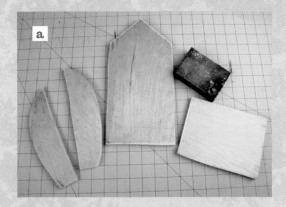

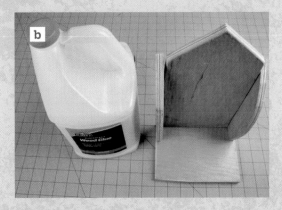

HERE'S HOW

1. Enlarge and trace the patterns provided on page 374 onto plywood, then cut them out with a jigsaw.

2. Sand the wood pieces with your sandpaper or sanding block.

3. Using wood glue, adhere the pieces to the base piece, as shown in the photo.

4. Hot-glue rhinestones, glass chips, beads, buttons, and so on to your shrine until you can't fit any more on.

5. Fill in the areas in between the decorative items with glitter glue and let dry.

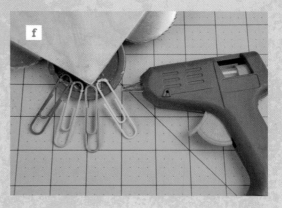

6 Fill in any leftover empty areas with Elmer's glue, sprinkle loose glitter on top, and let dry.

7 Paint any exposed wood.

8 Glue the bottoms of paper clips along the top of the shrine.

9 Write out your wishes on small pieces of paper and slip them in the paper clips.

SUGGESTION

Glue fortunes from fortune cookies or photos on the sides of your shrine if you like.

10 Place a small votive candle onto the base of the shrine and light it.

11 Make your wishes, blow out the candle, and get back to what you were doing!

MONEY SHRINE

If you believe in lucky pennies like I do, you'll probably like this shrine. And you'll enjoy it if, like me, you're one of those people who also is attracted to anything shiny. My eye instantly follows the sparkle, and because of that I have found tons of money on the streets of New York and Los Angeles. I always save my found money and put it in my money shrine in hopes that one day it will bring me an enormous amount of good luck. Who knows, maybe it already has.

YOU'LL NEED

- Pencil
- Scraps of 1/2-inch plywood
- Jigsaw
- Sandpaper or sanding block
- Elmer's wood glue
- Approximately 20 "Popsicle" craft sticks
- Hot glue gun and glue sticks
- Green Krylon Fusion for Plastic spray paint
- Laser color copies of currency (make sure to enlarge and/or change the colors of the currency for your copies using the copier settings, and steer clear of inkjet copiers since the ink on the copies will bleed)
- Elmer's glue
- Cup of water
- Small glass
- 1-inch paintbrush
- Minwax Polycrylic Protective Finish
- 10 shiny pennies

HERE'S HOW

1 Follow steps 1 through 3 for making the Wish Shrine on page 265.

2 With a glue gun, glue the ends of your craft sticks to the back of the top of your shrine so they fan out about 3 inches from the top.

3 When the glue is dry, spray-paint the entire structure, including the craft sticks, in green.

4 Cut your copied currency into the shapes you'll need to create the desired look for your shrine. (I made stripes along the sides and glued whole bills on the back and bottom of my shrine, but you can do something totally different.)

5 Water down some Elmer's glue just a bit so it's easy to spread and brush glue on the back of your currency. Glue the pieces in place.

6 Now cover the glass with pieces of currency by gluing it to the sides.

7 Clear-coat the entire shrine and the covered glass and let dry.

8 Glue the shiny pennies on your shrine with a hot glue gun to add some pizzazz.

9 Put a votive in the glass and place in the middle of the base. Light the candle, wish for a million dollars, blow the candle out, and wait for a bank error in your favor.

BABY IN A BOX FORTUNE-TELLER

I'm not really sure why I made this, but I'm glad I did. It sure gives people something to talk about when they come over!

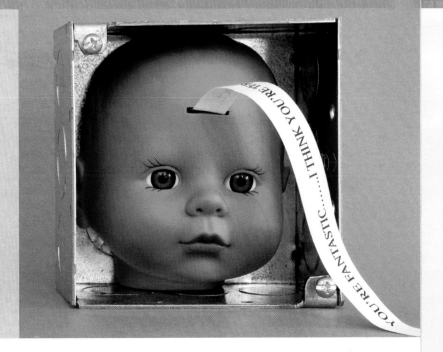

YOU'LL NEED

- Plastic baby doll head small enough to fit in a 4-inch by 4-inch box
- X-ACTO knife
- Home printer
- Scissors
- Clear tape or Elmer's glue
- One 4-inch by 4-inch metal electrical box
- E-6000 glue

HERE'S HOW

1. Remove the doll head from the body and cut off the back half of the head so it comfortably fits in your 4-inch by 4-inch box.

2. Type out tons of fortunes, print them out, cut them into thin strips, then glue or tape the strips together end to end to make 1 long strip.

3. Roll up your strip of fortunes and set them aside.

4. With the X-ACTO knife, cut a horizontal slit on the forehead of your baby, just large enough for the strip of fortunes to glide through easily.

5. Put the roll of fortunes inside the head, leaving the first fortune poking through the slit.

6. Glue the baby head to the back of the box with E-6000 and let the glue dry.

7. Invite some friends over to have their fortunes told by a baby head.

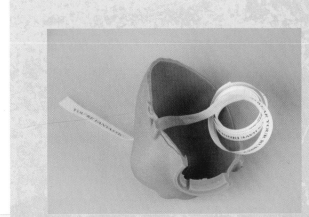

MAGIC MOJO DOLLS

We all have talismans. Some people prefer a four-leaf clover, some a rabbit's foot (gross!), while others hold on to a wishing stone or a jar of lucky pennies. I have my magic mojo dolls, who watch over me and look darn cool in my house. All of my friends want them, and as I started making them for my pals they began to evolve into elaborate creations. Here is the most popular version.

YOU'LL NEED

- 1 twig 12 inches long plus several smaller twigs
- Yarn
- Hot glue gun and glue sticks
- Faux butterflies (if you can't find any, make your own out of paper)
- Wire plant basket or small wire lampshade frame
- 5 yards of fine-gauge wire
- Wire cutters
- Upper half of a doll (including arms and head!)
- Gold, brown, and black Krylon Fusion for Plastic spray paint
- Glitter
- Elmer's glue
- *Optional:* E-6000 glue

HERE'S HOW

1 Cover your 12-inch-long twig with yarn by tying a knot around one end and wrapping the yarn around and

around the twig all the way down to the other end and then tying another knot.

2 Hot-glue a couple of butterflies on one end of the yarn-covered twig and let the glue dry. (Run around the house casting magic spells on your friends and/or kids.)

3 Add wire to the basket to make it more interesting, wrapping wire around and through the basket wires, twisting the ends around the basket wires to hold them in place.

4 Place the basket facedown on the table, and using E-6000, wire, or hot glue (whatever you think is easiest), affix the doll torso to the top of your wire basket.

5 Once your doll is secured to the base, spray-paint it black, gold, and brown to give it an antique look. (You could use other colors too—these are just my favorite combination.)

6 Spread some Elmer's on the doll's head and around the area where it joins the wire basket, then sprinkle glitter on top.

7 Hot-glue some butterflies and short twigs to the underside of the wire basket to give it a wild look.

8 Attach the yarn-covered stick to the hand of the mojo doll by wiring it in place.

9 Tell anyone that if they cross you, this little fairy will come to life and cause chaos!

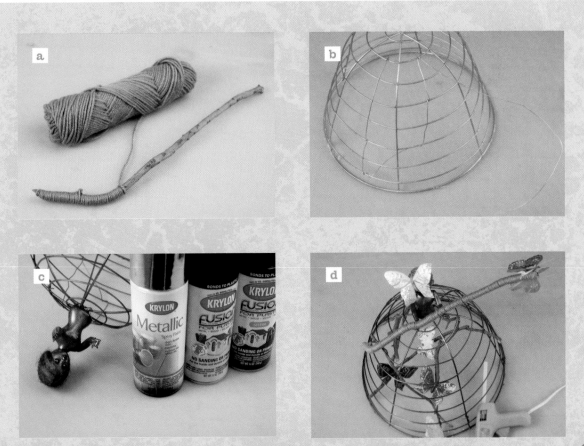

99-CENT-STORE SHADOW BOX

I had a feeling the words "99-cent store" would get your attention, since most shadow boxes cost an arm and a leg. Rather than paying top dollar, I head to the 99-cent store and pick up four or five identical frames and glue them together, and voilà, for four or five dollars, I have a shadow box to store special items.

YOU'LL NEED

- 4 or 5 flat frames from the 99-cent store
- E-6000 glue
- Krylon Fusion for Plastic spray paint in any color
- Hot glue gun and glue sticks
- Stuff to put in your shadow boxes
- *Optional:* Fabric or decorative paper to make your backing a little fancier

HERE'S HOW

1 Remove the glass and backings from each frame.

2 Glue all but one of the frames together, back to front, using E-6000. I repeat, *make sure not to glue on the last frame yet!*

3 Spray-paint all of the frames, including the frame you set aside.

4 Replace the glass in your single frame and add some hot glue around the edges of the glass so it'll stay in place. This will be the front of your shadow box.

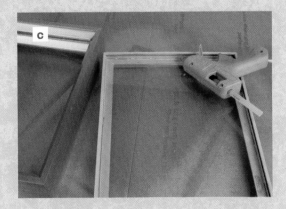

5 Glue your frame with the glass on top of the stack of frames with E-6000.

6 Fill your shadow box with whatever you'd like.

7 Use the original backing of one of your frames or cut a piece of cardboard the size of your frames and glue it on the back of your shadow box.

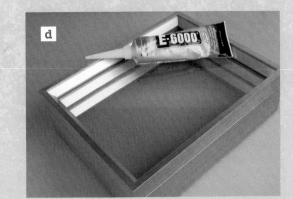

SUGGESTION

> Get creative with the backing. Spray-paint it the color of your frame, or cover it in fabric or decorative paper.

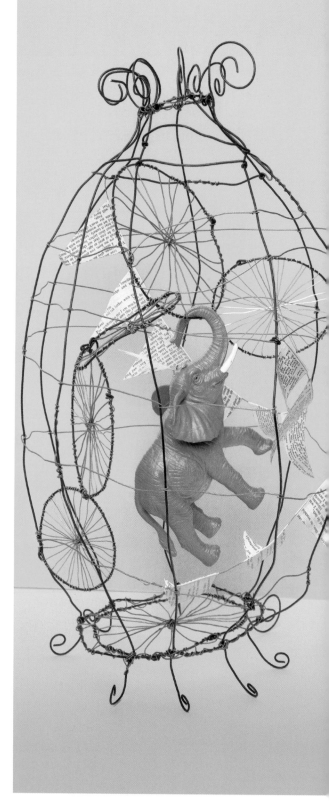

TABLETOP TERRIFIC

I like my tabletops to be covered with stuff—cool coasters, vases, books, little sculptures I've collected over the years ... I think without these my tables look naked. I find too that people feel more comfortable when they visit a home filled with fun objects. It gives them something to talk about and to look at. This chapter offers some projects that are sure to inject a little personality into your home and spice up your underdressed tabletops. I loved making all of them, and I love the way my home looks with the extra knickknacks. Now, if I could just stop bumping into my tables and knocking stuff over, I'd be golden!

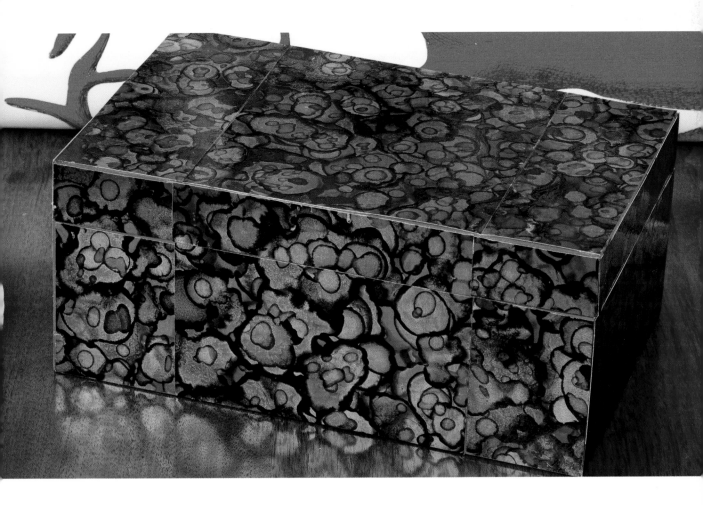

MAYBE MALACHITE BOX

I've always wanted to try alcohol inks on a project, and I finally just jumped in and started experimenting and discovered that my favorite use for these inks is on aluminum flashing. You could use this technique to cover everything, from tabletops and frames to mirrors and dressers.

YOU'LL NEED

- Ranger Alcohol Ink in 2 colors (I used Bottle and Stream, but any two shades of green or blue would work)
- Aluminum flashing
- Flat wood box to cover
- Green Krylon spray paint
- Minwax Polycrylic Protective Finish
- 1-inch paintbrush
- Ruler
- Permanent marker
- Tin shears
- E-6000 glue

HERE'S HOW

1 Squeeze droplets of your first ink color on your sheet of flashing and watch how it bleeds and spreads.

DON'T WORRY

About how it goes on. I think the sloppier the better! Just make sure to cover the entire piece of flashing.

2 When the first coat of ink is dry, make smaller dots on the flashing with the other color. It will bleed and form more circles with dark edges.

3 When that coat is dry, add smaller dots and lines of ink over the existing ones. Trust me, you'll get the hang of it and develop your own technique.

4 While the ink dries, paint your box with green Krylon spray paint.

5 Using a paintbrush, apply clear coat to the painted flashing to protect it.

6 On the nonpainted side of the flashing, measure and mark off the pieces you'll need to cover your box, and cut out the pieces with tin shears.

7 Glue your painted pieces to the box with E-6000.

HINT

Place something heavy on top of the metal pieces while the glue dries to ensure a strong bond.

OPTIONAL

Clear-coat the box again for an extra-hard surface.

STRIPED PVC PIPE VASE

PVC pipe is supercool, easy to cut, cheap, and comes in all different sizes. It's also good for whacking your assistant when they give you flack. I'm just sayin'. Anyway, I was totally inspired by this project and decided to paint it instead of just leaving it plain white, but you could leave yours plain or use a rainbow of colors. Just have fun with it—you really can't go wrong.

YOU'LL NEED

- 10 feet of 1-inch PVC pipe
- Handsaw
- Sanding block
- Damp cloth and dry cloth
- Blue painter's tape
- 7 (1-inch) PVC caps
- Krylon Fusion for Plastic spray paint
- E-6000 glue
- 8 inches of 1-inch black or white elastic
- Straight pin
- Hot glue gun and glue sticks

HERE'S HOW

1. Cut your PVC pipe into 7 sections, each 17 inches long.

2. Sand the rough edges until they're smooth, then sand the rest of each pipe to remove dirt and any markings that you don't like.

3. Wipe the pipes off with a damp cloth and dry them.

4. Tape off stripes on each piece of pipe using blue painter's tape.

5. Spray-paint the pipes and let them dry. Then, carefully remove the tape.

6. Squeeze some E-6000 in the bottom of each cap and put 1 on 1 end of each piece of pipe.

7. Gather all of the pipes together and wrap elastic tightly around the bunch, securing the ends with a straight pin. Hot-glue the elastic in place.

8. Arrange your pipes however you want, fill them with water, and add flowers.

CIRCUS ELEPHANT AND HORSE SCULPTURES

I like how these sculptures make it look like I've trapped a tiny elephant inside a birdcage and a tiny horse inside of a ball. My nephew was obsessed with them, so as soon as I finished photographing them for the book, I gave them to him to keep in his room. I admit I'm a little bummed because I really liked them! Guess I'll have to make a couple more.

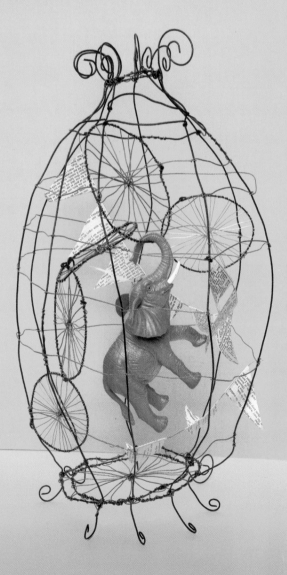

YOU'LL NEED

FOR BOTH
- Rebar tie
- Wire cutters
- Needle-nose pliers
- Fine-gauge wire
- Glitter glue
- 2 small feathers
- 2 rhinestones
- Elmer's glue
- E-6000 glue

FOR THE ELEPHANT
- Book pages
- Scissors
- Small plastic elephant
- Glitter glue

FOR THE HORSE
- Small plastic horse

HERE'S HOW
FOR THE ELEPHANT

1. Cut 8 pieces of rebar tie, each 22 inches long. These will become the vertical wires for your cage.

2. Cut 2 more pieces of rebar tie, an 8-inch piece and a 20-inch piece, then bend the 2 wires into circles by making a hook on each end of each wire, linking the loops, and squeezing them together with pliers, as shown in the photo. These circles will be the top (smaller circle) and bottom (bigger circle) of your sculpture.

3. Insert one end of a 22-inch wire into the large circle, leaving 4 inches out, and the other end into the small circle, leaving 4 inches out. Wrap the ends around the circles and loop the 4-inch ends into loose spirals that point away from the circles, as shown in the photo. Repeat with the rest of the 22-inch wires.

4. Secure the vertical wires in place by wrapping fine-gauge wire around the circles and where the vertical wires intersect them, as shown in the photo.

5. To complete your cage, attach the end of the wire to the top circle, then wrap around and through the vertical wires, working from top to bottom.

6. To create the "bicycle rim and spokes," cut 3 pieces of rebar wire, each 12 inches long and 3 pieces 9 inches long.

7. Make the "rims" the same way you made your circles in step 3.

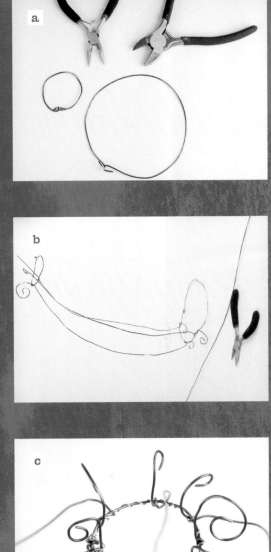

8. To make the "spokes," wrap small-gauge wire back and forth across each rim, from one end to the other, crossing the center of the circle each time and wrapping the wire around the rim every time you meet it. Keep crisscrossing until the rims are packed with spokes.

9. Center a large bicycle rim and spokes piece on the base of the cage, and wire it in place using small-gauge wire. Make sure it's secure.

10. Using the small-gauge wire, link your 5 remaining bicycle rim and spokes pieces together in a row. Then, using pieces of the small-gauge wire like a wire twist tie, attach them to the top of the cage on the inside.

11. To create the strand of flags, fold book pages in half, then cut small triangles along the folds (when unfolded they will be diamond-shaped). Cut 2 strands of small-gauge wire, each 9 inches. Spread Elmer's glue on one side of your diamonds, and glue them to the wire by lining up the wire along the fold line and folding the diamonds into triangles.

12. Add a feather, rhinestone, and some glitter glue to the head of your plastic elephant to dress it up a bit.

13. Hang your elephant by looping its trunk through the top bicycle rim and spokes piece.

DON°T WORRY

If your elephant doesn't have a raised trunk. It will look just as neat standing on the bottom of the cage.

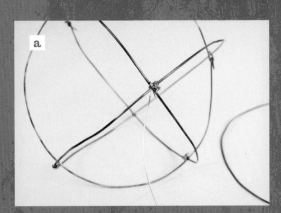

14 Place your strands of book page flags inside wherever you think they will look nice, and secure them by twisting the end of each strand to the sides of the cage.

HERE'S HOW
FOR THE HORSE

1 Using wire cutters, cut 7 pieces of rebar tie, each 19 inches long, and make each into a circle by following step 3 for making the elephant sculpture.

2 Put 1 circle inside another at a perpendicular angle, and attach the 2 circles with small-gauge wire where the edges meet.

3 Keep adding circles and attaching them to each other with the small-gauge wire until you've made a sphere, as shown in the photo.

NOTE

> Each sphere will be a little different—just keep adding circles until you get the effect you want.

4 To create your "bicycle rim and spokes" piece, cut an 11-inch piece of rebar tie and follow steps 8 and 9 for making the elephant.

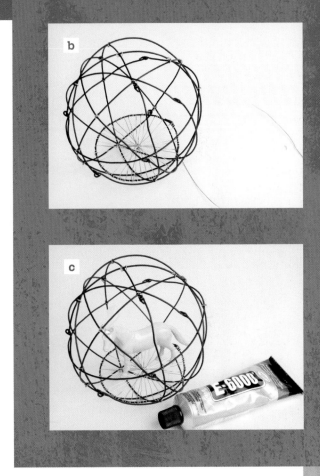

5 Attach the bicycle rim and spokes piece at the bottom of the sphere on the inside, twisting small pieces of wire around where the edge of the rim meets the sphere.

6 Glue a feather and rhinestone on your horse's head to dress it up a bit, then glue your horse on top of the bicycle wheel using E-6000.

PUNK ROCK BOWL

When I was making this bowl I kept putting it on my head. It just seemed like something Dr. Frankenstein would do to help with his experiments, and since I was experimenting, I figured I'd employ some mad scientist moves, too.

YOU'LL NEED

- 4 plastic office folders
- Scissors
- Clear tape
- Plaster of Paris
- Mixing bowl for plaster
- Two bowls that comfortably fit inside of each other (mine were 8 inches and 6 inches in diameter)
- Heavy-duty sanding block
- Hot glue gun and glue sticks
- Caulk
- Krylon spray paint in silver and gray

HERE'S HOW

1. Cut the office folders into 19 rectangles, each 5 inches by 4 inches.

2. Roll the rectangles into cone shapes and place some tape on the loose edges so they hold their shape. Place more tape over the small hole in the bottom of each cone.

3. Make about 3 cups of plaster of Paris in a bowl, following the instructions on the packaging.

4. Quickly pour the plaster in the large bowl until it's about halfway full, then push the smaller bowl inside the larger bowl. You might have to put some weights inside the smaller bowl to keep it from floating up.

5. Quickly fill the cones with the leftover plaster.

6. Let the plaster dry thoroughly, then remove your new plaster bowl from between the 2 bowls and the plaster cones from the plastic molds.

7. Sand the rough edges off the bowl and the cones.

8. Pick 3 cones that are exactly the same size to use as the cones that your bowl will rest on. Glue these 3 cones to the bottom of the bowl with a generous amount of hot glue.

9. Squeeze caulk around where the tops of the cones meet the bottom of the bowl, and smooth with your fingers.

10. Continue adding cones and caulk around the base of the bowl until it resembles a spiky sea creature.

11. Hold the spray paint can about 15 inches away from your bowl, and lightly spray your vase silver and then gray, without letting the silver dry in between coats. Let the paint dry.

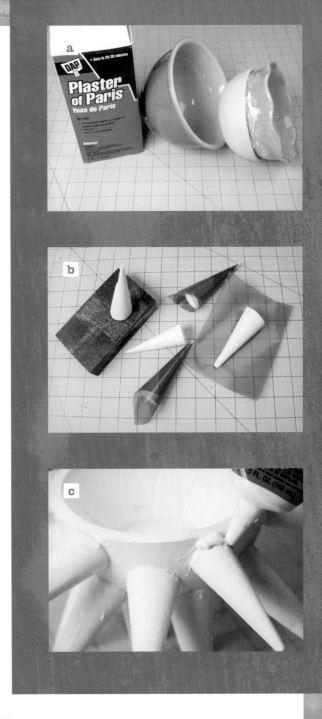

285

MAGAZINE-EMBELLISHED JEWEL BOX

Ever since the third grade I've loved to cover things in macaroni! My poor mom had a serious collection of macaroni-adorned treasure boxes. Lucky for her, I've learned to cover boxes in different things over the years, and I think these magazine jewels are the perfect adult version of macaroni. Have fun making this project. I'll see you at recess!

YOU'LL NEED

- A few old magazines
- Scissors
- Elmer's glue
- Needle-nose pliers
- Plain wooden box or cigar box
- Krylon spray paint in any color
- Metallic gold paint (not spray)
- Paintbrush

HERE'S HOW

1 To make the straight straws, cut the magazine pages into 6-inch by 4-inch strips. You are going to need a lot of these, I'd say at least 150.

2 Taking 1 corner of a strip, start to roll the strip into a small tube. Glue the ends down with a tiny dot of Elmer's glue. Continue until you have tons of straws.

HINT

> I like to make these while watching a movie because it makes the time fly.

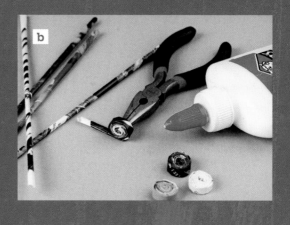

3 To make the paper spirals, cut magazine pages into 11-inch by 1½-inch strips and roll them into small tubes, gluing down the ends with a tiny dot of Elmer's. Then grab one end of the tube with the tip of your needle-nose pliers and twist the tube around it to create a spiral. Dab a dot of Elmer's glue on the end of the tube to hold your spiral in place.

4 Make spirals in a few different sizes by adding tubes to continue your spirals, making sure to tack down the tube ends with glue.

5 Lay out your design on the top of your box, then start gluing the spirals in place.

6 Fill in the remaining space on your box top and sides with straight straws. Cut the tubes to size if necessary.

7 Once your straws are in place and the glue has dried, spray-paint your box with color.

8 When the spray paint is dry, lightly brush over your box with metallic paint to give it some added dimension.

RESIN PAPERWEIGHT

I have about 100 glass tealight holders at home, and I would bet twenty bucks you have a few in your house right now, too. Why not use some by making these pretty pieces for your desktop?

YOU'LL NEED

- Small glass tealight holder
- Small image that'll fit inside the bottom of your light
- Scissors
- Elmer's glue
- Cup of water
- Small paintbrush
- Glitter
- Clear resin (ICE Resin is great!)

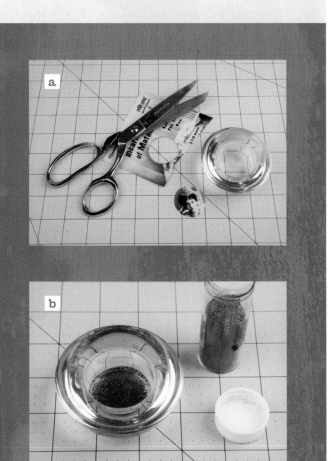

HERE'S HOW

1 Clean your tealight holder until it sparkles.

2 Cut your image so that it fits perfectly on the bottom of the holder.

3 Slightly water down some Elmer's glue. With a paintbrush, lightly apply glue to the front of your image, then glue it facedown to the bottom of the tealight holder and let the glue dry.

4 Sprinkle a thin layer of glitter in the holder, then take it outside and mix enough resin to fill the holder. Follow the instructions on the package carefully.

5 Fill your container with resin and let it dry overnight outside in a covered area so nothing gets inside.

WINDSTORM PLACE CARD HOLDERS

After a huge windstorm, I was left with some rather large branches to haul out of my yard. I was cutting them up to make them easier to move when I had a craft attack: *What can I make out of these branches? What can I do with these little pieces?* I took the wooden disks inside, and the next thing you know I had these place card holders ready to go for my next dinner party.

YOU'LL NEED

- Safety goggles
- Jigsaw
- 1 branch, 2 to 3 inches in diameter
- Drill with a 1/16-inch drill bit
- 8 inches of medium-gauge wire per place card holder
- Needle-nose pliers

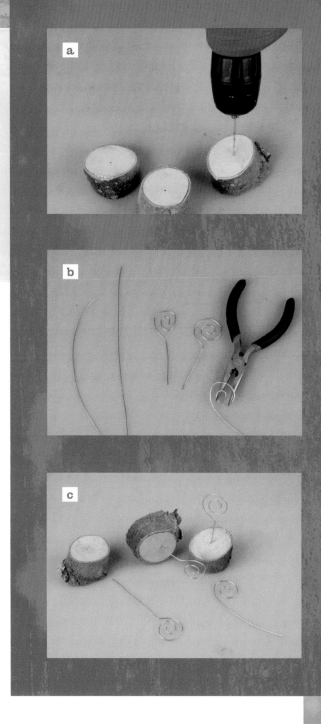

HERE'S HOW

1. Put on safety goggles and cut your branch into disks 1 inch to 1 1/2 inches thick.

2. Drill a hole in the center of each disk.

3. Cut an 8-inch piece of wire. With your pliers, make a spiral in the wire, leaving about 3 inches at 1 end straight.

4. Push the straight part of the wire into the drilled hole.

5. Write your dinner guest's name on a piece of paper and tuck it in between the circles in the spiral.

THAT'S SHOE BIZ

Like most of my female friends, I enjoy hanging out in the I Love Shoes department. I can't help it. I see a pair of cool kicks, and two seconds later I'm pulling out my credit card. Worst-case scenario, I'll see a pair of Ferragamo loafers, and two seconds and $500 later I'm on my bedroom floor, stroking them and smelling the new leather in a happy daze. (If anyone ever filmed me doing this I would be an instant YouTube sensation).

Unfortunately, that new-shoe feeling doesn't last forever, and eventually even the most fabulous pair inevitably ends up in the back of your closet in need of some crafty love. Well, on the next few pages you'll find some ideas that I hope will inspire you to spruce up a neglected pair of shoes that still have some life and save a few bucks you can put toward your next new pair. So get out that glue, sisters (and brothers), and let's make some shoe magic.

SCRAP LACE–COVERED SHOES AND BAG

I know you have several purses and pairs of shoes under your bed that you just can't get rid of, and that you probably have some scraps of lace sitting somewhere just waiting to be put to use. Well, let's put those items together!

YOU'LL NEED

FOR BOTH
- Scissors
- E-6000 glue
- Toothpicks
- Damp cloth and dry towel

FOR THE SHOES
- 1 pair of shoes
- For the colorful shoes: ⅛ yard each of 5 different kinds of lace and lace trim
- For the black and gray shoes: 1 yard of black lace trim

FOR THE BAG
- 1 purse
- ¼ yard each of 5 different kinds of lace and lace trim

HERE'S HOW

1 Clean your shoes or purse with a damp cloth, making sure to remove all dirt and grime so that your adhesives will work properly, then dry with a towel.

2 Cut your lace into small pieces. Try keeping the elements of the pattern intact so you can create a design on your shoe or purse.

3 Dab E-6000 on the back of the lace pieces, then adhere them to your shoes or purse.

4 As soon as the glue is dry, tack down any remaining loose pieces of lace with a toothpick and dab on more E-6000.

CAMEO PUMPS

I think you're going to go crazy with this project once you get the hang of it. You can put any image in your cameo, so your shoes can make a statement while you keep your mouth shut. How great is that?

YOU'LL NEED

- 1 yard of 1½-inch ribbon
- Straight pins
- Sewing machine and matching thread
- 2 cameos (see page 342)
- Hot glue gun and glue sticks
- Shoes that need sprucing up
- E-6000 glue
- Damp cloth and dry towel

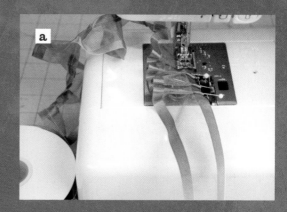

HERE'S HOW

1. Follow the instructions for making the cameos on page 343.

2. Pleat your ribbon by making little folds in the fabric and pinning them in place (½-inch pleats every ½ inch will work well for this project).

3. Sew your pleats in place by stitching along one side of your ribbon, about ¼ inch from the edge.

4. Cut your pleating in half. You'll use half for each shoe.

5. Form 2 rings out of each half of your pleating, and use a few straight pins to hold the shape.

6. Hot-glue a cameo in the middle of each pleated ribbon ring. When the glue is dry, remove the pins.

7. Glue your ribbon-ringed cameos to your shoe with E-6000 and let dry.

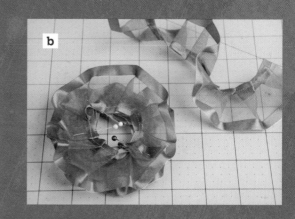

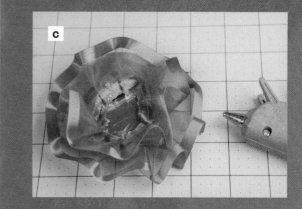

FABULOUS FLOWER FABRIC DÉCOUPAGE SHOES AND PURSE

Chance are, you have a pair of shoes or a purse that have been taken out of rotation because of a major scuff or scratch that you just can't fix. Here's how you can cover up the flaw and have a brand-new accessory in no time. All you need is a little bit of printed fabric and some imagination.

YOU'LL NEED

- A pair of shoes and/or purse that needs some love
- Damp cloth and dry towel
- Cotton fabric with a terrific flower print that you can easily cut out (you could also use a print that features interesting shapes)
- Sharp scissors
- Minwax Polycrylic Protective Finish
- 1/2-inch flat paintbrush

HERE'S HOW

1. Clean your shoes or purse with a damp cloth, making sure to remove all dirt and grime so that your adhesives will work properly, then dry with a towel.

2. Cut out flowers from your fabric. Try to get as much detail as you can.

3. Paint a bit of clear coat on an area on your shoe or purse that you want to cover, place a flower over it, and paint more clear coat on top.

4. Continue until you've covered your shoes or purse with as many flowers as you want, and then let the clear coat dry.

5. Add 3 more layers of clear coat, making sure to let dry between each application.

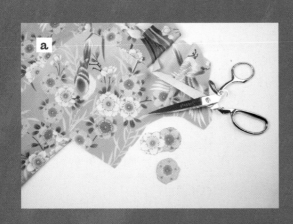

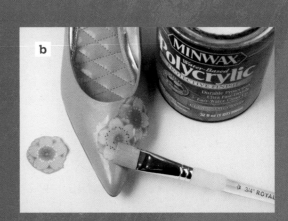

ZIPPER PUMPS

Zippers have made their way into fashion over the past year and I don't think they are going away for a while. That's fine with me because I think they add a punk edge to any item, but if you're not a zipper fan like me, don't worry—you can make this project with ribbon, a strip of fabric, or even some chain.

YOU'LL NEED

- 2 yards of metal zipper
- Scissors
- Hot glue gun and glue sticks
- Pair of pumps
- E-6000 glue
- Toothpick
- Clothespins
- Damp cloth and dry towel

HERE'S HOW

1 Clean your shoes with a damp cloth, making sure to remove all dirt and grime so that your adhesives will work properly, then dry with a towel.

2 Take 10 inches of zipper and roll it into a spiral, running a line of hot glue along the inside of the spiral as you roll.

3 Using a generous amount of E-6000, glue the spiral to the front of your shoe.

4 Cut 2 portions of zipper, 1 long enough to wrap around the mouth of your shoe and the other about $\frac{1}{2}$ inch longer than the first.

5 With your glue gun, lightly tack the shorter length of the zipper all the way around the mouth of the shoe, with the ends meeting the sides of the spiral and the teeth pointing up.

6 Add the longer zipper piece just below the first.

7 With a toothpick, add some E-6000 in between where you tacked, then put a few clothespins around the mouth of your shoe to hold the zippers in place while the glue dries.

8 Repeat to decorate your other shoe.

9 Go out and strut your stuff!

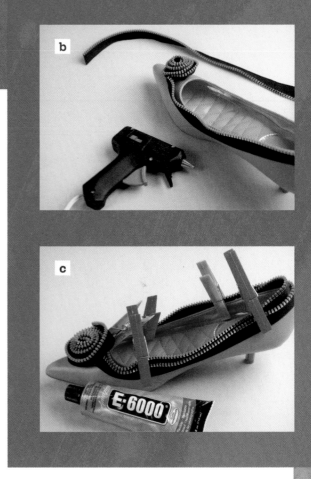

DOROTHY'S OTHER SHOES AND MATCHING CUFF

I would bet a thousand dollars that Dorothy would have tossed Toto to the flying monkeys for these shoes and matching cuff. I can hear her now, "Screw these ruby red slippers, I'm going for something that will get me a date with one of those hot Munchkins!" Click your heels three times and start crafting.

YOU'LL NEED

FOR BOTH

- E-6000 glue
- Chunky silver glitter
- Toothpicks
- Rhinestones in several colors and sizes
- Damp cloth and dry towel

FOR THE SHOES

- A plain pair of pumps you want to spruce up

FOR THE CUFF

- Plain metal cuff

HERE'S HOW
FOR THE SHOES

1. Clean your shoes or cuff with a damp cloth, making sure to remove all dirt and grime so that your adhesives will work properly, then dry with a towel.

2. Cover the shoes in a layer of E-6000 and sprinkle chunky glitter on top. Let the glue dry.

3. Using a generous amount of E-6000, apply rhinestones and sequins on the heel, toe, and around the mouth of the shoes in a pattern that you like. Let the glue dry for about an hour.

4. With a toothpick, add more glue around the rhinestones and sprinkle more glitter on top of the glue. Cover any bare spots with more glue and glitter, and let the shoes dry.

5. Shake off any excess glitter, then hit the yellow brick road.

HERE'S HOW
FOR THE CUFF

1. Spread a generous amount of E-6000 on the cuff, then apply enough rhinestones to cover the top and sides.

2. As soon as all of the rhinestones are in place, sprinkle glitter in between the stones to cover any metal that's still showing.

3. With a toothpick and E-6000, add some more rhinestones in between and on top of the first layer to add dimension. Let the glue dry.

SHOESTRING SHOE

I know it's hard to believe, but with just a pair of shoes, some spray paint, and some string, these super cool pumps can be yours. Try this technique to add life to a beat-up pair of heels or create a fun pair of shoes that can spice up any all-black ensemble.

YOU'LL NEED

- Shoes that are crying out for some crafty love
- Newspaper
- Yarn
- Krylon Fusion for Plastic spray paint in at least 1 color
- Damp cloth and dry towel

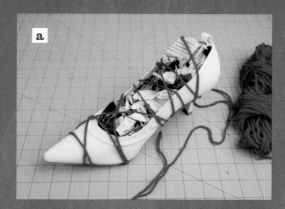

HERE'S HOW

1. Clean your shoes with a damp cloth, making sure to remove all dirt and grime so that your adhesives will work properly, then dry with a towel.

2. Stuff your shoes with newspaper to protect the insides from paint.

3. Wrap your shoes in yarn, crisscrossing at random and making sure to wrap some string around every part of each shoe.

4. Go outside and place the shoes on a large sheet of newspaper.

5. Spray-paint your shoes and let the paint dry.

6. Remove the yarn and admire your handiwork.

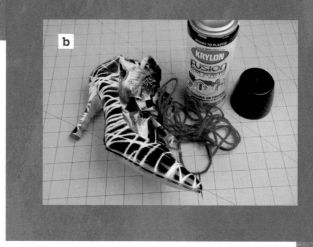

SUGGESTION

Repeat with additional colors for a really fun effect. Just make sure that you use contrasting spray paint every time you change up the color, alternating between a light color and then a dark color, then a light and then a dark. . . .

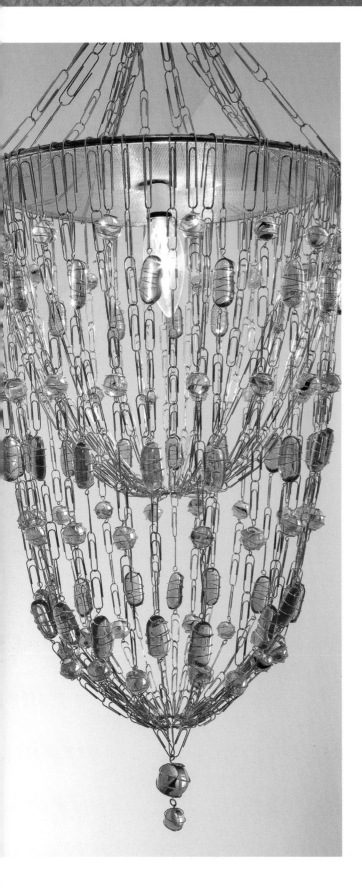

THE LIGHT FANTASTIC

I love, love, love lamps. I must have twenty in the living room alone. They eliminate hideous overhead lighting, which makes everyone look terrible, and there's such variety—they can cast the perfect glow to set any mood—colorful lights and shades for festive occasions, dim and serious for romantic evenings. Even when I'm home alone and want to get into a certain mind-set, lighting is the first thing I tweak.

In this chapter I've included a few ideas and techniques that I hope will put you in the right mood. Just remember to use energy-efficient cool lightbulbs when making these projects. They're much better for the environment and for the glue and materials you'll use to put the lamps together.

IMPORTANT

I'm serious about using energy-efficient cool bulbs! Some of these projects should not be exposed to the heat a conventional bulb gives off. So head to the store and stock up on eco-friendly, cool bulbs before you even turn this page. You heard me, go!

LULU LAMP

This project reminded me of the first time I did macramé. I was with my aunt Lulu, who was letting me help her make a hanging planter. We spent a lovely Saturday afternoon tying twine and watching it take shape while she drank boxed wine and I had a Coke. Aunt Lulu had a talent for macramé for sure, but sadly, I didn't take to it. That said, I do love braiding and twisting fabric strands together, and this project reminded me of her. So here's to you, Aunt Lulu!

YOU'LL NEED

- 1 yard each of 3 different fabrics in complementary colors
- Scissors
- Hot glue gun and glue sticks
- Wire plant basket
- Cord and socket set
- Nylon zip tie
- Energy-efficient cool bulb—Do not make this project with any other type of bulb!
- *Optional:* Sewing machine with matching thread

HERE'S HOW

1. Cut 14 strips of each fabric, 2 inches wide, along the width of the fabric. (Most fabric is either 45 inches or 60 inches wide, so your strips will probably be 2" × 45" or 2" × 60", but it doesn't matter if they're longer or shorter.)

2. Take 1 strip of each piece of fabric and braid them together. Secure the ends by either stitching across the 3 pieces or hot-gluing them together. Repeat until you've made 13 braids.

3. With the wire basket's mouth down on your workspace, crisscross your 3 leftover fabric strips on top so they lie flat, and hot-glue them to the wires, as shown in the photo. Be sure to glue the ends of the strips securely to the mouth of the basket.

4. Cut a hole in the strips at the center of the top of the lamp. Place your socket inside

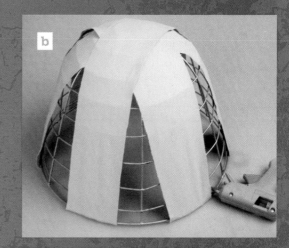

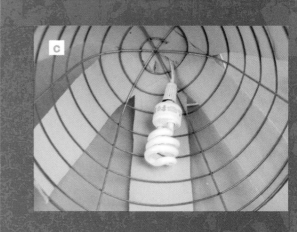

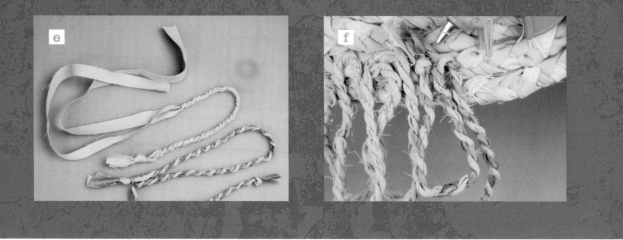

the top of the basket, and thread the cord through the top. Secure the socket in place with a nylon zip tie.

5. With your basket's mouth down on the table, twist your braids in a spiral pattern starting in the center of the top, and glue them in place. Continue working around and down the basket toward the mouth, adding braids as you go, until the entire basket is covered.

6. Cut 8 strips of fabric from each of your 3 fabrics, each $1/2$ inch wide.

7. Tie the ends of 2 pieces together, and trap the tied ends in a drawer or under something very heavy.

8. Twist each of the pieces clockwise while simultaneously twisting each color counterclockwise to form a ropelike strand, and then tie a knot on the end to finish it. Repeat until you have 8 twisted strands.

9. Glue the end of 1 of your twisted strands to the mouth of your lamp. Let it hang down about 4 inches, then loop it back up and tack the loop in place. Continue creating a 4-inch looped fringe with your strands until it goes all the way around the mouth. Make additional twisted strands if you need them.

10. Make some more twisted strands and glue them around the lamp in between the braids to cover up any gaps and to add texture.

11. Make another twisted strand and glue 1 end to the top of your lamp in the middle of the spiral so you can poke a hanging hook through it later.

12. Attach your energy-saving cool bulb to the socket, and hang your light.

BEER CAN BETTY PARTY LIGHTS

I call these Beer Can Betty Party Lights because whenever I need an aluminum can for a project I call up my neighbor Betty. She's always throwing parties and she saves the empty beer cans for me. Hopefully the beer (or soda) lovers in your life will save some cans for you so you can make these, too.

YOU'LL NEED

- 20 or so beer cans
- Scissors
- Large nail and Phillips screwdriver
- Silver Krylon spray paint
- Elmer's glue
- Small paintbrush
- Silver glitter
- String of colored lights
- E-6000 glue

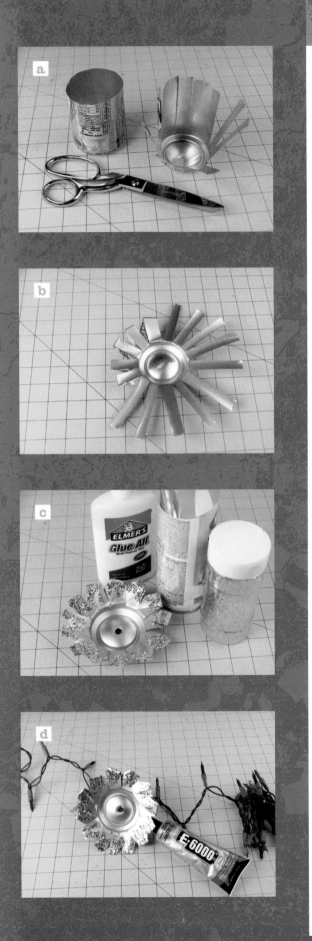

HERE'S HOW

1 Cut the tops off your beer cans about 1 inch down from the lid so that you have a "beer cup" about $3^{1}/_{2}$ inches high.

2 Cut the sides of the cans into $^{1}/_{2}$-inch-wide vertical strips.

3 Bend the strips outward so each can looks like a starburst.

4 Fold each strip under and slightly sideways, so that the top of the strip is hidden under the base of the next strip.

5 Poke a hole in the center of each can with your large nail, and then work it open with the screwdriver until it's big enough for a lightbulb to fit through.

6 Spray the cans all over with silver spray paint and let them dry.

7 Paint Elmer's glue on the edges of your cans, sprinkle glitter on top, and let dry.

8 Slip your starbursts over the lightbulbs and add a dab of E-6000 to keep them in place.

9 Invite Betty over to help you party it up a little.

PAPER CLIP AND DUCT CAP LAMP

This is one of the projects I'm most proud of, and my friends dig it, which is always a good indication of a successful craft. It's made from only a few simple elements—paper clips, a duct cap from the hardware store, and two binder rings—and you can make it while watching TV and eating a very large bowl of peanut butter–filled pretzels.

YOU'LL NEED

- 1 8-inch-diameter duct cap
- Large nail and hammer
- Scrap piece of wood
- 330 small paper clips
- 104 large paper clips
- Stick-on battery-operated light
- Two binder rings that are 1½ inches in diameter

HERE'S HOW

1. Place the edge of your duct cap on the scrap wood, and working from the inside, tap 66 holes around the edge of the cap using a large nail and hammer. The holes should be about ⅜ of an inch apart.

2. Make 66 strands of paper clips, each consisting of 5 small clips hanging from 1 large clip.

3. Add the strands to the cap by poking the end of the large clips through the holes.

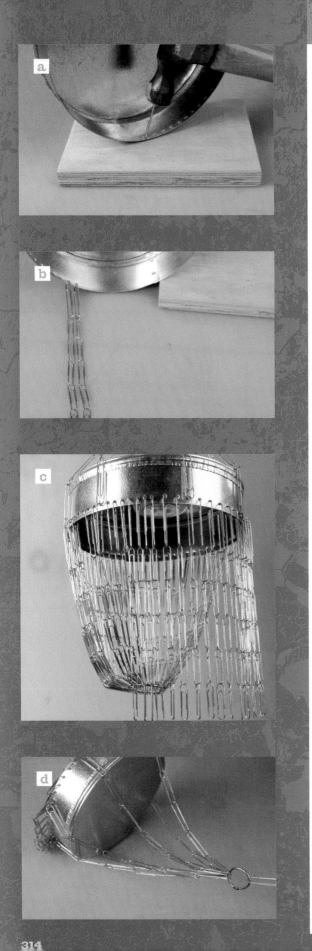

4. Stick the battery-operated light inside the duct cap, right in the center.

5. String the end clip on each paper clip strand through 1 of the binder rings and clasp the ring shut.

6. Make 6 strands of 6 large paper clips each, and evenly attach them around the duct cap, connecting each to the top of 1 of the large paper clips you put there earlier.

7. Attach the ends of the 8 strands you just added to another binder ring and clasp the ring shut.

8. Hang your lamp from the ring and enjoy the glow.

INDIA-INSPIRED UMBRELLA LIGHT COVER

I noticed these beautiful Indian and Moroccan upside-down umbrella lamps in tons of home décor magazines, and had no idea where to get one. Luckily, while cleaning out a closet I found a spare umbrella. I immediately started playing around with it, and here is the result. Problem solved!

YOU'LL NEED

- Umbrella in a color or pattern you like
- Heavy-duty wire cutters
- Hot glue gun and glue sticks
- Enough fringe to go around the edge of the umbrella (3½ yards is enough for an average-size umbrella)

- 2 to 3 yards of several additional decorative trims (lace, embroidered ribbon, anything you can think of)
- Scissors
- 4¼ yards of ribbon (for hanging your creation)
- Tassel for the center of the umbrella
- Eco-friendly cool bulb hanging from the ceiling and in need of a cover

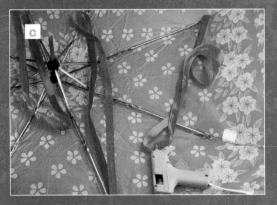

HERE'S HOW

1 Open your umbrella.

2 With heavy-duty wire cutters, cut the shaft of the umbrella about 6 inches above the runner. Make sure not to cut too near the top spring (this is what keeps the umbrella locked open).

HINT

> The runner is the little piece above the handle you push to open your umbrella.

3 Hot-glue a layer of fringe all the way around the outer edge of the umbrella.

4 Hot-glue another ring of trim evenly all the way around the umbrella, about 4 inches closer to the center than your first.

5 Continue adding layers of trim until you are satisfied.

6 Cut 4 pieces of ribbon, each 1 yard long.

7 Inside the top of your umbrella there are 8 stretchers that extend when you open it. String 1 yard of ribbon through the outermost piece of every other stretcher, and hot-glue the opposite ends together in the center of your umbrella so you've formed 4 big loops.

8 Thread the extra $\frac{1}{4}$-yard-long piece of ribbon through the loops and tie the ends in a knot to form a loop from which you can hang your umbrella cover.

9 Hot-glue a tassel in the center of the outside of the umbrella cover. Let the glue dry.

10 Hang your umbrella cover from a hook on a high ceiling.

PAPER CLIP AND GLASS PENDANT LAMP

Do you ever just want to mix together a bunch of different materials and see what happens? Well, that's how this project came about. If you don't need another lamp, the marble-wrapping technique employed here can be used for making jewelry or a window treatment, and paper clips can be used to hang other hand-made artwork in the sunlight on your porch. Let your imagination run wild!

YOU'LL NEED

- 12 yards of medium-gauge wire
- Needle-nose pliers with wire cutter
- 65 small marbles, plus 1 large marble
- 48 flat glass chips
- 104 large paper clips (get 150 to be safe)
- 720 small paper clips (get 750 to be safe)
- 1 splatter lid about 10$\frac{1}{2}$ inches in diameter
- 3 binder rings, 1$\frac{1}{2}$ inches in diameter
- 1 cord and socket set

HERE'S HOW

1 Cut a 3-inch piece of wire and create a small loop at the end with needle-nose pliers.

2 Wrap the wire around a small marble 3 times, and then create another small loop at the other end of your wire. This will probably take you a few tries, but you'll get the hang of it.

3 Repeat the previous two steps for all but 1 small marble, then use the same technique with 5-inch pieces of wire to wrap all of your glass chips.

4 To make the strands that will go on the top part of your chandelier (which the body hangs from), make 8 strands of 5 large paper clips and 8 strands of 8 small paper clips.

5 Remove the handle of the splatter lid. (These are usually screwed on with a Phillips head screw.)

6 Clip the strands of large paper clips evenly around the edge of the splatter lid by hooking the ends of the paper clip strands around the rim and through the screen.

7 Attach all of the other ends of the strands to an office clip. Hang your partially finished chandelier to continue work on the next stages.

8 For the outer body of the chandelier, make 16 strands following this pattern: 1 large paperclip + 1 wrapped marble + 3 small paperclips + 1 wrapped marble + 3 paperclips + 1 wrapped marble + 3 small paperclips + 1 wrapped marble + 3 paperclips.

Now make 16 strands following this pattern: 1 large paperclip + 1 small paperclip + 1 wrapped glass chip + 3 small paperclips + 1 wrapped chip + 3 small paperclips + 1 wrapped chip + 4 small paper clips.

9 For the inner body of the chandelier, make 32 strands following this pattern: 1 large paper clip + 8 small paper clips.

10 Hang your strands evenly all the way around the rim of the splatter lid. Alternate hanging the marble and glass chip strands, and a paper clip strand goes in between each.

11 Gather the ends of the 32 paper clip strands and attach them to a binder ring. This will create the inner body of your chandelier.

12 Gather the ends of the glass chip and marble strands, and attach them to a binder ring to create the outer body of your chandelier.

13 Take the remaining 8 strands of 8 small paper clips and drape them between the large clips that you used to hang your chandelier, then attach one end to the top binder ring and the other end to the large clips around the edge that create the body of your chandelier.

14 Wire your cord and socket set in the hole in the middle of the splatter lid where the handle of the lid used to be.

15 To make the bobble at the bottom of the chandelier, wrap 6 inches of wire around your large marble and 1 remaining small marble, and attach them to a binder ring with 3 evenly spaced paper clips.

ZIP TIE LAMPSHADE

I thought this project was going to take months to finish. It did take several hours, but not as many as I thought, and once I got the hang of it I started to really enjoy the process. I find repetitive motions are always enhanced by watching a movie, so I recommend renting something good when you tackle this one!

YOU'LL NEED

- 400 large (7 to 8 inches long) zip ties
- Scissors
- 1,000 small (3 to 4 inches long) zip ties
- Wire lampshade base
- Black Krylon Fusion for Plastic spray paint

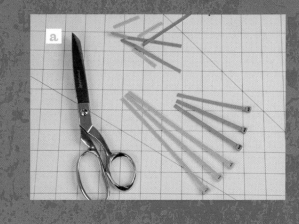

HERE'S HOW

1. Cut off the ends of 3 large zip ties, keeping them as long as you can.

2. Cut off about 3 inches of 3 more large zip ties.

3. Fasten these 6 ties into teardrop shapes by inserting the ends into the mouths.

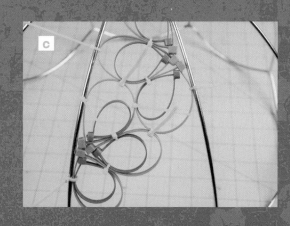

4. Place a small teardrop in the center of each large teardrop and arrange the large teardrops so they connect at their points, as shown in the photo.

5. Using 2 small ties, connect the teardrops together so every teardrop—large and small—is held in place.

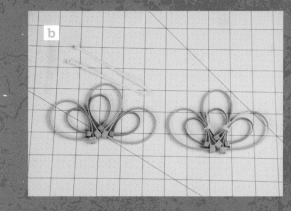

6. Using small ties, connect the teardrop cluster to a wire on your lampshade.

7. Repeat the above steps until you've covered the entire lampshade.

8. Spray the shade with Krylon Fusion spray paint, making sure to hit all angles.

SERVING SPOON CANDELIER

I know that you might look at this and think, "What a weirdo!" Though I am a weirdo, I can assure you that this "candelier" will bring much joy to your life, and even more romance to your dinners. So when you're done making out with your other half after a dinner of spaghetti and meatballs under this contraption, call me and just try to say it wasn't magical.

DON'T WORRY

The sizes of your spoons may vary a little bit. I think that just makes the project look more interesting.

YOU'LL NEED

- 5 stainless steel strainer spoons that are about 14 inches long from the end of handle to tip of spoon

- 5 large stainless steel mixing spoons that are about 14 inches long from end of handle to tip of spoon

- 1 silver wire trivet, 8 inches in diameter

- Four chain dog collars, about 16 inches long (could be longer or shorter, it's up to you)

- 1 binder ring, 2$\frac{1}{2}$ inches in diameter

- 4 binder rings, 1 inch in diameter

- E-6000 glue

- 1 large silver plastic Christmas tree ornament

- 12 inches of silver chain with jump rings or 12 inches of fine-gauge wire

- Pliers, if you use a chain and jump rings

- 4 small office clips

HERE'S HOW

1 Bend the handles of the strainer spoons backward 3 inches from the tip, almost all the way to the rest of the handle.

2 Bend the handles of the large serving spoons backward 4 inches from the tip, almost all the way to the rest of the handle.

3 Hang the spoons and strainers from their bent handles on the outer wire of the wire trivet, and note how far you'll have to bend each spoon to form a horizontal surface on which to rest your candles. Remove the spoons and strainers and bend accordingly.

4 Attach 1 end of each of the 4 chain dog collars to the large 2^1/$_2$-inch binder ring. This will be the top of your candelier.

5 Attach the other ends of the chain dog collars evenly around the metal trivet, 90 degrees apart, using the 4 small office clips.

6 Hang the partially finished candelier before you continue to work.

7 Arrange the spoons around the outer wire of the trivet. Once your spoons are in place, add a gob of E-6000 under the bent handles where they touch the trivet to keep them from moving. Let the glue dry.

8 Hang the Christmas ornament from the center of the trivet in between all of the hanging spoons, using your silver chain and a jump ring or a piece of wire.

9 Hang your candelier in its final location, place a tealight on each spoon, and light the candles.

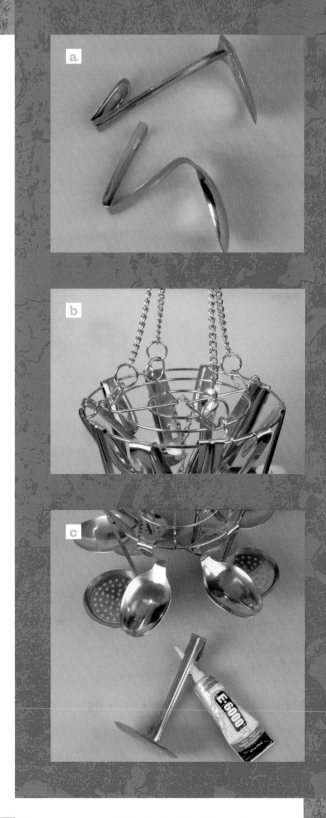

VENETIAN MASK LAMP

All right, I know this is creepy, but I love it. I was on the fence about including this in the book, but then I thought, what the heck. I know there is *someone* out there who will appreciate this project!

YOU'LL NEED

- Ruler
- Cord and socket set
- Drill with ¼-inch drill bit
- 2 large clear plastic bowls
- X-ACTO knife
- 3 plastic masks that will fit inside your bowls when glued together
- Fine-gauge wire
- Dremel tool
- E-6000 glue
- 1 energy-efficient cool bulb

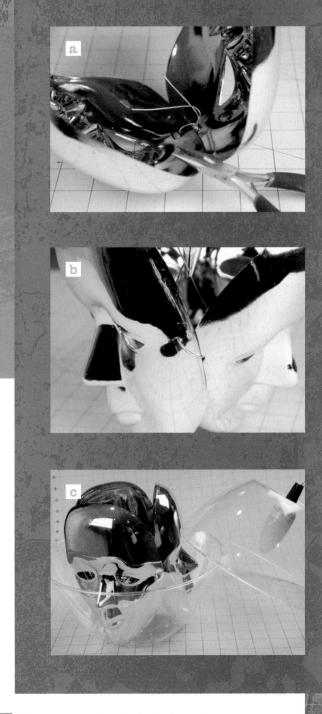

HERE'S HOW

1 Measure the diameter of your socket. Carefully drill a hole in the bottom of 1 of the plastic bowls the same size as the socket measurement so that the socket will fit comfortably in the hole.

2 With the Dremel, cut a larger hole in the bottom of the second clear bowl, big enough for you to fit your hand through to change the bulb.

3 With your knife, cut small holes in the temples of each mask.

4 Cut 3 pieces of wire, each 3 inches long, and maneuver your needle-nose pliers to wire the masks together, using the wire pieces like twist ties.

5 Place the masks inside the bowl with the larger hole.

6 Glue the second bowl on top of the first, trapping the masks in place.

7 Slip your socket in the hole at the top and glue it into place with E-6000. Let the glue dry.

8 Reach your hand in through the bottom bowl and put your bulb in the socket.

9 Hang your lamp from a hook in the ceiling. Spooky!

MOTHER NATURE CHANDELIER

I have a huge tent in my backyard for when I entertain in the summer. It's pretty plain, but I dress it up for special occasions. One of my favorite ways to spruce it up is by creating huge, arty chandeliers to hang from the center. This chandelier was made for an afternoon lunch I hosted in honor of a friend's birthday. She loved it, and promptly asked me if the chandelier could be one of her birthday presents.

YOU'LL NEED

- 2 identical round wire plant baskets
- A bunch of thick branches
- Small handsaw or jigsaw
- 3 feet of fine-gauge wire
- Needle-nose pliers with wire cutter
- Hot glue gun and glue sticks
- A few faux butterflies
- Several faux flowers
- 2 feet of small chain

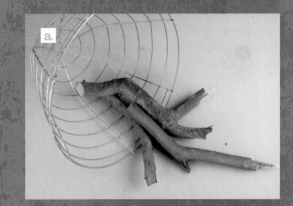

HERE'S HOW

1. Place your baskets mouth-to-mouth and note the dimensions of the space inside. Then cut your branches accordingly, bearing in mind that you'll want to bundle them in an artistic way.

2. Create your branch arrangement, and wire the branches together so that they stay put.

3. Using your hot glue gun, add faux butterflies, leaves, and flowers to the branches. Let the glue dry, then place the arrangement inside one plant basket and place the other on top.

4. Cut about 10 pieces of small-gauge wire, 5 inches long. Wire the mouths of the baskets together with the wire, using pliers to bend them like twist ties.

5. With your pliers, loosen the link on one end of your chain and hook it onto the

top of the chandelier where the wires intersect. Close the link back up.

6. Hang your chandelier from the chain and enjoy!

ORIGAMI CRANE CHANDELIER

When I moved into my first apartment I was in my twenties; I had nothing. And when I say nothing, I mean *nothing*. I didn't care, because I knew that with a little creativity my apartment would be the envy of the complex, and three weeks later it was. Contributing to my little flat's charm was the enormous paper origami chandelier I made with notebook paper and some large twigs I'd found on the street. This is a more colorful version, which I know will add charm to your space.

YOU'LL NEED

- Hollow plastic hand fixture (try AcmeDisplay.com)
- Drill with ¹/₂-inch drill bit
- Fine sandpaper
- Black Krylon spray paint
- 6-inch by 6-inch square of wood for base
- Krylon Metallics gold spray paint
- Cord and socket set with chandelier bulb-size socket
- E-6000 glue
- Eco-friendly cool bulb with a chandelier base

HERE'S HOW

1. Drill a hole in the top of the hand using a ¹/₂-inch bit.

2. Drill a similar hole through the base of the hand (where your cord will exit).

3. Sand the holes to smooth out the edges and get rid of any small pieces.

4. If necessary, spray the fixture with the black paint to give it a nice even finish, and let dry.

5. Sand your wood base, and spray it with gold paint.

6. Wire your lamp according to the instructions that came with it, threading the cord through the holes so that the socket sits in the hand.

7. Glue the base of the hand to the center of the lamp base with E-6000.

8. Screw in a bulb and pat yourself on the back.

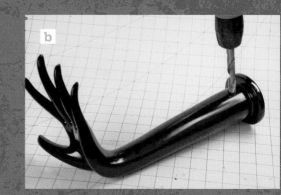

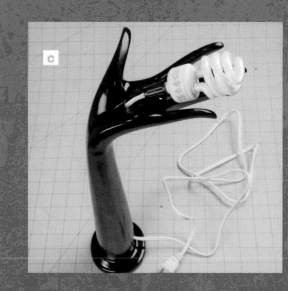

WRISTFUL THINKING

From what I've read, there was a time when wrists were considered quite sexy. Around 1900 that's about all the skin women ever exposed, so I guess you took what you could get. Now, of course, we're in an age in which superstars wear underwear and pretty much nothing else out in public, and I must say, when I see them, all I can think about is how they must be freezing. In this chapter you'll learn some ways to call attention to the forgotten wrist and, hopefully, get some action. At the very least, I think these projects might get your hand kissed by a gentleman.

QUILLED TIN JEWELRY

One of the very first crafts I attempted when I was a kid was quilling (my parents used crafts to calm me and my brothers so we wouldn't raise the roof). Recently, after attending an exhibition of quilling from the turn of the century, I was inspired to try it again, and this is what I came up with.

YOU'LL NEED
FOR BOTH
- 3 (5" x 7") sheets of aluminum flashing
- Tin shears or heavy-duty scissors
- Regular needle-nose pliers
- Long needle-nose pliers
- E-6000 glue

FOR THE BRACELET
- Plain silver cuff

FOR THE EARRINGS
- Earring wires
- Jump rings

HERE'S HOW
FOR THE BRACELET

1 Cut up aluminum flashing into 25 strips, each ¼ inch wide and 5 inches long.

2 Grab 1 end of a strip with the regular pliers and curl it around the needle-nose pliers until you get to the center of the strip. Now grab the other end of the strip and curl it in the opposite direction (the curls should form an S). This hides the sharp edges so you can wear your bracelet without worrying about poking somebody.

3 Make as many curly S's as you need for your design.

HINT

> I varied the size of my S's a little by trimming a few of my strips. Feel free to do the same.

4 Glue your curly S's on the cuff with E-6000 glue.

HERE'S HOW
FOR THE EARRINGS

1 Follow steps 1 through 3 for making the bracelet.

2 Cut 2 more strips of flashing. Fold 1 strip in half, then curl each end around the needle-nose pliers, twisting each end in the opposite direction, stopping about $1/2$ inch from the center of your strip on both sides. This is the top of your earring. Repeat for the other strip to make your other earring top.

3 Glue a few curly S's to the curls on the tops of your earrings, and keep adding S's until you've achieved your desired shape.

4 When the glue has dried, loop a jump ring through the tops of each earring, add earring wire, and put on your new jewelry.

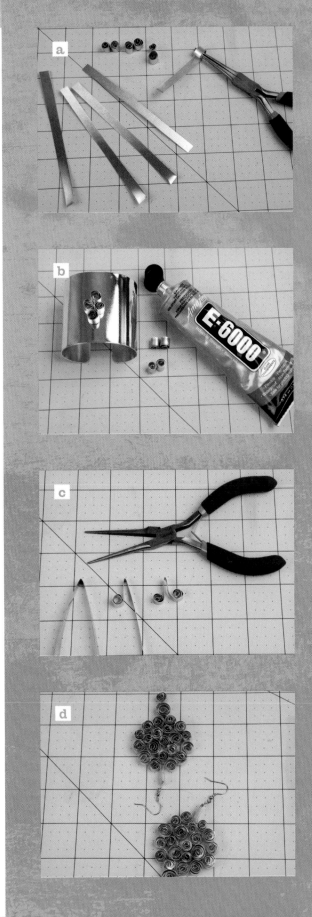

ZIP TIE LINK BRACELET

These are just plain fun to make and they cost about as much as a gumball.
Make a hundred of them, wear them all up and down your arm, and spark a new
fashion trend!

YOU'LL NEED

- Nylon zip ties, 3 inches or 8 inches long and in different colors
- Scissors
- 2 jump rings
- Pliers
- 1 large lobster claw closure

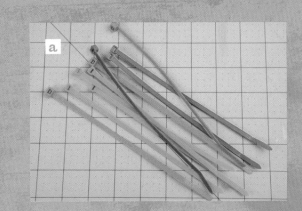

HERE'S HOW

1 Bend and secure a zip tie, creating a loop any size you like, and cut off the loose end. This will be your bracelet's first link and will determine the size you cut your other zip ties.

2 Slip the end of another zip tie through the finished link, and keep it going until you have enough to fit around your wrist.

3 Add a jump ring to 1 of your end links with pliers.

4 Add a jump ring with a lobster claw closure to the other end link.

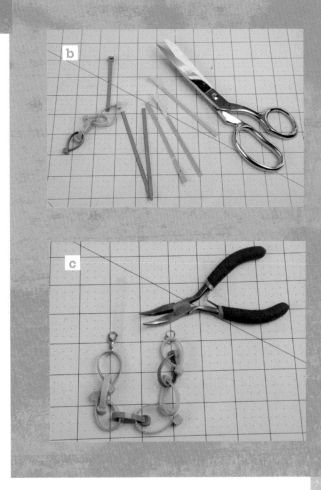

MEASURING TAPE BRACELET

I wear this bracelet when I'm sewing, but if you're hip and cool (which I'm not), then you could rock it with a funky outfit. I'll just stick to rocking it in my sewing room.

- 1 measuring tape
- Scissors
- Sewing machine with zigzag stitch and thread in a contrasting color
- Velcro sticky dots

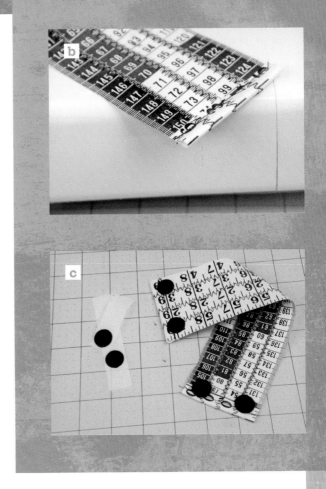

HERE'S HOW

1. Measure your wrist and add 1 1/2 inch for the ideal length of your bracelet (mine was 9 inches long).

2. Cut the measuring tape into 4 pieces, each the length that you calculated in step 1.

3. Zigzag-stitch the pieces together, long edge to long edge, side by side.

4. Fold each short end over 1/2 inch in opposite directions and straight-stitch the folds in place, making sure to backtack.

5. Stick your Velcro sticky dots on the ends of your bracelet where you folded the edges over, and you're ready to go.

RESIN RENAISSANCE CAMEO AND CAMEO CUFF

When I attend a party I make a beeline for the woman wearing the biggest jewelry, because I've learned that big jewelry equals *big* personality. This cuff just screams "I'm fun!" Even if you're not into big jewelry, the resin cameo may still be for you; cameos can be added to a lot of things in need of a little flair.

YOU'LL NEED

- Laser-printed image (I chose one of Renaissance women)
- Scissors
- Permanent marker
- Aluminum flashing
- Heavy-duty scissors or tin shears
- Elmer's glue
- Small bits of lace
- Seed pearls (or beads)
- Toothpicks
- Rhinestones
- Resin
- Cardboard
- Plastic lids from a juice container or cap from a bottle of water (these will serve as lifts for your pieces so they don't stick to your surface while they dry)
- X-ACTO knife
- E-6000
- Plain metal cuff

> If you're making a cuff, you'll want your image
> to be roughly the width of your cuff—maybe
> a little bigger or smaller—so you may need to
> reduce or enlarge it accordingly.

HERE'S HOW

1 Make a copy of your image using a laser
copier. (You may have to go to Staples for
a laser copy. See page 249.)

2 Cut out your image in the shape of an
oval, circle, or square.

3 Trace your image onto a piece of aluminum flashing in permanent marker, then
cut out the shape using heavy-duty scissors or tin shears.

4 Glue your image to the aluminum flashing with some Elmer's.

5 Apply tiny dabs of glue around the edge
of your image and add a pearl border.
Use a toothpick to spread your glue and
push the pearls into place.

6 Glue a bit of lace on the image to give it
some texture, and glue on some beads
and/or a rhinestone or two just for kicks.

7 *Go outside to finish this project!*

8 Mix a small amount of resin, following the
instructions on the package carefully.

9 Put down some cardboard to protect your
work surface, place your water bottle
lid on the cardboard, and balance the
cameo on the lid.

10 Pour resin over the cameo, making sure
it spreads all the way to the edge. Let the
cameos dry overnight.

DON'T WORRY

> If some resin drips off the edge of your
> cameo. After it dries you can remove it with
> an X-ACTO knife.

11 Check the underside or your cameo for
drips and scrape off any excess with an
X-ACTO knife. Your cameo is now ready for
action.

12 To complete the bracelet, glue the cameo
to the metal cuff with a generous amount
of E-6000. Let the glue dry, then wear it out
only if you plan on being the life of the party!

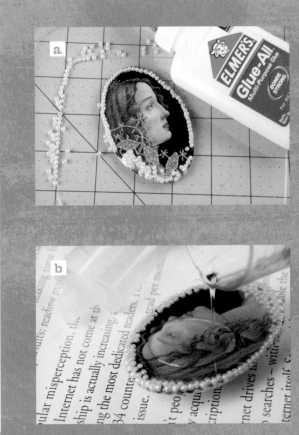

THIMBLE BRACELET

Nothing says "I like to sew" like a thimble bracelet clanking around your wrist. Trust me, this is one noisy piece of jewelry, so don't wear it to church or you'll get some seriously dirty looks from all of the people who are trying not to end up downstairs with the devil. But if heaven to you is getting crafty with your sewing machine, this is the project for you.

YOU'LL NEED

- 20 metal thimbles
- Awl
- 20 flathead pins (including some about 1¹/₂ inches long)
- 2 pairs of needle-nose pliers with wire cutter
- 22 jump rings
- Length of chain that fits your wrist
- 1 lobster claw clasp

HERE'S HOW

1 Place your thimbles with mouths down on your workspace. Poke a hole with the awl in the top of each thimble, just big enough for a pin to fit through.

2 Poke a flathead pin through the top of each thimble, with the head catching where your fingertip would be. Cut and curl the pointed end of the pin into a loop with needle-nose pliers.

3 Thread a jump ring through the loop and attach the thimble to your bracelet chain.

4 Continue adding thimbles until your bracelet is clanking away.

5 Add your lobster claw at one end of your chain with a jump ring, then add an extra jump ring at the other end of your chain to complete the clasp.

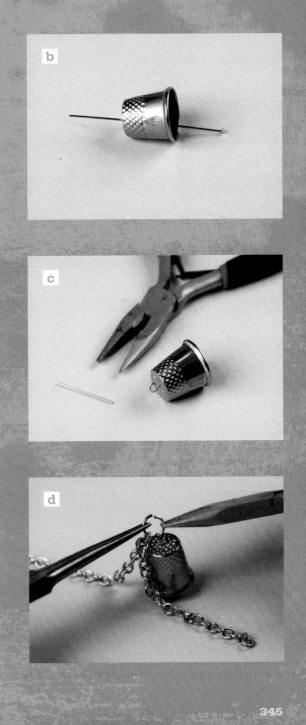

LADY ESTHER CUFF

These bracelets were made with my friend Esther in mind. I often think she was born in the wrong time and should have been part of high society during the Victorian era instead, though I'm glad she's part of my life in the here and now!

YOU'LL NEED

- 1 yard of 1-inch black satin ribbon
- Scissors
- ¼ yard of black netting (less would work, but most stores won't sell it in smaller quantities)
- Several hundred small, flat-back rhinestones
- E-6000 glue
- Toothpicks
- Black felt
- Black Velcro dots
- Sewing machine with black thread

HERE'S HOW

1. Cut 2 lengths of ribbon, each 11 inches long.

2. Cut 2 pieces of netting, each 2 inches by 8 inches.

3. Lay your ribbon pieces on your sewing machine side by side, with one overlapping the other ¼ inch.

4. Sew the ribbons together, leaving 1½ inches at each end unsewn.

5. Center the netting on top of the ribbon piece and stitch it on.

6. Fold a pleat in each end of the bracelet where the netting ends. Pin the pleats in place and stitch across them.

7. Add a Velcro dot to each end of the bracelet, one on the outside and one on the inside.

8. Determine how big and what shape you want the decoration on your cuff to be and cut it out of the heavy black felt.

9. Using a toothpick and E-6000 glue, fill in your decorative piece with rhinestones. Let the glue dry.

10. Glue the decorative piece on top of the netting in the center of your cuff with E-6000 and let dry.

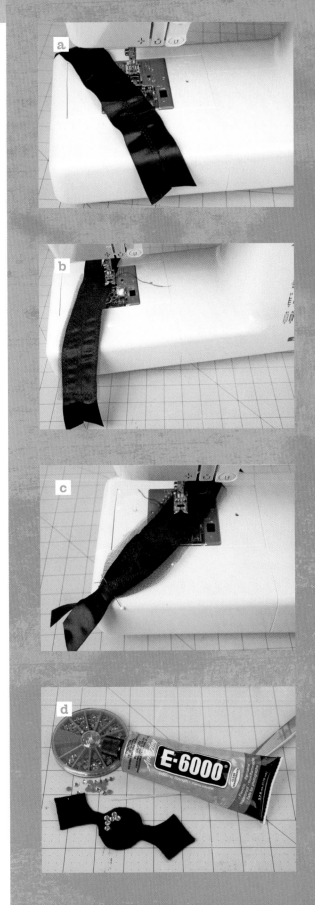

METAL FLOWER BRACELET

I think this bracelet is so cool because the flowers are made from metal and yet they still look delicate. This technique could also be used to make a beautiful brooch, a pendant, or a hat pin.

YOU'LL NEED

- Fine-point permanent marker
- 8-inch by 8-inch square of thin aluminum flashing
- Tin shears or heavy-duty scissors
- E-6000 glue
- Wire cutters or Dremel tool
- Needle-nose pliers
- Round silver buttons
- Clear tape
- Plain metal cuff

HERE'S HOW

1. Enlarge and trace the patterns provided on page 362 onto aluminum flashing with a fine-point marker, and cut the flower shapes out with tin shears or heavy-duty scissors, making sure to dull sharp points by cutting them off.

2. Layer the flower shapes, and glue them together with E-6000 to make your flowers.

3. With wire cutters or a Dremel, remove the shanks from the back of your buttons. Use pliers to hold the buttons while you do this!

4. Glue a button in the center of each flower and let dry.

5. Arrange the flowers on the metal cuff.

6. Glue the flowers to the cuff with E-6000. Use clear tape to hold the flowers in place while they dry.

7. When the glue is dry, remove the tape and admire your new jewelry.

MARKER CAP BRACELET

Do you have an old set of beautifully colorful markers that are dried up but you keep them anyway because they look good in the jar/drawer/desk organizer? I did too, but not anymore—I took off the caps and made this fab bracelet for myself.

YOU'LL NEED

- Approximately 18 marker caps
- X-ACTO knife
- 2 yards of heavy-duty cord
- 1 large lobster claw closure

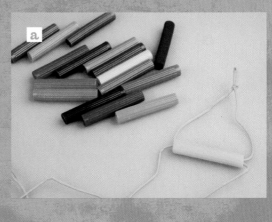

HERE'S HOW

1 Cut off the tips of the marker caps to make them into hollow tubes. Try to cut them all the same size.

HINT

> Leave the caps on the markers while you do step 1 so you can keep your fingers on your noncutting hand far away from the blade.

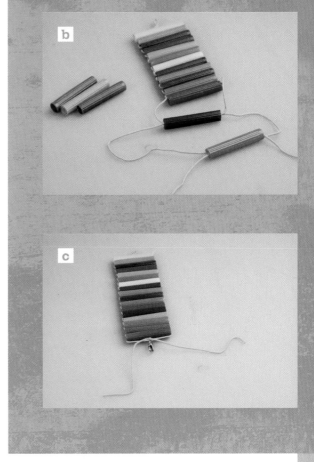

2 Tie a knot with a loop in the middle of your cord exactly at the 1-yard mark.

3 Put 1 end of your cord through 1 end of a cap tube and the other end of the cord through the other end and pull until the string is taut.

4 Position the knot so it's centered against the side of the first tube.

5 Repeat steps 3 and 4 until you've used all of your caps.

6 Once the last cap is in place, tie your cord in a very secure knot, centered against the middle of the last cap.

7 String on the lobster claw closure and tie another knot so it stays in place.

8 Cut the excess cord and tuck the ends inside the last cap (you might want to dab some glue on the ends to keep them in place) or let the strings hang loose for a more casual look.

THINGS I USED FOR THE PROJECTS IN THIS BOOK

These items are great to have around the house for whenever you get inspired. If, like me, you love a bargain, look for the items marked here with an asterisk at your local 99-cent store and get some bang for your crafty bucks.

Aluminum flashing: This comes in a roll in different widths. It's great for the tin projects because it's easy to cut and holds its shape when it's bent. Also, it doesn't rust!

*Ball point pins: These will help you hold tiny things in place. The long ones are especially handy.

Books, old and discarded: You can use the paper for all sorts of things. Cut up pages for découpage projects, mount artwork on a book-page background, use the covers for card stock—there are tons of possibilities.

*Buckets with lids: Great for storing large batches of papier-mâché and for keeping water and sponges nearby while you work.

*Buttons: Start collecting these now and always try to have tons around. Get them anywhere and glue them on anything. They are decorative, great for flower centers, and neat for mosaic projects.

*Clothespins, wood and plastic: Wooden clothespins are perfect for gluing around and on projects to give them a handmade feel, and the plastic ones are great little clamps for holding things together while they dry.

*Craft paper: You know, the brown stuff that looks like what they use to make paper bags out of. Perfect for patterns.

Decorative scissors: You can get these in so many different shapes at arts and crafts stores, and you will want them all. They give your paper projects beautiful borders. Fiskars makes a terrific selection of scissors that last and last.

Drill and drill bits: Get a good drill. Mine is from Skil, and it's sturdy and strong. A nice selection of drill bits will last you forever, as long as you take care of them (Black & Decker make a great set). Stay away from cheap tools; they just don't last! (Also see Dremel, page 358)

E-6000 (see Goop).

(Elmer's) glue: The basic white stuff is great for all craft projects, especially dé-coupage.

(Elmer's) wood glue: For small wood projects, where getting a small nail in place is almost impossible, this stuff will really keep your work together. It's also great for securing pieces of furniture that might be wobbly. Just fill in the cracks, and you'll see what a difference it makes! I use it all the time on old furniture.

*Extension cords: Let's just say that sometimes your glue gun does not quite reach your worktable.

Fabric scraps: I save all of mine and eventually use every last one.

*Faux flowers and leaves: Stick them in vases, use them for jewelry, spruce up a headband . . . always have tons around, they will come in handy.

Felt: Just a great fabric that does not fray at the edges. Perfect for putting on the underside of your projects to protect your table-tops, and great for graphic fabric projects, such as pillows and tablecloths.

Fiskars cutting mat: This is a piece of plastic that you can use your craft knife on, over and over again, without harming it. It's perfect for all of the precise cutting you do. It also has a 1-inch square grid for easy measuring.

Glitter glue: Michaels arts and crafts stores have a great selection of this stuff. Glitter glue is perfect for sprucing up any project. I love it and never leave the house without some in my backpack!

Glue sticks: What did we do without them? Perfect for greeting card and envelope projects. A nice clean way to use glue.

Google.com (image search feature): If you're looking for a picture of a Union Jack to make a pillow pattern or need an image of Frieda Kahlo to transfer onto a pillow, just get on your computer and do an image search. It's an easy way to find inspiration for your projects.

Goop glue: Goop has a huge selection of different glues that bond everything. The E-6000 is the best and sticks just about any-thing to anything.

Hammer: A must for every toolbox. Try a smaller craft hammer for tiny nails and projects.

*Hot glue gun: You can get these anywhere. Although I am not a huge fan of the hot glue gun, there are great things you can do with it, and as long as you use another adhesive along with it, it's perfect for keeping something in place.

ICE Resin: Great for jewelry projects, this is a super product that'll make your crafts last.

Jigsaw with different size blades: I use a Skil jigsaw with a scroll blade for many of my projects.

Level: This is a must in any home and for any craft project—from making tables to hanging pictures. You can pick up a level anywhere these days. Get a small one that is no more than 1 inch long.

Magazines: Old magazines are full of inspiring pictures and great ideas for new projects.

Metallic spray paints, gold and silver: As any southern girl will tell you, everything looks better sprayed silver and gold. Krylon's Metallics are my favorite.

Minwax Polycrylic Protective Finish: Hands down the best clear coat on the market.

Mod Podge: This is a great sealer that leaves a nice finish on your projects.

Needle-nose pliers: Super for picking up tiny things and bending small wires.

Newspapers: You need these to keep your work area clean, for papier-mâché, and for inspiration.

*Night-lights, plug-in: One of the easiest ways to light a project is to plug in a night-light to the end of an extension cord. It's safe and gives off a very nice low-wattage glow.

OOK: What is an OOK, you ask? It's a self-leveling sawtooth hanger made by a company called OOK, and it's great for hanging your projects.

*Paintbrushes: Get them anywhere, in lots of sizes, and make sure you take care of them.

Paint chips: It's always good to have color references around you, and paint chips allow you to see what colors work well together.

Paint thinner: This stuff is flammable, so be careful. It's great for getting rid of all kinds of messes, and can even remove some gooey glue. Just dab a bit on a cotton swab, and you have a very useful item.

*Paper clips: In case you need a wire hook, these are handy to have around. Just unbend them and twist them into shape. They're also great materials to use in your crafts—

I always have gold, silver, and multicolor ones around.

Paper cutter: Perfect for making straight edges and long cuts. It's also great for cutting several sheets at once. Get one at Staples for a good price.

Paper shredder: I got mine on sale at Staples for 15 dollars. Great for making huge batches of paper strips for your papier-mâché projects.

Paper towels and old rags: The more messes I create, the more I'll need them. You'll need a lot of cleanup supplies on hand.

*Pencils: You can never have enough pencils. You'll use them for marking measurements, tracing, sketching, outlining. . . .

Pinking shears: Shears with notched blades; used to finish edges of cloth with a zigzag cut for decoration or to prevent raveling or fraying. I love them! I have one pair for paper and one pair for fabric.

Plaid acrylic paints: Great colors, perfect for any craft project. Nice quality, too.

Plaster of Paris: Experiment and have fun with this stuff. I like to fill old plastic dolls with it and make them into sculptures.

Plywood, birch, ¼ inch, ½ inch, ¾ inch, and 1 inch thick: Great for all of your wood projects. Birch plywood has a nice finish and is a higher grade than other plywood.

*Popsicle sticks and wooden coffee stirrers: Use these and lots of Elmer's wood glue to make sculptures, frames, trivets, what-have-you.

*Q-tips: Perfect for dabbing on small bits of glue or taking off a little drip of paint while you work.

Rebar tie: This bendable wire comes in handy when you want to create wire structures or hold things in place.

Recycled containers: C'mon, how many times do you need somewhere to store your brushes and pencils? Use what you have around the house.

Ribbon: Great for finishing edges on projects, hanging picture frames the old-fashioned way, and embellishing pretty much anything. Keep lots of different kinds on hand—satin, grosgrain, faille—and stock a variety of widths.

Rocks to use as paperweights: It's always good to have some smooth rocks on hand to hold things down while you work. I work outside a lot, and I just gather some and keep them beautifully arranged in a corner somewhere. You will be surprised at how handy they are.

*Rulers: Have a few of these on hand at all times. You will need them for everything. Be sure to get a metal ruler for making cuts with your craft knives.

*Safety goggles or glasses: It doesn't matter if you are only drilling or sawing or hammering for one second. You need to protect your eyes!

Sandpaper: I like to scrape smooth items before I add glue or paint to them. The rough surface will give the glue something to stick to, and a little sandpaper is perfect for scoring.

Scissors for paper and fabric: Invest in good fabric scissors (Fiskars and Gingher make great ones). For paper, it's good to have several pairs, so you don't have to waste your time sharpening.

Scraps of wood: Check out the scrap pile of a local woodworker to see if you can get a bag of scrap wood for a good price.

Screwdriver set: No home should be without a set of screwdrivers. Paint the tops of the Phillips-head screwdrivers one color so that you know what you are picking up from the toolbox. I swear, whenever I want a Phillips I get a flathead, and vice versa!

*Screws and nails: Small, long, fat, wood, metal, these will always be useful.

*Scrubbers: You know how messy you can be. Always have some small ones on hand.

Sewing machine: Need I say more?

(Sharpie) permanent markers: These will write on most any surface, so try to have them around. I like to use them on metal.

Snap-in socket-and-cord set with switch: These are great for all of your lamp projects. They use a candelabra bulb (a smaller bulb), and they are safe to use and don't need wiring.

Spray adhesive: Elmer's makes a wonderful spray adhesive. It's a spray glue that gives a nice, even coat of glue on your projects. There are strong- and light-tack ones, and depending on the tack, you can reposition your work until it dries, which is very helpful when you're découpaging images.

*Spray bottle: Next time you empty out a spray bottle of glass cleaner, save it and fill it with water for your workroom. Spraying water on your projects that use paint can produce wonderful effects. It can cloud ink and make spray paint gather and dry into terrific patterns.

Staple gun, heavy duty: JT21 is great for small upholstery projects, and the staples are easy to pull out if you make a mistake.

*Stapler: You'd be surprised how you can use your stapler for projects in ways other than stapling a pile of papers together.

Sticky felt: Great for adhering to the bottoms of your projects so that they don't scratch the surfaces of your tables. Also great for appliqués so that you don't have to use pins while you are sewing.

*Tape: Painter's tape, masking tape, clear tape. You need them all! Have plenty around for your projects.

Tin snips: Hand shears for cutting sheet metal. There are so many beautiful projects in this book that use sheets of aluminum. You will want to have a nice pair of tin snips that make cuts with a serrated edge so that the edges are not sharp.

Turpentine: Great for cleaning oil-based paint off brushes.

*Twine: From tying up your recycled newspapers into bundles to wrapping a lampshade, twine is your friend, and now it comes in fantastic colors. Stock up and use it!

Wire cutters: Get a pair with spring action. They are much easier to work with. This way, you have more control when you are working on your projects.

*Wire, fine, medium, and heavy gauge: I'm constantly wiring things together and twisting wires into sculptures and other structures. Keep some around for everyday use and in case you get inspired.

Wood fill: Comes in a tube, great for cracks in your wood.

*Work gloves in cotton, canvas, leather, and rubber: Find a pair that fits so that you can really use your fingers.

*X-ACTO knife: You need tons of these. Use them for making clean cuts, scoring, and preserving as much detail as you can while cutting out images.

RESOURCE GUIDE

A.C. Moore
www.ACMoore.com
A.C. Moore is a fantastic retailer that offers a huge variety of arts, crafts, and floral products. I can always find whatever I need for my projects here, and I usually end up buying tons of additional items that I just want. (The buyers for this store have a great eye.) If there isn't an A. C. Moore in your area just visit their website and order on-line.

Benjamin Moore Paints
www.benjaminmoore.com
Amazing colors, great quality, low VOC. I love these paints and use them in my home and on all of my home décor projects. I highly recommend them.

The Container Store
www.containerstore.com
I rely on this place to keep myself organized and when I want to find containers for all of my creations.

Dollar Stores and 99-Cent Stores
What a great resource for just about anything you might need. Glass plates,

candles, toothpicks, Popsicle sticks—you name it. You can't depend on the stock, but more often than not, you will find a piece of your crafting puzzle there for only a buck.

Dremel
www.dremel.com
You need to have a Dremel in your toolbox. There are very few craft projects I make that aren't made easier with this handy little tool. Great for cutting, sanding, grinding, and drilling small holes.

Eclectic Products, Inc.
www.eclecticproducts.com
The makers of E-6000 and Goop glue products. You cannot go wrong with the products found on this website. Their comprehensive line of adhesives work better than any other glues out there, and they have a sticky solution for any project you might be tackling.

Elmer's
www.elmers.com
You can find these glues almost anywhere, but just in case you want to see what else the company makes

and sells in bulk, this is a good place to start. I like to buy the white glue by the gallon, since I use so much of it.

Fiskars
www.fiskars.com
An amazing company that makes everything from wonderful sewing scissors and decorative hole punches to paper cutters and pinking shears. Check out the website for all of their products and where to buy them. They are of great quality, and I use them for all of my craft projects!

Glu-Stix.com
This is the most comprehensive hot glue gun site on the web. Calling their toll-free customer service line (1-877-770-5500) connects you directly to one of their "glue professionals," who are there every day to help customers find the right glue or gun for every purpose.

Goodwill Stores and Salvation Army Stores
www.goodwill.org
www.salvationarmy.org
If you need a table and you're prepared to add a

little pizzazz to it, this is the place to look. Same goes for if you're looking for a chair to spruce up and paint. The money goes to a good cause, and it's fun to recycle something. Check out these places before you head off to a furniture store for something brand new.

The Home Depot
www.homedepot.com
You can get anything here, from lamp-making parts to lumber. It's also a great place to roam around and get inspired.

ICE Resin
www.iceresin.com
This company makes excellent resin that's perfect for any project. Check out their website for more info about their products and crafty inspiration.

Jo-Ann Fabric and Craft Stores
www.joann.com
Terrific national fabric chain with wonderful remnants at great prices. They carry every sewing supply you could ever need!

Krylon
www.krylon.com
Krylon products are available everywhere. They are the best craft paints and spray paints around. The paints dry easily and make a great finish and Krylon has everything you can imagine, from frosted-glass paint to reflective paint to make your own mirrors.

The Lamp Shop
www.lampshop.com
This is the best site I've found for lamp parts, if you are making your own lamp-

shades. You'll be inspired by just looking at their website!

Lowe's
www.lowes.com
It's a joy to shop at Lowe's. It's organized, the staff is knowledgeable, and you can find just about anything you need there for your projects.

Michaels
www.michaelscrafts.com
A nationwide craft-supply store that has everything. I was there constantly while working on this book, and you will learn to love it too.

Minwax
www.minwax.com
For amazing products to finish all of your wood projects, try Minwax. They make beautiful stains and wonderful protective finishes. I won't use any other brand on my wood projects.

Olfa
www.olfa.com
A great manufacturer of cutting mats and blades. Check out their site for locations and products.

Oriental Trading Company, Inc.
www.orientaltrading.com
More than 25,000 fun products for every occasion! Great online resource for craft supplies. If you can't find something, try this site.

Pearl River
www.pearlriver.com
The perfect place for all your Asian craft materials, from lanterns to fabrics. If you

are going for an Asian theme, start by checking out this site. They ship everywhere, and the prices are great!

Plaid
www.plaidonline.com

I've been a fan of Plaid products for too many years to count. The quality of their amazing products (which include Mod Podge, which I give an A++) is unmatched. Visit their website for wonderful craft ideas and to learn about terrific uses for their products.

Ross
www.rossstores.com

Ross has an amazing home décor section. I like it because you can often find beautiful sheets that are easily turned into window treatments and tablecloths in a snap. It's also a great place to find a throw pillow or a vase at a very reasonable price. Frames are of good quality and inexpensive here, too.

Skil
www.skil.com

These are the only power tools I use for my projects. They are of good quality, fairly priced, and powerful. The sanders are my favorite because you can handle them easily, and the drills are fantastic. I promise that you will be happy with any Skil tool you purchase.

Staples
www.staples.com

Get your copying done here. Staples has the papers and other things you might need, so if you're trying to cross a lot of things off your list at once, Staples is the way to go. Look for sales on things like glue sticks and pencils when the school year starts.

Strathmore Papers
www.strathmoreartist.com

When you are creating something and you want it to last, use quality products. Papers especially, because in time they will change. Not Strathmore products, though. They are high-quality papers that will last a lifetime. I love the watercolor blocks, and I always have a Strathmore sketchbook with me. The paper is smooth, and you can erase and erase all you want and it won't tear.

Your Grocery Store

I know this is obvious, but I like to be thorough.

Your Trash Bin!

I believe that we should recycle as much as we can, so why not start by using what we discard to make our projects? Cans, yogurt cups, plastic soda bottles—you name it, they are all perfect starts to many projects.

Moroccan Thumbtack Tabletop
(Enlarge 10%)

Cut eight of each pattern in tin

Metal and Wire Bugs
(Enlarge 15%)

Mix and match

Metal Flower Bracelet

Cut one of each pattern in paper

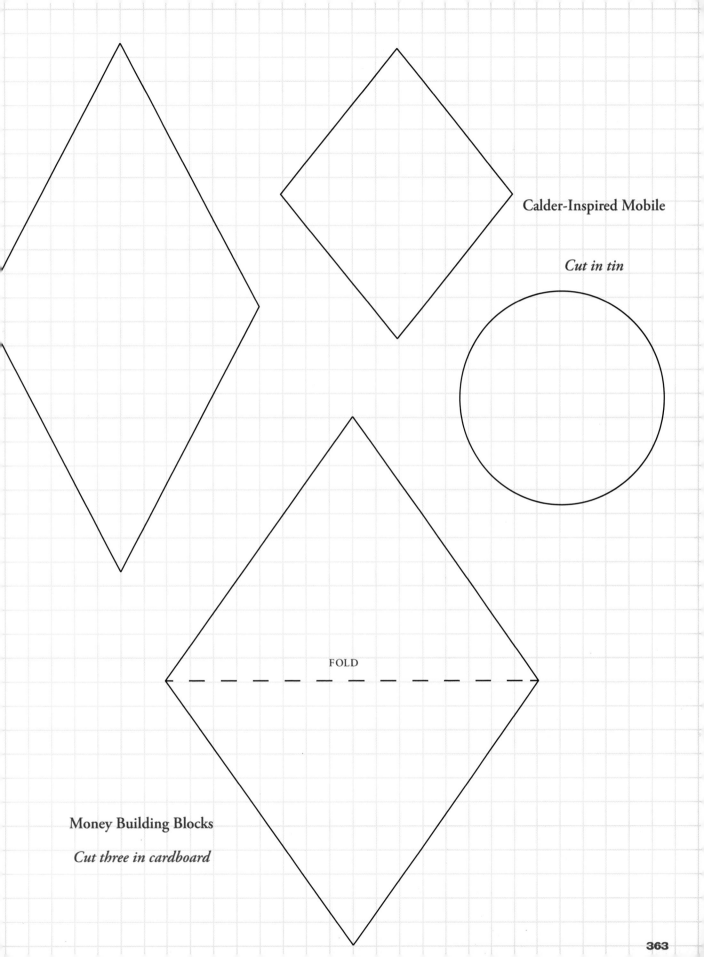

Calder-Inspired Mobile

Cut in tin

FOLD

Money Building Blocks

Cut three in cardboard

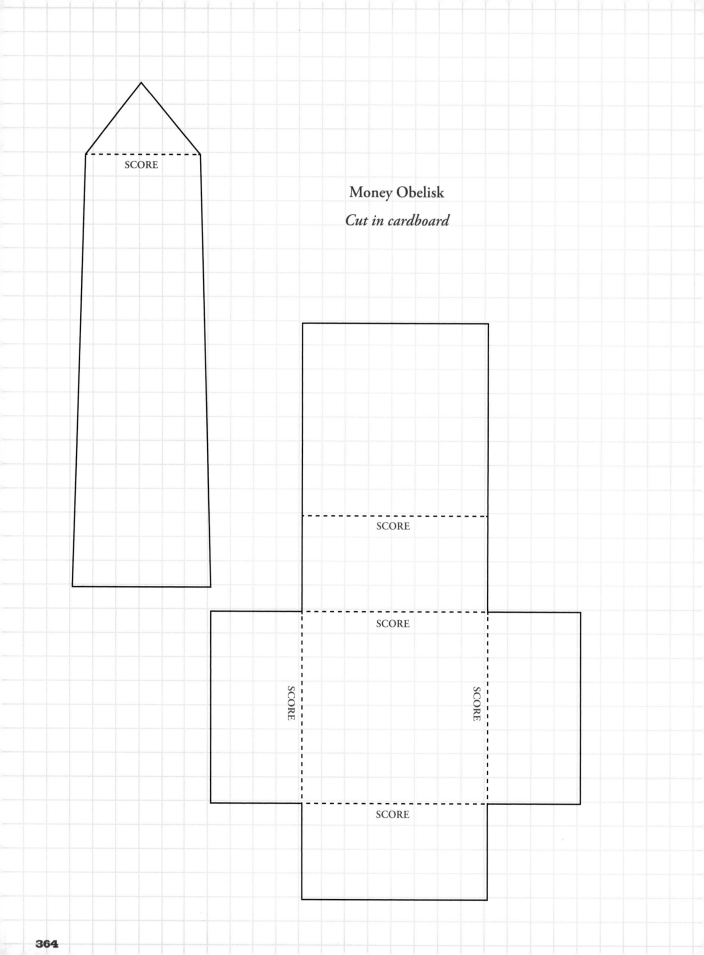

SCORE

Money Obelisk

Cut in cardboard

SCORE

SCORE

SCORE

SCORE

SCORE

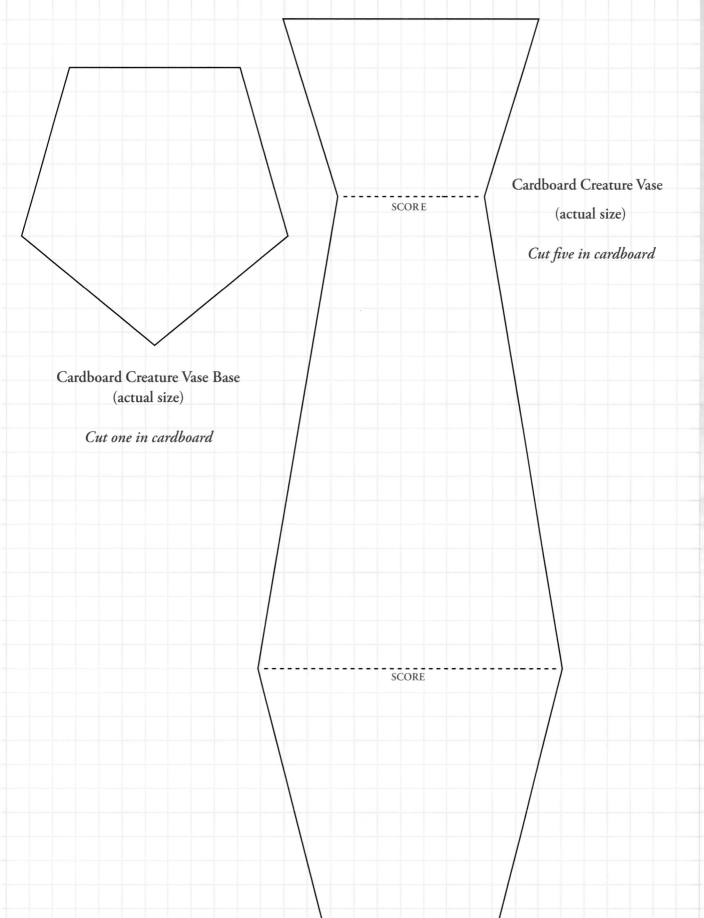

Cardboard Creature Vase Base
(actual size)

Cut one in cardboard

SCORE

Cardboard Creature Vase
(actual size)

Cut five in cardboard

SCORE

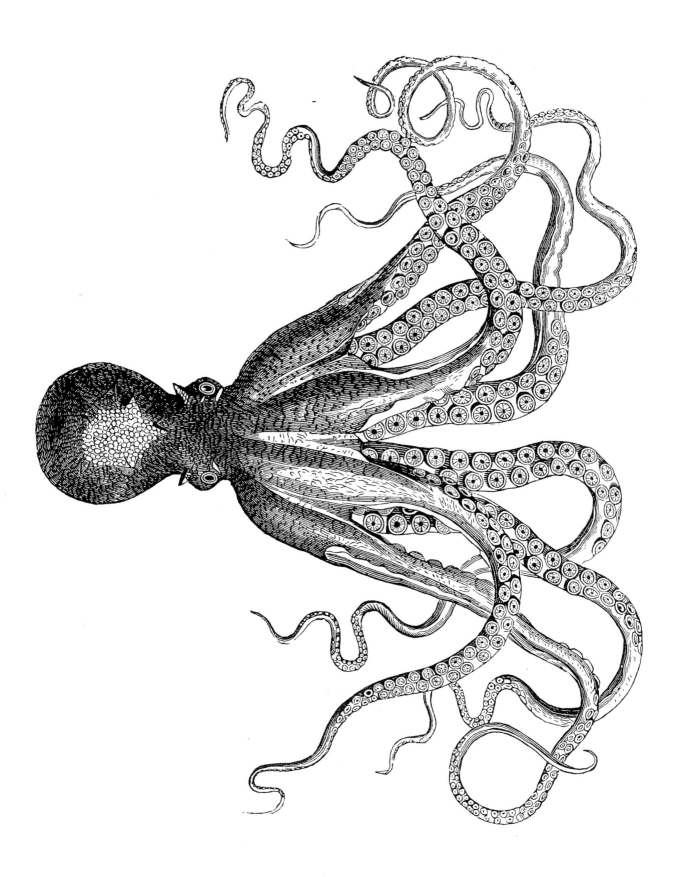

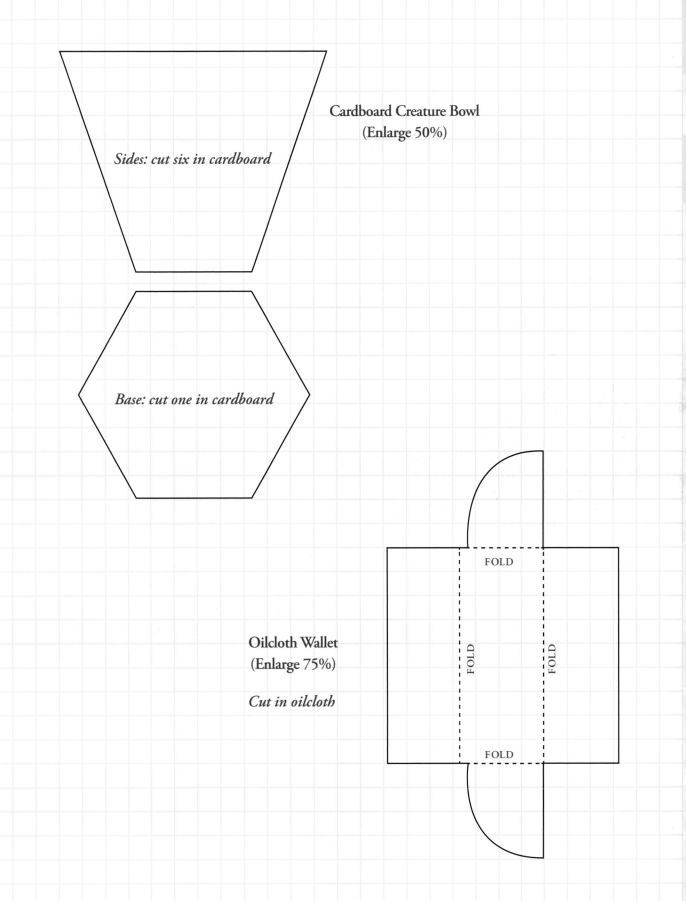

Sides: cut six in cardboard

Cardboard Creature Bowl
(Enlarge 50%)

Base: cut one in cardboard

Oilcloth Wallet
(Enlarge 75%)

Cut in oilcloth

FOLD

FOLD

FOLD

FOLD

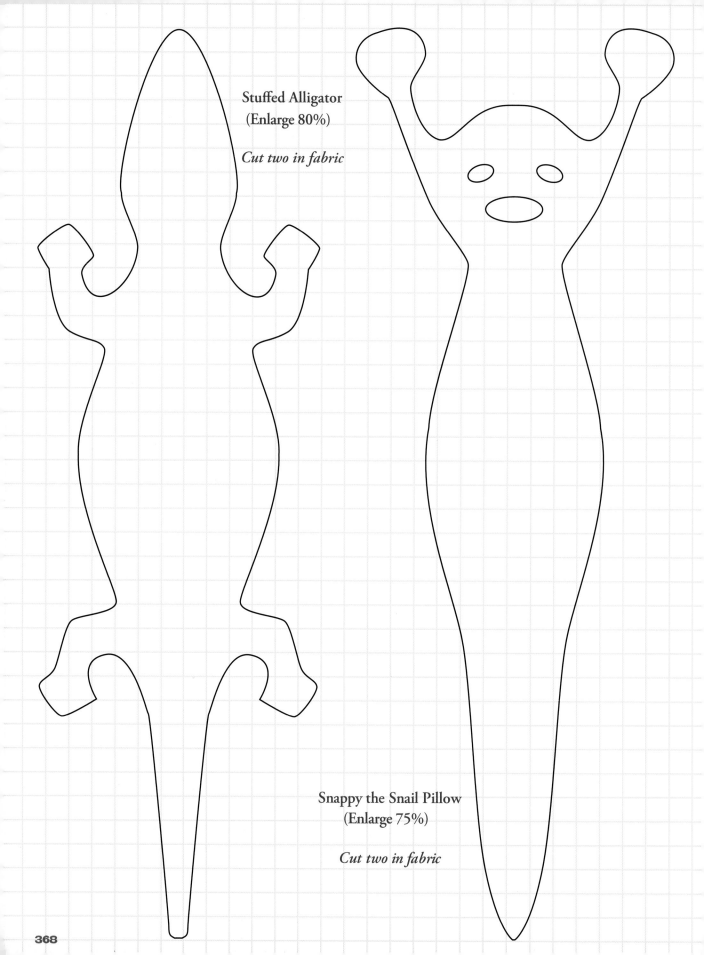

Stuffed Alligator
(Enlarge 80%)

Cut two in fabric

Snappy the Snail Pillow
(Enlarge 75%)

Cut two in fabric

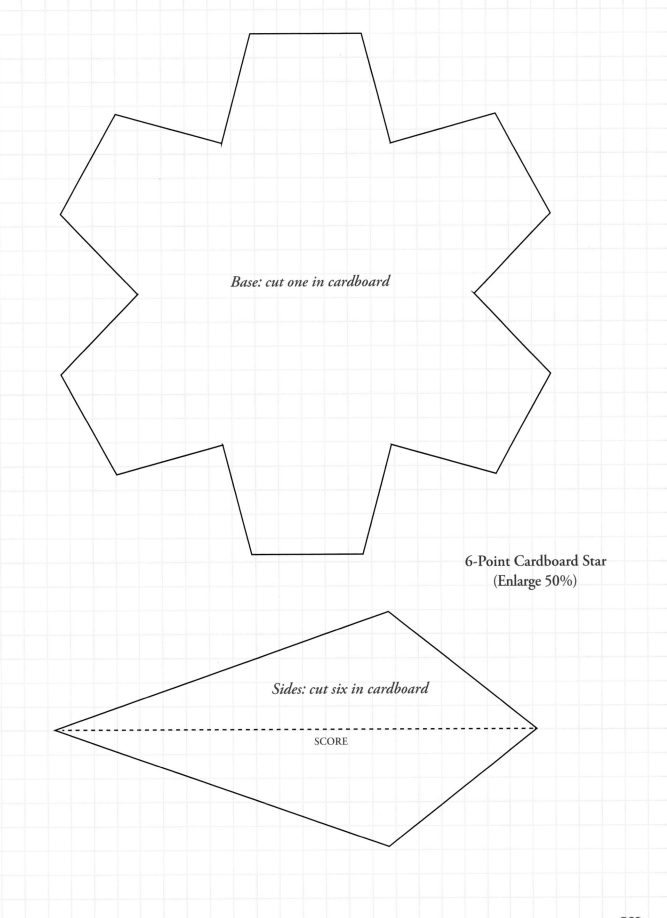

Base: *cut one in cardboard*

6-Point Cardboard Star
(Enlarge 50%)

Sides: *cut six in cardboard*

SCORE

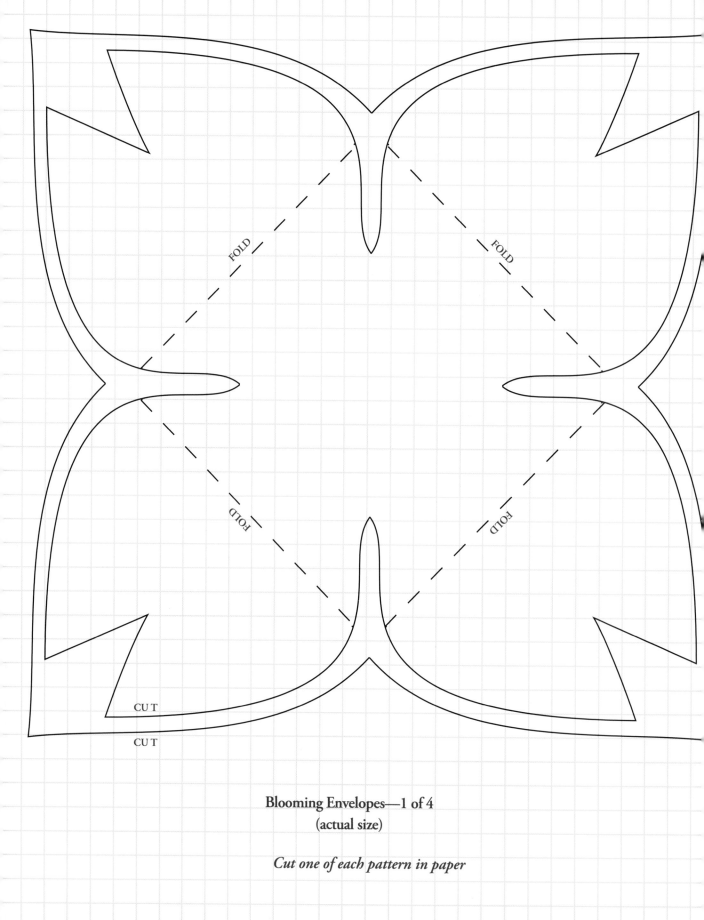

FOLD

FOLD

FOLD

FOLD

CUT

CUT

CUT

Blooming Envelopes—1 of 4
(actual size)

Cut one of each pattern in paper

CUT

CUT

Blooming Envelopes—2 of 4
(actual size)

Cut one of each pattern in paper

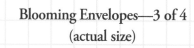

Blooming Envelopes—3 of 4
(actual size)

Cut one in paper

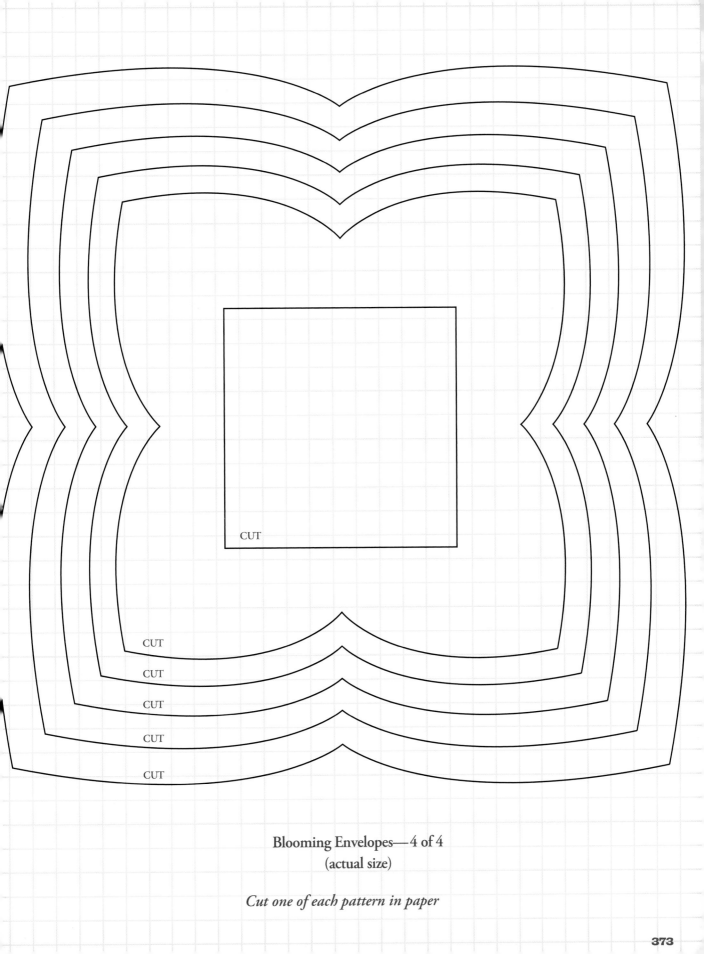

CUT

CUT

CUT

CUT

CUT

CUT

Blooming Envelopes—4 of 4
(actual size)

Cut one of each pattern in paper

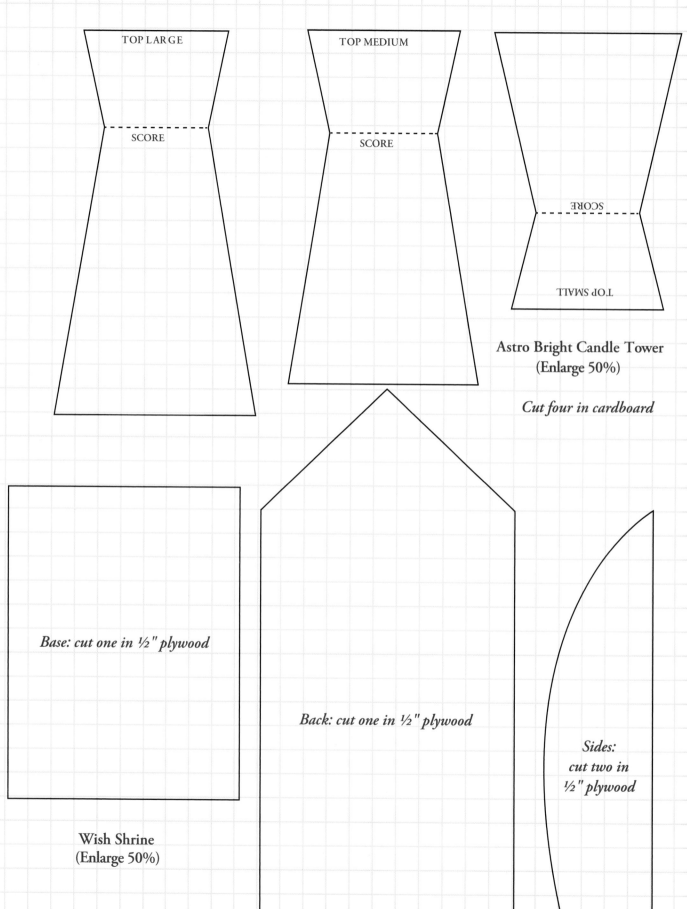

TOP LARGE

SCORE

TOP MEDIUM

SCORE

SCORE

TOP SMALL

Astro Bright Candle Tower
(Enlarge 50%)

Cut four in cardboard

Base: cut one in ½" plywood

Back: cut one in ½" plywood

Sides:
cut two in
½" plywood

Wish Shrine
(Enlarge 50%)

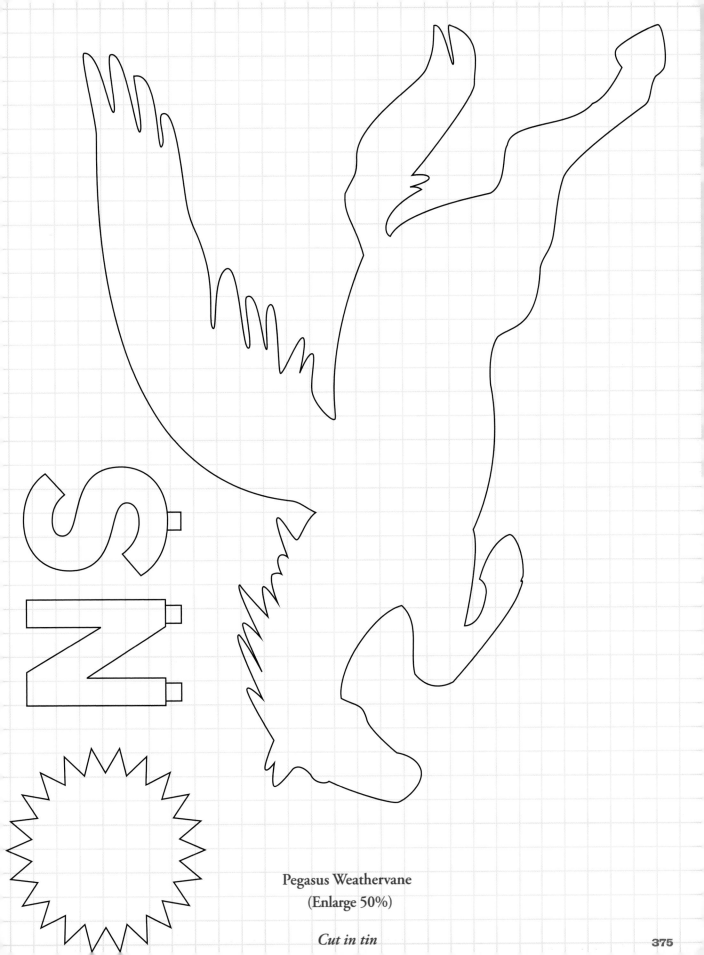

Pegasus Weathervane
(Enlarge 50%)

Cut in tin

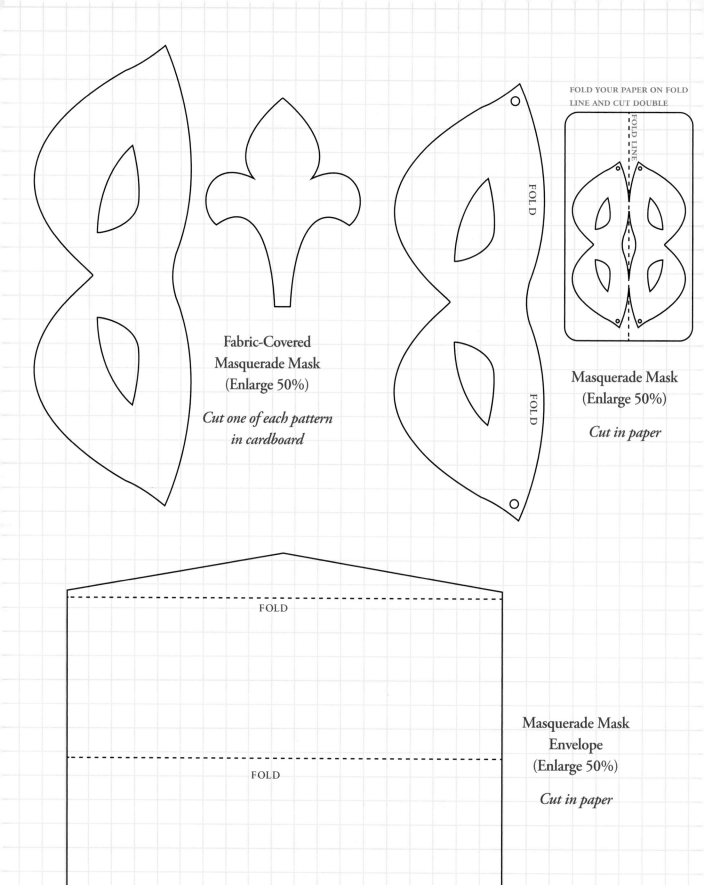

Fabric-Covered Masquerade Mask (Enlarge 50%)

Cut one of each pattern in cardboard

FOLD YOUR PAPER ON FOLD LINE AND CUT DOUBLE

FOLD LINE

FOLD

FOLD

Masquerade Mask (Enlarge 50%)

Cut in paper

FOLD

FOLD

Masquerade Mask Envelope (Enlarge 50%)

Cut in paper

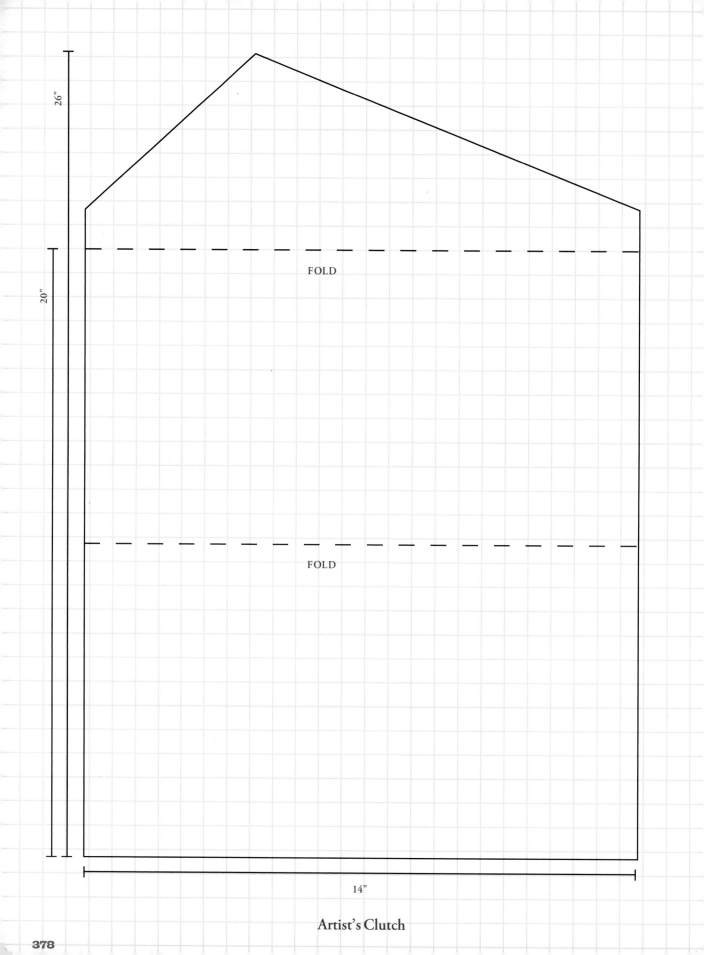

26"

20"

FOLD

FOLD

14"

Artist's Clutch

GOT A CRAFTY QUESTION?
STILL ITCHING FOR INSPIRATION?
VISIT MARK ON THE WEB AT:

WWW.MARKMONTANO.COM
MARKMONTANOBLOGS.BLOGSPOT.COM
WWW.BIGASSCRAFTS.COM
TWITTER.COM/MARKMONTANO

"Mark Montano is the glittering godfather of all things paper, paint and glue. Whether you are into fashion, home improvement or self-expression, *The Big-Ass Book of Crafts* is the ultimate go-to manual to have at your fingertips."

—Kathy Cano-Murillo,
The Crafty Chica

And don't forget to check out
The Big-Ass Book of Crafts!

OVER 150 CRAFTS TO FILL YOUR HOME, GIVE TO FRIENDS, DECORATE THE YARD, OR SEND TO MOM.

THE BIG-ASS BOOK OF CRAFTS

BY MARK MONTANO